Java
A Practical Guide

Dedications

For Roz.

TR.

The reality of this book is that it couldn't have been written without the incredible effort that JavaSoft has put into making Java as ubiquitous as it is. Quite remarkable how much interest there is in the industry regarding this language.

But there are people who need to be thanked. Terry Ridge, my co-author, is one of the most talented programmers I've ever had the fortune to work with. Also, he has the patience of a saint for putting up with me.

I'd like to thank Carol Pedley for her support during 1996, and for giving me the drive to actually complete a project I desperately wanted to finish.

And to my daughter, Katherine Louise, who is far too young to program any language, but gives her father a reason to finish one book and start another one.

NF.

Java
A Practical Guide

NEIL FAWCETT
AND
TERRY RIDGE

Butterworth-Heinemann
Linacre House, Jordan Hill, Oxford OX2 8DP
A division of Reed Educational and Professional Publishing Ltd

$\mathcal{R}$ A member of the Reed Elsevier plc group

OXFORD BOSTON JOHANNESBURG
MELBOURNE NEW DELHI SINGAPORE

First published 1997

©1997 Neil Fawcett and Terry Ridge

British Library Cataloguing in Publication Data

A catalogue record for this book is available from the British Library.

ISBN 07506 3344 1

Designed and typeset by ReadyText, Bath

Printed in Great Britain

Contents

Part 1

Understanding the fundamentals

The Wonderful World of Java

An Introduction

Welcome to *Java: A Practical Guide*. This book and CD-ROM are intended to provide you with all of the information, data and knowledge that you need in order to enter into the exciting and ever growing world of the Java programming language that was invented by JavaSoft some two years ago.

Java itself is far more than just an object oriented programming language and in addition to helping you gain first hand knowledge of how to build applications, applets and exciting interactive content for the World Wide Web (WWW), this book will identify exactly what Java is, what a JavaOS is, what Java Beans means to the average mortal and how Java will grow to impact much of the business and consumer worlds over the coming years.

Many in the computer industry believe that Java represents an exciting step forward in the world of programming, and in order for you to play a role in this brave new world you need some help. *Java: A Practical Guide* will give you that knowledge, helping you learn about a programming language that has started a revolution in software creation and has garnered industry support from all and sundry.

We have gone to a lot of trouble to ensure that this book and CD guide you carefully through the Java language, step by step introducing the tips and techniques that will enable you to develop your own applications, your own Web applets or to simply add to your programming knowledge. It has been written from a programmer's perspective and takes a logical look at all of the components of the language, explains the syntax of the language, offers advice and copious code examples.

This book has been written with you in mind. It does not expect you to be a rocket scientist (although if you are then Java will seem like a walk in the park) and will look to you to have had some experience in structured programming, be it C or Visual Basic, but will never assume that something does not need to be explained. By the end of it you will be able to develop your own applications, confident in the knowledge that you have embraced the Java language and all its features.

A wide use of programming examples and an in depth guide to the Java Application Programming Interfaces (APIs) will constantly help you embrace the various components of Java. A chapter that reviews the concept of object oriented programming will enable you to visualise in your own mind how a modular, component-based application can be built, how classes and subclasses work and so on. The book will also discuss the different object approach to programming that JavaSoft has taken with Java in comparison to the C++ programming language.

Many topics are included within the confines of this book. They include:

- A Guide to Getting Started
- Object Oriented Programming: What is it?
- The Java Development Kit (JDK)
- JavaBeans
- What is the Java Virtual Machine (JVM)?
- Fundamentals of the Java Language
- Class Creation
- Developing Java applets for Web Use
- The Graphical User Interface
- Graphics manipulation
- How to handle I/O calls

and much, much more.

With this book and your own capability the Java language will be unleashed. The power of this language is immense, and given a helping hand you will see just how exciting programming in Java can be!

So who should be reading this book?

Exploring Java is effectively aimed at anybody interested in learning the Java language. However, there are a few questions you should be asking yourself before you opt to buy this guide. Firstly, have you ever programmed before? If the answer to this question is no then you may find yourself getting into trouble.

Now we're not saying that you won't be able to program in Java, just that you may well find yourself in too deep. Whilst this book has been written to help you learn all aspects of the Java language it does expect the reader to have programmed before. Writing software in an object oriented programming language like Java is not a simple exercise.

Whilst there are some in the computer industry that allege that Java is a language that anybody can master, with some claiming that even non-programmers can use it, this is not necessarily true. There are utilities on the market, such as Jamba from AimTech, that are designed to allow the non-programmer to assemble applets that can be embedded into a document that has been created using the HyperText Markup Language (HTML).

Now that's fine if that's all you want to do. But the Java language goes beyond that. Taking the JDK that JavaSoft provides and writing an application, whether it is a full blown program or applet for use on the Web, is not something that a non-programmer can do. Java is an easy language once you understand its design and methodology, but its not something you can embrace easily without having programmed before.

So now you've read this, and decided that you want to own this book despite the warning. Both the authors hope you find this book an informative and fun guide to the Java language. So let's move on.

When this book was written its ideal reader was selected: the Visual Basic (VB) programmer. The corporate arena is populated with programmers who have adopted the Microsoft language. Whilst VB is not the most elegant of languages it is, without a shadow of a doubt, very successful. Companies in there 1,000s have turned to it to generate applications for their business use.

It could be a simple database application, say holding a telephone directory, or it could be an advanced article tracking system which uses databases spread across multiple servers and hosts data for several hundred users. VB is, as Microsoft rightly crows about, almost ubiquitous in the business world. That is a business world that deploys Windows as its standard desktop operating system, and to date around 60m copies of Windows in its various incarnations have been shipped.

With the VB programmer in mind this book makes assumptions about a reader's ability. We are not here to give you a complete beginner guide and then expect you to walk away and create a Java application for distribution across the Internet or a corporate intranet. A VB programmer is more than likely able to make the jump across the programming gulf to embrace Java as their next language. If you are a C or C++ programmer then this book will become a great add-on to your existing knowledge of writing modular code and you should be up and running with Java pretty quickly.

Organisation: How This Book is put together

The whole purpose of *Java: A Practical Guide* is to give you the best resource available to learning Java. Therefore it has been put together in what we believe is the optimum way of learning the different parts of the language. It effectively splits into two parts which cover the following:

Part 1 – Understanding the fundamentals

This section contains the following chapters:

- *Chapter 1* is the introduction to the book that you are currently reading.
- *Chapter 2* provides an introduction to Java and the Internet. It explains the origin of the language and how it actually manages to run on all the different platforms.
- *Chapter 3* is all about Java Beans, which Java calls "an architecture and platform neutral API for creating and using dynamic Java components."
- *Chapter 4* is a discussion of Object Oriented Programming (OOP) concepts, and introduces some of the concepts that you will meet in the later chapters.
- *Chapter 5* is a guide to the Java Development Kit (JDK) and how you can install, test and then write a simple application and applet using it. The object is to get you started and to prompt you into understanding how the Java interpreter works and how the command line syntax of the JDK can be used.

Part 2 – Programming in Java

This part of the book effectively splits the language into its various components and looks at them one at a time, explaining their operation and use. You could view this part of the book as slicing up the anatomy of the Java language into bite size chunks that can be easily digested. Here is a short summary of the contents of each chapter:

- *Chapter 6* looks at the basics of the Java programming language: the structure of a Java program, statements, variables, literals, constants, expressions and operators. C and C++ programmers will find this very straightforward.

- *Chapter 7* continues with the fundamentals of Java, covering the program control flow statements: conditional statement like `if` and `switch`, and loops, such as the `for` loop and the `while` loop.

- *Chapter 8* discusses how Java implements object oriented programming techniques and covers the definition of classes and how to create new objects. Instance variables and methods are discussed and an introduction is provided to packages and interfaces.

- *Chapter 9* concentrates on strings and arrays. We look at the usual issues concerning strings: concatenations, comparisons, and substrings, and explain how arrays are created and manipulated.

- *Chapter 10* begins our look at Java applets. We take another look at the simple applet we included in the Getting started chapter and explain how applets are structured. The use of the HTML <APPLET> tag is demonstrated and the lifecycle of an applet is investigated.

- *Chapter 11* shows how text is displayed and introduces Java's colour capabilities. The standard fonts and styles are explained, as well as the methods for obtaining font information.

- *Chapter 12* concentrates on Java'a ability to draw graphical shapes. Examples of all the usual shapes are provided, including lines, rectangles, ovals, circles, arcs and polygons. A set of example methods for improving the built-in ones are included.

- *Chapter 13* is all about mouse and keyboard events and how you use them to allow the user to interact with your applets or applications.

- *Chapter 14* explains how you can download, manipulate and display images. A summary of the sound capabilities of Java is also given.

- *Chapter 15* is all about animation. It begins with an introduction to threads, and how they are indispensible when it comes to running threads in applets. Double Buffering, a method for elinating screen flicker, is explained. Four example applets are used to illustrate both text and image animation.

- *Chapter 16* is by far the largest chapter in this book. It covers just about everything you need to know about designing graphical user interfaces in Java. The following GUI building blocks – components and containers – are explained and the use of layout managers to position them within applets and windows is discussed.

- *Chapter 17* covers exception handling – the way that Java deals with errors that occur in your programs.

- *Chapter 18* looks at threads and multithreading in a little more detail. The difference between the Thread class and the Runnable interface is explained. We also talk about thread priorities, thread states, thread groups and synchronisation.

- *Chapter 19* concentrates on input and output. The two main classes – InputStream and OutputStream and their subclasses are covered in detail.

- *Chapter 20* looks at the Java networking class and shows how you can use various communications protocols to transfer data across the internet.

- The *appendices* include all the class hierarchy diagrams, a reference section for the tools provided with the JDK and a summary of the new features included with version 1.1 of the JDK.

With all that over and done with we hope you enjoy this book and welcome to the world of Java programming!

2

Introduction to Java and the Internet

The Internet

The birthplace of the Java programming language is undoubtedly the Internet, that giant network of networks that links together millions of people around the world (estimates have it that some 50m people are now linked to this entity) via a computer, modem and telephone. Over the years the Internet has grown at a staggering rate and has begun to influence the way companies look at how they will do business in the future. Just about every software developer now talks of Web-enabled applications, and most business users of computers around the world are paranoid about how/why they should use the Internet or an intranet.

Now whilst the Internet and the World Wide Web (WWW) existed without Java this programming language has had a major impact on both. You could say that Java has revolutionised the Internet and Web, that it kick started a series of changes that have dramatically altered the electronic landscape that is the Internet.

Where once you accessed the Web and were greeted with a static, quite often boring set of Web pages that are based around the Hyper-Text Markup Language (HTML). Java means that you could now access the same page and be graced with an application downloading that allows you to enter data. Alternatively, you could initiate a search for some data, or simply display an animation that has been written in the Java language.

Now you might be asking what all the interest in Java is all about? Why has it revolutionised the Internet? Why is it such a clever language?

Plus a myriad of other questions. If you're not asking these questions then all well and good, just keep reading. If you are, then hang on a moment and keep reading as well because all will become clear eventually: we promise.

There have over the years been several languages that were supposed to have revolutionised the software industry as we know it. Languages like SmallTalk and C++ were supposed to bring with them an entirely new model of developing software. Well they did and they didn't, but that's neither here nor there at the moment, although we can thank the invention of C++ for the arrival of the Java language.

SmallTalk and C++ did instigate the concept of modular programming and for that we must also thank them. It is this concept that Java builds on: blocks of code that is assembled and reused. But more of that later.

While Microsoft's Visual Basic (VB) did indeed revolutionise the market for writing applications that run on the Windows operating system, be it Windows 3.11 or Windows 95, it does have its major restrictions. VB is clumsy, not that powerful (although Microsoft has made a great change with version 5.0 of the language) and restricted to the world of Windows.

But the Internet is not a Windows only technology. The Internet embraces all computing platforms, be it the Apple Macintosh, Windows-based PCs or Unix workstations. In fact, even IBM's ancient MVS operating system which runs on its massive mainframe computers will support a Java Virtual Machine (JVM) which will allow it to run applications written using Java.

If you talk to JavaSoft it talks of the Java Platform, but what does it mean by this? In the world of computers there are a massive number of architectures with which we must deal with on a daily basis. You have Windows (16 and 32-bit), OS/2, Unix, Sun Microsystems Solaris Unix, Apple Macintosh, IBM MVS mainframes, IBM AS/400 midrange Unix-based computers, Novell Netware and a whole load of others.

That is one large problem to contend with. Now add to this the idea of writing software for all of these different operating systems, and the different implementations of the operating system on different hardware. The problem is the binary file that is created when a programming language generates an application. This binary file is machine-specific and therefore if you write a business application, say a financial package, if you want it to run on Windows and the Apple Macintosh you basically have to write two quite different versions.

Now add to this an even greater problem: the Internet. You don't get much more cross-platform than the Internet. All sorts of operating systems, all sorts of hardware and different Web browsing software. What a nightmare the industry was faced with.

When Sun Microsystems looked at the issue of cross-platform software development it took an interesting approach. How do you write an application that will run anywhere, no matter what operating system, without needing the binary to be changed? The answer is the Java Platform, and that's one reason you are reading this book now.

JavaSoft looks at the problem of software portability from what it calls *bytecode*. The way that this works is that the Java compiler creates not a binary file but a bytecode file which is not specific to any underlying physical hardware, but is created for what is known as a Java Virtual Machine (JVM). So wherever the Java Platform is written to work a Java bytecode file can operate.

So the next question is where is the Java Platform in existence? Java-Soft has moved to make sure that anyone who is anyone has made a Java JVM available for their operating system or Web browser application. These include Microsoft with Windows 95, Windows NT, IBM with OS/2 and MVS, Apple with its Macintosh MacOS software, Netscape with its Navigator software, Microsoft with its Internet Explorer 3.0 software, Novell with Netware and so on.

The way that it works is that a bytecode file created once can be deployed on any one of these operating systems or Web browsers. It's designed to offer what JavaSoft calls "Write Once, Run anywhere" capability. Each underlying hardware platform has to have had a JVM written to run on it, and this JVM must adhere to a rigid specification that JavaSoft and Sun Microsystems has laid down.

The net result is that you end up with a common, standard, uniform programming interface for generating applets and applications on any hardware platform. Well that's the theory. A developer writes an application to adhere to the Java JVM application programming interface (API) and then compiles it. Not to the hardware or a specific operating system, but to a consistent API. The bytecode does the rest because that bytecode, via the JVM, becomes specific to the hardware/operating system that it is running on.

So what is Java all about? What you have is an object oriented, multi-threaded, dynamically linked application written using Java that should run just about anywhere you want it to. Java is a very neat operating system. It has built-in security features (although many argue that Java is not that secure, but let's not worry about that for the time being), exception handling and automatic garbage collection.

Now there is a problem with Java and its JVM. Performance! By virtue of its design a bytecode compiler will never generate an application as fast as a native compiler for, say, an Intel microprocessor. So if you write an application in Visual C++ for Windows and then the same application in Java the C++ one will beat it in terms of raw performance. But there is a way around this issue. It's called a Just In Time (JIT) compiler. The JIT compiler is a clever component of Java because what it does is convert the Java bytecodes into machine language specific to the platform its running on.

Another way to create even faster code is to develop what are known as native methods – methods that have been written in C, C++ or another language which compiles to an underlying operating system – for speed and additional functionality.

Now the Java Platform is really the beginning of the Java road map and is composed of two fundamental parts:

- The Java Virtual Machine
- The Java Application Programming Interface (API)

To hear JavaSoft talk these two components provide a developer (that's you) with the fundamentals to deploy end-user runtime applications for the Internet and the intranet. Now when JavaSoft first thought about its plans for Java it really only impacted the world of the Web, although these days Java is potentially going to revolutionise all areas of software development, not just the Internet.

The Java Base Platform, as we have described so far, can be safely viewed as the bare minimum that developers need to aim for in order for their applications and applets to run safely. Inside this is the minimum set of APIs needed to run an application written in Java on any platform that supports a JVM. Developers who write to this minimum set should feel confident in their programs running anywhere without the need for extra class libraries.

As you read this book more and more APIs are being defined for the Java language. As time moves on and Java becomes more successful so the Java Base Platform will expand to encompass these extra APIs and this will be reflected with new and more powerful versions of the Java JDK.

The following is a list of companies and their products that have so far licensed the Java Base Platform from JavaSoft in order to run Java software. They are:

- **Windows**
  Microsoft   *Windows 95, Windows NT*
  IBM   *Windows 3.1*

- **Macintosh**
  Apple Computer   *MacOS*

- **OS/2**
  IBM   *OS/2*

- **Unix**
  Hewlett-Packard   *HPUX*
  Hitachi   *Hitachi OS*
  IBM   *AIX*
  Silicon Graphics   *Irix*
  SunSoft, Sun Microsystems   *Solaris*
  The Santa Cruz Operation   *Unixware*
  Tandem Computers   *Non-Stop Kernel*

- **Network OS**
  Novell   *NetWare 4.0*

- **Mainframe OS**
  IBM   *MVS*

The Future

JavaSoft has a lot of ideas and plans for Java and there is talk of having the software running all over the place. It may sound amusing, but there is no reason why you couldn't see Java inside a toaster or a television some day. JavaSoft is working on what it calls Embedded Java, which should see the software available for such devices as Network Computers (NCs), the new breed of business computers making an impact in the business world, set-top boxes, printers, copiers, smart cards and cellular phones.

Sun Microelectronics is also working on a family of microprocessor chips that can be embedded inside electronic devices to help them run Java. There are three at the moment: the picoJava, microJava and UltraJava families. The first of these, picoJava, is actually a standard specification for the design of a microprocessor that supports the Java

JVM, and this design will be made available to other electronic companies to design chips around. The chip is designed to meet the needs of the Java language, that is multithreading and garbage collection.

The other two chip designs are also based on the picoJava design and will have built-in support for the Java JVM and Java APIs embedded inside the silicon and vary wildly in design needs, ranging from their memory, communications and I/O needs.

On the software side – no hardware here – is what has become known as the JavaOS. The JavaOS is basically an operating system that implements the Java Base Platform for running Java-powered applets and applications. The JavaOS is designed to run on Network Computers and other embedded applications, such as printers, copiers and industrial controllers. The JavaOS will be widely ported to a range of microprocessors, including Sun's own chips.

Back to the language

As languages go Java is very powerful and relatively easy to program. Let's recap. Java is an object oriented language, statically typed, multithreaded, dynamically linked, and has an automatic garbage collection.

The basic syntax of Java is based around that of C and C++, so any programmer that has used either of these languages will pick Java up very easily. However, there is much less redundancy built-into Java which means that developers should be able to easily read another programmer's code. An example of this is the fact that Java has no user-defined operator overloading, as can be found in the C++ language. This is a major issue with C++ which in many ways is a sloppy language, with one programmer having a nightmare understanding the code construction of a second programmer.

Like the symbolic programming language Smalltalk, Java is object oriented, that much we have ascertained, uses a class hierarchy, single inheritance and dynamic linking. For numeric programming Java uses platform-independent data types, uses array bounds-checking and its arithmetic is IEEE defined. The result of all of this, which will mean little to many people, is that as languages go Java has a good grounding for letting developers create stable numerical algorithms. In many instances, expressions, statements and operators are almost identical to those as in the C language.

Given that Java has multithreading capability built-in, and uses a strong model of how thread-critical code can be synchronised in order to avoid timing problems, Java is well positioned to become the language with which a whole generation of new concurrent applications and services are created.

3

JavaBeans: Sun's grand new strategy for Java software creation

Introduction

Over the past few years, the concept of constructing applications by assembling re-usable software components has raised itself as a productive and accepted way to develop custom applications.

If you want to take a sideswipe at Microsoft you can talk of first generation products such as Microsoft's Visual Basic taking a step towards modular programming. With Visual Basic Microsoft introduced us to VBX components and a "forms-based" application assembly process, which did prove useful in bolting applications together quickly and easily.

Visual Basic has since been followed by products such as Borland's Delphi which further enhanced the basic component assembly application development model by adding more powerful data access components and object-oriented component extension capabilities.

But what JavaSoft is offering with Java Beans is a whole new concept, and to coin an expression that the computer industry loves, an entirely new paradigm shift.

JavaSoft calls Java Beans "an architecture and platform neutral API for creating and using dynamic Java components. Java Beans build on the strengths of the component assembly development model established by these pioneering products, and extends the power further. Application developers will be able to use a variety of development tools to assemble custom applications from fully portable Java Beans."

When you talk to JavaSoft it discusses several topics with Java Beans:

- How Java Beans extend and enhance the capabilities of the portable Java Platform
- The key elements that make up a software component model
- Highlights of Java Bean functional capabilities
- How to prepare for Java Beans
- How Java Beans Extend the Java Platform

Java Beans builds on Java's Strengths

Java has quickly established itself as the industry standard platform for building fully portable Internet and Corporate Intranet applets and applications. The Java platform provides a number of advantages to developers for these types of applications:

- *Fully portable platform:* language, libraries and virtual machine's pervasive presence of the Java platform in browsers, and soon within operating systems themselves, allows developers to write application functionality once and deploy the application broadly on a wide variety of OS and hardware platforms.
- *Powerful and compact environment:* The Java platform provides developers with the full power of an object-oriented language while eliminating the complexity, housekeeping and heavier weight object creation and registration processes required by other language and programming model environments. The lightweight runtime can be incorporated in chips for embedded systems, in PDAs as well as client and server class PCs and workstations where Java is becoming increasingly pervasive.
- *Network aware:* From its inception, the Java platform has been network aware. TCP/IP support is built in. Security mechanisms which allow full protection from applet interference with client-side data are built-in.

Finally, the platform was designed to allow applets to be built from self-describing classes which can be easily downloaded to the client-environment without the need for heavy weight installation or registration processes.

Java Beans build on all of these strengths and extends the Java platform further.

How to extend the Java Platform

Today Java applets provide a simple static component model. Applets can be placed on Web pages; however, they cannot interact with the page or with other Java applets on the page.

Java Beans enhance the Java platform by allowing richer, more dynamic interaction. Java Beans allow developers to define independent components that can be used and re-used in a variety of combinations to compose new applications inside a variety of Browser and non-Browser environments. (e.g., HotJava, Netscape Navigator, Internet Explorer, Visual Basic forms, and Claris Works).

Java Beans components can be GUI widgets, non-visual functions and services, applets and more full scale applications. Each of these components can be built by different developers at separate times. Java Beans components do not need to be part of the same application build. Instead, they communicate dynamically.

For example, let's look at a Web site which provides on-line banking services. The web site might start out allowing a user to view historical interest rate data using a graph format. This web page would include two Java Beans components: an interest rate data retrieval component and a charting component. The interest rate retrieval component retrieves data on interest rates. It then interacts dynamically with the charting component to make a graph of the data.

At some point in the future, the web site developer could add a new component that lets customers retrieve historical account balance information. The account balance data in turn can be charted by re-using the existing charting component. The developer does not need to re-build a new application that combines all three elements as one whole. Instead, the developer only needs to add the new account balance retrieval component.

Since Java Beans is part of the Java platform, the new component will be able to communicate with the older chart component dynamically as needed. Note that the charting and interest rate retrieval components could be provided by commercial software developers, and the account retrieval component might be custom built for the particular bank.

Thus, Java Beans further enhance the Java platform by adding new levels of dynamism, flexibility and re-use.

The Power of Java Beans

In keeping with the design philosophy and strengths of Java, Java Beans will be easy to build and use, compact for network deployment, and of course fully portable.

Java Beans will enable tool vendors to build more powerful, highly productive Java assembly tools. Java Beans will empower application developers to add even more exciting levels of interactivity and richer functionality to their Internet and Intranet applications.

Finally, developers will be able to re-use Java Beans in a number of popular environments, thus extending their usefulness.

4

Object Oriented Technology: What does it mean?

The Business Dilemma!

Companies are drowning. They are drowning in a flood of information that is flowing into them from a wide variety of sources. Despite the fact that computers continue to improve in speed and power at a rapid rate and are capable of handling this data, the software programs are not progressing at the same pace and are desperately struggling to cope. To be blunt, there is a software crisis!

The world of computers has long been beset by problems of keeping up with the latest technologies and integrating old systems with new. Creating new applications can be a minefield of time-consuming labour with poor end results.

For those looking to replace or update legacy systems, or integrate new technology into them, many of the PC terms can seem irrelevant and full of empty promises. One of the hottest terms in the PC market today is Object Oriented (OO) technology. But what is it, and how can it help you?

The cost of development is often difficult, or nearly impossible to calculate, but two things are certain: the cost goes up the more lines of code that are needed, and the more corrections that have to be hunted down and rewritten.

The basic claims of OO technology is simple: it simplifies development, reduces the amount of code that needs to be written and makes testing and maintenance easier. Altogether it makes for an easier life. It makes sense that, if these claims are true, OO technology reduces the cost of development.

Without a shadow of a doubt OO is the most exciting technology to hit the software industry, yet probably the single most misunderstood development in software to date. Programming has always been a long-winded painful process, so how can this OO technology deliver such a holy grail?

Once you get past the hype, you encounter the simplicity of OO technology: Rapid Application Development (RAD) and reuse. Why build something three times when you've already done the programming work somewhere else? RAD and reuse are two of the biggest buzzwords in the software industry at the moment.

OO technology takes the programming emphasis away from the lines of code that are written, and focuses on the various elements of the program, treating them as objects. Once the program objects have been determined by aligning them with the business objectives and the needs of the user, the links between the objects can be mapped out, with repetitive programming functions simply using the same object or piece of code.

As the legacy systems that are used throughout large companies have grown, they have evolved into large unstructured databases that are immensely difficult to define and control. The programs always contain duplicated logic and 'modularisation' is limited. Objects can help to untangle this web of logic and program calls, and provide a clear route to maintaining software, giving a clear view over logic and files in accordance with the business processes. Objects provide the flexibility to handle all data behaviour from simple data retrieval to complex logic.

The method behind the OO approach has been proved to help companies get the development right, if not first time, then certainly faster than projects could otherwise be completed. OO programming offers a formal design for correctness and completeness based around the business requirements, and the program structure. By its very nature OO technology allows programmers to produce flexible interfaces to proven systems.

The business benefits of OO are clear. Save time and money programming applications, reshape software to better meet the needs of users, and to better handle the flow of information through an organisation.

Through the embracing of OO technology the term 'legacy system' will eventually vanish.

A company's software should never be left behind by the information its users want access to. Because it is assembled in pieces an application should evolve on an ongoing basis.

The world of the Internet is driving the evolution of OO-based software, with applications being assembled in 'chunks' to better serve a distributed world. The term 'applets' has been coined and the online world has kick-started a revolution which will permeate its way throughout the entire software industry.

The components of OO

IT managers and departments are faced with an almost overwhelming task – to keep up with the amount of data that their companies are now producing. If you lack power in hardware the solution is simple, buy some faster, bigger systems. If you lack functionality in your software, or your databases are growing out of control the solution can take months to find, let alone produce.

And as new hardware is purchased, IT departments are running to catch up to get the software to use the full potential of the new machines.

Not since the initial days of the first BASIC program have software development projects been easy to implement. If a project does come in on time, or even on budget, there are still problems that lie ahead. With typical programming methods, even the best constructed systems confront IT managers with an iron curtain when the need arises to enhance them and add more functionality.

The basic problem of creating good working programs is keeping track of what is required, and how the different elements of the program will interact. As the size of the project grows, so does the difficulty in performing this basic but essential task. The solution, so we are told, is to break large programs into small components that can be designed and tracked far easier. Okay, and so we have modular programming – there's nothing new there. And so object oriented technology is born – it harks back to the 1950s' subroutines.

And why go back to the principles of the 1950s that have been superceded by other methods of programming? Because for all the so-called benefits that 4GL's and modern programming disciplines have promised, most programs are still built by hand, one instruction at a time. While other construction methods are available, they often produce bug-ridden software that's difficult, if not almost impossible to adapt or maintain.

But of course the data structures have become so much more complicated since the days of the subroutine. And if that was all that was needed then we wouldn't be where we are today. Software must be capable of handling a huge number of different types and sources of data, which is more often than not required by several different users, in different formats, by different parts of the program. DBMSs (database management systems) are around to help, but you still need to integrate your program with them.

The biggest challenge to IT departments today is future proofing the company's investment in technology. While for hardware it means making the right purchasing decisions, for software it means having programs that can change with the company's business.

The next step

The first object oriented programming language was developed in the late 1960s and was called Simula. This language – coupled with the invention of the subroutine back in the 1950s – were the beginnings of object oriented programming.

The most difficult problem when programming is controlling how different parts of the program interact with each other. Stopping conflicts, making sure that instructions are executed correctly, and that they can be executed at all. The basic problem with most programming is that ten lines of code to perform one task can work perfectly fine on their own, but getting them to work with ten lines of code written to perform another task that operates at the same time can cause problems. Multiply this by the thousands of tasks that are required in a business system and you see the inherent problems of programming.

So let's take the elements of OO one at a time and discuss how it all works.

The first piece to understand is, what is an Object?

"An object, simply put, can be thought of as a software "package" that is basically composed of a collection of related procedures and data. In the world of an object-oriented software approach, you can give these procedures a special name by which they can be known from here on in; they are called methods."

"The concept, and the beauty of an object, is its simple yet powerful design. The strength of **Objects** is that they make ideal software modules because they can be defined and maintained independently from one another, with each forming a neat, self-contained universe. Everything an object "knows" is expressed through its **variables**. Which leaves everything it can do to be expressed via its **methods**."

Each object contains the instructions to carry out a certain task, along with all the information and data required to do that. The key to the success of object technology is the way that the objects interact with one another. They send each other messages asking them to carry out their tasks.

This means that all one object needs to know about another is what its name is, and any additional information that tailors that object's task. For example, a boat may move from A to B picking up cargo. That boat would be an object and the tasks that it is capable of performing would be included in that object as "methods". Also included in that object would be the necessary "variables" such as the size of the boat; the maximum cargo it could carry; and its the speed, range etc.

But in the real world, things are rarely that simple. One occurrence of an object is unlikely to be sufficient. It is much more likely that several of the same types of object will be required that vary only in a small detail, but are capable of performing the same tasks.

It defeats the point somewhat if you have to redefine the same tasks and instructions in every occurrence of that object. This is where classes come in.

All the methods and variables of that type of object are grouped together to define exactly how that object may behave. These make the class that confines these objects. The objects (instances) within that class, themselves only contain their particular values for the variables in the way that they are unique.

The objects will receive a message to perform a task, and get the necessary information for that method from the class. The object will then apply its own variables to that method.

Objects, messages and classes form the basis of object oriented technology, and it was from the Simula programming techniques that objects, messages, classes and various other associated object oriented principles were born. Whilst Simula never achieved huge success as a programming language the principles that it was based on have been the foundations of a number of everyday languages

Messages

So here we have our objects, with certain variables and methods which apply to its operation and existence. These objects exist together and need each other in order to function. Objects can have a wide variety of effects on each other, including creation, destruction, forcing an action and so on. But how do objects interact with each other.

The answer is messages. Quite simply they send each other a simple message that asks them to carry out a specific method. A message is constructed of two main pieces of information: the name of the object that is then followed by a method that the object is known to be able to perform. Any other information that is needed, such as data elements that help an object perform a method, can be further expressed and these are simply known as **parameters**. The only other information you need to know is that the object that sent a message is known as the **sender** and the one that received it the **receiver**.

So if we continue our example of a cargo boat the following message could be issued by an object:

`boat10moveTopier2`

In this example the receiver object is called `boat10` and what is happening is that a method, in this case `moveTo`, has been issued which asks the boat object to move to `pier2`, with the `pier2` data being a parameter.

Classes

Now although an object may well take a wide number of forms the methods and variables within it may not differ that much from one object to another. What you don't want to happen is keep defining object after object and all the data that goes with it. So what you end up with is the ability to define a **class** of object. You can best think of a class as a kind of template that can be used to define the methods and variables that apply to a particular example of an object.

By doing this you only need to define the methods and variables of an object once, in what is known as the definition of the class. The next stage of this example is to understand that all objects that belong to a class, and known as **instances** of the class, contain only their specific values for any variables defined.

So back to our example of a cargo boat. You could define a class of boat object that represents every possible boat in the fleet, maybe you could call it AllCargoBoats, and this class would therefore contain the definitions of its methods and variables. But the individual boats in the fleet would be defined as instances of that class and then given a unique name (such as boat10, boat12 or boat16).

The way that these objects would work is that each instance has data values which pertain to its size, type, contents and so on. So when one of these boats receives a message from another object to perform a method, it would look to its class (which has already been defined at the initial creation of the object) for a definition of the method and then apply that method to the data that it holds locally.

So to sum it up, you can think of an object as the instance of a class.

OK, now let's complicate things a little. A class can also be affected by the definitions of another class. An example being, as with our original boat metaphor, of a class for a cargo boat, which we called AllCargoBoats. But this of another class which we want to be another kind of boat, which we call AllCargoBoatsBlue. In this case the class could be defined as all of the methods and variables that appeared in the first class, plus another detail: the colour Blue. This is known as **inheritance** and is a central part to object oriented programming, indeed without inheritance object programming would be neither possible or as powerful.

You can view inheritance as an automated mechanism by which one class of an object can be defined as a special case of a more general class, with its methods and variables being automatically included. This class of a class is known as a **subclass** with the first class from which the subclass has been defined being known as the **superclass**. Now subclasses are not unintelligent, and although they inherit methods and variables, they may also define their own methods and variables and if prompted to do so can override inherited characteristics.

Again keeping to our example of a cargo boat we could define a superclass, with the name AllCargoBoats and then we could define several subclasses, which we could call RoundCargoBoat, SquareCargoBoat and so on. All would inherit the methods and variables of the superclass, but also have the option to override the parent's definitions with its own.

Now as you start to make and destroy classes so you end up creating a sort of nested order, which is generally referred to as a **class hierarchy**. Through this structure the inheritance of methods and variables can be automatically rippled through all levels of classes and subclasses. You could argue that the true, core strength of an object oriented programming language is its class hierarchy.

Modular programming: madness or solution to a nightmare?

So we've gone through the pieces of an object, what forms it and what makes it tick. So let's introduce another term: **encapsulation**. This is the term that is applied to the simple packaging of data and procedures together. You can think of encapsulation as the hiding of information, and builds on the methods inside structured programming of information-hiding. Indeed in the OO world this mechanism is vastly superior to that of structured programming in that information is better pulled together and more effectively hides their details.

But what does this mean? Simply put, encapsulation is a mechanism whereby the data inside an object is only interfered with by an object's methods, with the methods prompted by messages sent from other objects. The core of this is that objects are protected. The first level of protection comes from the fact that one object cannot corrupt the variables of a second or a third object, it can merely force a method to act upon the variables.

The idea being that given that an application will undoubtedly be made up of many objects and classes, at some point an object is likely to damage the variable information of another object, by handling it incorrectly or whatever, if it had direct access. But this cannot happen because of encapsulation.

The second level of protection comes from making life much easier for objects to interact with other objects. The amount of information needed is reduced massively by encapsulation. All an object needs to know is how to ask a second object a question, or issue a message. It doesn't have to worry about how the data inside an object is stored or how it works, that's taken care of by the method which is encapsulated inside an object.

Polymorphism

The last advantage that OOP has over structured programming is known as polymorphism. The idea of polymorphism is that a class can contain methods which have the same name but with *different* parameters. A message can be sent to an object wich can react differently depending on the *signature* of the method employed – the name and parameter list of a method is known as it's signature.

For example, you might have a rectangle object that draws itself by applying the draw() method. Polymorphism allows you to define two draw() methods – one with no parameters, which draws a rectangle with a line thickness of one; and a second with an integer parameter which causes the rectangle to be drawn with a line thickness equal to the value of the integer argument.

The compiler works out which method should be called by searching upwards through the class hierarchy for a method with the correct signature. It uses the concept of late binding to include code which will determine which method should be run when the program is actually executed.

5

The JDK – Getting Started with Java

What you will need

To compile Java source code into what those familiar with Java refer to as bytecode files which a Java interpreter can run you will need the Java Developers Kit (JDK) from Sun. As well as a compiler the JDK also contains a stand-alone Java interpreter and other tools to aid the development process. It is the creation of bytecode that gives the Java language its ability to run across several operating systems effectively unchanged.

The JDK also includes a program called AppletViewer which will allow you to test any Java applets you write. However, the AppletViewer does not display anything else you might have included in the HTML page so, to obtain full interaction between a HTML page and a Java applet you will need a Web browser that is Java-aware. At the moment the main Java-enabled browsers are Netscape Navigator version 2 and above and Microsoft's Internet Explorer 3.

Platform availability

At the time of writing the JDK version 1.0.2 is available for the following platforms:

- Microsoft Windows 95/NT
- Sun Solaris 2.3, 2.4, 2.5 SPARC
- Sun Solaris 2.5 X86
- Mac OS

Note   This is the version of Java that we have used for this book. To find out the new features that are included in version 1.1 and an important note regarding the conversion of 1.0.2 source files to the 1.1 API, see Appendix C.

The JDK version 1.1 has just been released for the following platforms:

- Microsoft Windows 95/NT
- Sun Solaris 2.4, 2.5 SPARC
- Sun Solaris 2.5 X86

Obtaining and installing the JDK

The CD

The CD supplied with this book includes both Windows 95/NT versions. See Appendix D for installation instructions.

Downloading the JDK

The JDK can be downloaded from the JavaSoft site at Sun Microsystems: `http://java.sun.com` Full instructions are given for downloading the JDK for your particular platform and various ftp sites around the world are listed which won't be quite as busy as the main Sun site. Sun Microsystems and its software subsidiary JavaSoft are very open to making the SDK available to all and sundry.

Unpacking the file

The downloaded JDK is a self-extracting archive file. The archive file should be executed from the root directory of the C: drive. It will extract the JDK files into a parent directory that is simply called `Java`. If you want to place the JDK in a different directory, create it and run the archive file from that directory. The files will then be unpacked into a Java directory under your chosen directory name.

Note   Two ZIP files will be created when you unpack the archive: `src.zip` and `lib\classes.zip`. The `src.zip` file contains source code for some of the Java class libraries and may be unzipped if you want to examine the source. The `classes.zip` file ***must not*** be unzipped however.

= zipped

Environment variables

After the files have been unpacked you must edit the AUTOEXEC.BAT file to add the Java\bin directory to the path. (If you unpacked the JDK into a different directory you will obviously need to include that directory name in the Path statement.) Please make sure that you follow this closely, as an error in this Path entry will stop the JDK from working.

A CLASSPATH environment variable must also be included in your AUTOEXEC.BAT file. This should be defined as:

```
CLASSPATH=C:\JAVA\LIB\CLASSES.ZIP
```

Once you have made the changes to the AUTOEXEC.BAT file you must reboot your computer for the changes to take effect. Again if you made the host directory name different when you installed Java you must make sure that your Java CLASSPATH entry matches.

Your first Java application

We will begin by creating a stand-alone Java application. The following commands must be run from the command line. First of all, create a directory under your main Java directory called JavaApps. Enter the following program source code using any text editor you are comfortable with: this could be from within Windows 95 using Notepad or Wordpad, or even from MS-DOS using the EDITOR.EXE file which is normally used to edit the CONFIG.SYS or AUTOEXEC.BAT files. The file must be saved as plain ASCII text.

Listing 5.1: *A simple application to display a line of text*

```
Class FirstJavaApp
    {
    public static void main (String args[ ])
        {
        System.out.println("My First Java Application.");
        }
    }
```

Once you have entered the code, save the file as FirstJavaApp.java in the directory \Java\JavaApps.

Don't be too concerned about what the program code means at the moment – it will be explained in future chapters. The aim of this section is to familiarise you with the process of entering the source code for a Java application, compiling it and running the program using the Java Interpreter. It will also confirm that the JDK has been set up properly.

To compile the source code enter the following command from the \Java\JavaApps directory:

```
javac FirstJavaApp.java
```

If the file has compiled without any errors a Java bytecode file called FirstJavaApp.class will have been created in the directory. If the compiler reports an error, check that you have entered the code exactly as it is shown above and re-compile it. You must be specific about how you enter the file inside your text editor – Java is a programming language that requires its syntax to be closely followed.

To run the Java application you have just created you need to use the Java Interpreter that is included in the JDK. Enter the following command:

```
java FirstJavaApp
```

You should then see the text "My First Java Application" displayed on the screen. Alright so this is far from a marvellous piece of programming but you just took your first step down the world of Java programming that must be worth something. Having now checked that the JDK is installed and working you are ready to move on to something far more complex. But for the immediate future don't be too concerned that you are not totally understanding of what is going on. This will become clear in later chapters.

Your first Java applet

We will now compile and run a Java applet – the Java programs that can be embedded in Web pages, downloaded and displayed by Java-aware Web browsers. Although the Java language is fundamentally a full-blown development tool that can be used to assemble applications in their own rights, it is the Internet and the World Wide Web (WWW) which offers a massive arena of development for Java. In many cases it is the creation of applets that will give you experience writing code using the Java JDK.

You see, while Java is a full blown language it needs to mature a little more before the vast majority of programmers start knocking together BIG applications in Java. Where most programmers start is in the creation of applets, which can be thought of as an entry point into Java programming.

In the world of business users the Internet and Web have made great headway. From humble beginnings the Web has infiltrated its way into many companies and these companies are investing heavily in the assembly of Web sites or internal intranets. In a bid to automate these Web sites the Java language is being employed to create applets that are appearing all over the world.

But let's move on. Create another directory under your main Java directory and call it JavaApplets. Enter the following code using your text editor:

Listing 5.2: *A simple applet to display a line of text on a Web page – see Figures 5.1 and 5.2*

```
import java.awt.Graphics;
public class FirstJavaApplet extends java.applet.Applet
    {
    public void paint(Graphics g)
        {
        g.drawString("My First Java Applet", 20, 25);
        }
    }
```

Save as FirstJavaApplet.java in the \Java\JavaApplets directory.

Java applets are compiled in the same way as Java applications – by running the Java compiler javac. Enter the following command from the \Java\JavaApplets directory:

```
javac FirstJavaApplet.java
```

If the file has compiled without any errors a Java bytecode file called FirstJavaApplet.class will have been created in the directory. If the compiler reports an error, check that you have entered the code exactly as it is shown above and re-compile it. As with any language syntax is critical and commands must always be entered correctly, with brackets and commas and so on in place.

To test the applet you will have to create a HTML page. Enter the following text and save it in a file called FirstJavaApplet.html:

```
<HTML>
<HEAD>
<TITLE>Java applet test page</TITLE>
</HEAD>
<BODY>
```

```
<H1>A test page for my Java applet<BR>
</H1>
<P>
This is the output from a Java applet:<BR>
<BR>
<APPLET CODE="FirstJavaApplet.class" WIDTH=150 HEIGHT=50>
</APPLET>
</BODY>
</HTML>
```

You can see the results of running this Java applet by using either the AppletViewer program or the Netscape Web Browser or Microsoft Internet Explorer 3.0.

Using the AppletViewer

From the \Java\JavaApplets directory enter the following command:

```
appletviewer FirstJavaApplet.html
```

Here is what you should see:

Figure 5.1:

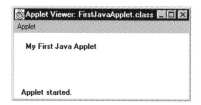

As you can see the HTML page was read by AppletViewer and interpreted for the screen. Again this is far from being a killer application, but demonstrates a couple of the features of Java, such as calling a graphics class library to display the text. What you have just done is create a cross platform application, albeit a simple one. You did not need to know how to create and display that text inside Windows, Unix or any other operating system that has Java support embedded into it. The power of Java becomes clear!

Using Netscape Navigator 3.0

Start the Netscape Web browser and from the File menu, select Open File. Move to the \Java\JavaApplets directory and choose the FirstJavaApplet HTML page. The page should look something like this:

Figure 5.2:

Tools of the trade

The JDK comes with a variety of tools that allow you to compile your applications or applets. They are as follows:

- **java** – the Java Interpreter
- **javac** – the Java Compiler
- **javadoc** – the Java API Documentation Generator
- **javah** – C Header and Stub File Generator
- **javap** – the Java Class File Disassembler
- **jdb** – the Java Debugger
- **appletviewer** – the Java Applet Viewer

The documentation for these programs has been included in Appendix B.

Summary

This chapter has covered installation of the Java Developer's Kit and presented simple examples of a Java application and a Java applet. The purpose of including these example programs is to make sure that you have correctly installed the JDK and understand how to compile and run a Java program.

We now move on to an in-depth study of Java programming in the next section of the book.

Part 2

Programming in Java

6

Java Language Basics (Part 1)

Introduction

We begin our in-depth study of the Java programming language with a look the basics of the language. The topics discussed will include:

- the basic structure of a Java application
- statements;
- comments;
- variables;
- literals;
- keywords;
- conversions;
- constants;
- expressions;
- operators.

We will assume that you already know how to program in at least one other high-level language such as C, C++, Pascal or Visual Basic. Due to the similarity between Java and C or C++, users of those languages will probably only have to skim this chapter to pick up the small differences that do exist. As for the Visual Basic programmer, you will notice significant differences to what you are accustomed to, but as you follow this book it will become a lot clearer.

Basic Structure of a Java Application

We will start by looking at the simple Java application from the Getting Started chapter and explain the component parts of the program. We will not go into great detail concerning object-orientated concepts here (that will be covered in a later chapter) – the purpose of this section is to get you familiar with the *structure* of a Java program.

This is the code for the first application which displayed the line, My First Java Application, on the console:

```
class FirstJavaApp
    {
    public static void main (String args[ ])
        {
        System.out.println("My First Java Application.");
        }
    }
```

The first line `class FirstJavaApp` defines a class `FirstJavaApp`. The body of the class `FirstJavaApp` is contained in the first and last braces. One of the main differences between Java and other languages is that everything in a Java program must be inside one or more class definitions. This includes all functions or procedures (known as methods in Java) and all variables.

The four lines of code within the class define a method called `main()`. Every Java application must have a `main()` method as this is where the Java interpreter starts to run the program. (This does not, however, apply to Java applets. We will cover applets in detail later.) The name of the Java source code file must always be the same as the name of the class which contains the `main()` method, with the extension `.java`. In this instance, the name of the source code file is `FirstJavaApp.java`.

Note   The Java compiler is case-sensitive so the file name must be the same mixture of upper and lower case characters.

The modifier keywords, `public static void`, in the `main()` method definition will be explained when we talk about class definitions in the next chapter. The `main()` method has a single argument passed to it – `string args[]` – which is an array of strings. The string array consists of the command-line arguments typed after the class (ie. application) name. Unlike the similar arguments passed in C, the first string of the array is the first argument, not the name of the program itself.

The body of the `main()` method definition is, like the class definition, enclosed in braces. In this case, it only contains one statement, to display on the console the string:

```
"My First Java Application."
```

A full explanation of class definitions, variables and methods will be given in a later chapter.

Statements

All statements in Java must end with a semi-colon (`;`). The semi-colon is not used as a statement separator as it is in Pascal – it must follow every statement. As in C and C++ it is possible to denote an empty statement, which does nothing, by including a semi-colon by itself.

Statements may be combined into compound statements, or blocks, by enclosing them in braces:

```
{
statement 1;
statement 2;
statement 3;
statement 4;
}
```

Blocks can be used wherever a single statement is used.

Comments

Comments in programming code are indispensable and should be used as extensively as possible. As well as providing a lifeline for other programmers trying to understand your code, they can be extremely useful for reminding you what a particular block of coding does in your own programs. Comments are not included in the compiled program so there are no disadvantages involved.

There are three ways of adding comments in Java. The first, and simplest, method is a `//`, for comments that are only on one line:

```
class FirstJavaApp // This is my first Java program
  {
  public static void main (String args[ ])
    {
```

```
        // The following line displays a message
        System.out.println("My First Java Application.");
        }
    }
```

The comment can either follow some code or can be on a separate line. A carriage return or line feed marks the end of the comment.

The second type, for larger comments, is the use of /* at the start of a comment and */ to mark the end:

```
/* The following section of code will display a message to the
console and is the first Java program I have written */
class FirstJavaApp
    {
    public static void main (String args[ ])
        {
        System.out.println("My First Java Application.");
        }
    }
```

The third type of comment allows you to automatically generate documentation using the javadoc application. For this you have to use a /** at the start and a */ at the end of the comment. We will cover the javadoc application in the chapter on Java tools later in the book.

Variables

Variables are locations in memory that can be named and used to temporarily store information. Every variable must have a name and must also be declared as a particular data type. During the life of a program values may be assigned to variables and can be changed at any time.

There are three different kinds of variable in Java programming: *instance variables*, *class variables* and *local variables*.

object ..... = instance variable
globle   class variable
method   Local variable

- *Instance variables* are used within class definitions to define the properties of an object, ie. its current state.
- *Class variables* are also defined within classes but their values apply to the class itself and not to individual objects. They are the nearest thing to global variables in Java. We will be covering instance and class variables in the chapter on classes and objects in Java.

■ *Local variables* are declared within method definitions and behave like local variables in C. They will cease to exist once the method has finished executing them.

Variable Names

Variable names must follow the rules for all identifiers in Java – the following rules therefore also apply to names of classes and methods. They must begin with a letter ('A' to 'Z', 'a' to 'z'), an underscore character ('_') or a dollar sign ('$'). This may be followed by any combination of letters or digits ('0' to '9') and can be of any length. Symbols, such as '@' and '+' cannot be used.

All the characters in a variable name are significant. Variable names are also case-sensitive. Therefore, count, Count, COUNT and cOuNt are all different.

Variable Types

The type of a variable determines what kind of data can be stored in it and the range of values which can legally be assigned to that variable.

Java, like most other programming languages, is a strongly typed language. This means that all variables must be explicitly declared to be of a particular type before they can be used. (Visual Basic, on the other hand, allows variables to be declared implicitly, ie. the variable can be used in the program without it being declared beforehand.)

There are two main types of data in Java: *primitive* and *complex*.

■ *Primitive* types (also known as *simple* types) are the fundamental building blocks of Java. There are eight different types: four integer types, two floating-point types, a character type and a boolean type.

■ The *complex* (or *composite*) types consist of classes, arrays and interfaces. These are built on the primitive types and will be discussed in later chapters. This chapter will cover all the primitive types.

Integer types

Integers are whole numbers which cannot have fractional parts. There are four kinds of integer: byte, short, int and long. Their sizes are, respectively, 1 byte (8 bits), 2 bytes (16 bits), 4 bytes (32 bits) and 8 bytes (64 bits). All integers in Java are signed (ie. they can be positive or negative) and cannot be made unsigned. (There is no `unsigned` keyword as there is in C). The following table summarises the integer types.

Table 6.1: *Integer types*

Type	Size	Range from	Range to
byte	8 bits	-128	127
short	16 bits	-32768	32767
int	32 bits	-2147483648	2147483647
long	64 bits	-9223372036854775808	9223372036854775807

In C and C++ the size of an integer often depends on the operating system or the machine being used – an integer of type `int` might be 16 bits on one system and 32 bits on another. As it was designed to be platform independent, the storage allocated for each kind of integer in Java is fixed.

Floating-point types

To denote numbers with fractional parts, Java provides two kinds of floating-point types: `float` and `double`. They are also known as, respectively, single-precision and double-precision numbers. Floating-point types in Java are defined by the IEEE 754 specification. Table 6.2 shows the storage requirements and the possible range of values.

Table 6.2: *Floating point types*

Type	Size	Range from	Range to
float	32 bits	$\pm 3.40282347E+38$	$\pm 1.40239846E\text{-}45$
double	64 bits	$\pm 1.79769313486231570E+308$	$\pm 4.94065645841246544E\text{-}324$

Character type

The character type in Java, `char`, utilises the Unicode encoding scheme and requires 2 bytes.

The Unicode system was developed to handle all the possible characters in every language throughout the world and the 2-byte code provides 65,536 characters. This compares with the standard ASCII/

ANSI codes used in other languages, which only use a 1-byte code and allows for only 255 characters.

The first 255 characters of the Unicode character set are, in fact, the same as the standard ASCII set. Therefore, if you are only using Latin characters you won't have to work any differently. Normal characters such as 'A' or '$' are still valid in the Unicode system. To refer to characters using the Unicode code you have to prefix a 4 digit hexadecimal code with a \u. For instance, the character 'A' in the ASCII/ANSI character set is hex 41. In the Unicode scheme this character can be referenced using the code '\u0041'.

Boolean type

The boolean type is used for variables or expressions which can have the value `true` or `false`. The results of tests using the relational operators such as < and == are boolean values.

Note   Boolean variables can only have the values `true` and `false` in Java. In C there is no boolean type – a zero denotes false and a non-zero value denotes true. This means that you can use the result of a numerical computation in a test expression and, depending on whether the result of the expression is zero or non-zero, false or true will be indicated. In C++ the type `bool` has been added to provide true and false values but you can still use numbers in test conditions. That is not the case in Java – the result of a test expression must be `true` or `false`, numeric values cannot be used.

Declaring Variables

All variables must be declared before they can be used. When a variable is declared, Java reserves the required amount of space in memory, assigns that space a data type, and gives it the name you have used.

A variable declaration consists of the type of the variable followed by a name:

    type *varname*;

Here are some examples

```
int count;
float salary;
boolean hasPassed;
```

Although you can declare a variable anywhere in a block of code (as long as it is declared before it is first referenced), it is standard practice to declare all local variables at the start of a method definition:

```
public static void main (String args[ ])
    {
    int numFiles;
    char initial;
    ...
    }
```

A number of variables of the same type can be declared on one line as follows:

```
int numFiles, numDirs, numDrives;
double accBalance, overdraftLimit;
```

In a VB program the above code would result in the variables numDirs, numDrives and overdraftLimit, defaulting to type Variant. In Java, as in C and C++, all the variables take on the type specified at the start of a line.

Assigning Values to Variables

Local variables must be assigned an initial value before they can be referenced. (You will get a compiler error if you try accessing the value of an unassigned variable.) Java does not automatically set default values. This is not the case, however, with instance and class variables. The compiler assigns initial values to them depending on their type: all numeric variables are initialised to 0, characters are set to '\0' and boolean values are set to false. You may assign a value to a variable using the assignment operator, =.

The syntax is

```
varname = value;
```

For instance:

```
int numFiles; // variables must be declared first
boolean hasPassed;
char initial;
...
...
numFiles = 0; // and then assigned values
hasPassed = false;
```

```
initial = 'T';
```

Variables can be given values when they are declared:

```
int count = 1;
float interestRate = 10.75;
```

If you declare more than one variable on a line and give them all values you must be careful to do so explicitly:

```
int numFiles = 0, numDirs = 0, numDrives = 0;
```

The following will only assign a value to the variable k :

```
int i, j, k = 10;
```

Scope of variables

The scope of a variable determines the specific part of the program in which the variable is valid. A variable is only valid within the block in which it is declared. A block is surrounded braces { }. Therefore, if a variable is declared at the start of a class method definition it will be valid throughout the method (except in special circumstances explained shortly), and if it is declared at the start of a block of statements it will only be valid in that block. The following examples should illustrate the rules of scope:

```
class FirstJavaApp
   {
   public static void main (String args[ ])
      {
      int i; //this variable can be used within the main()
      // method
      ...
      }
   }
```

In this example the variable i declared in the main() method can only be referenced in that method because the second() method is not included in main(). Likewise, j is only valid in the second() method:

```
class AnotherExample
   {
   public static void main (String args[ ])
      {
      int i;   // this variable can be used within the main()
```

```
                // method but not in the second() method
        ...
   }
public void second ( )
   {
   int j;   // this variable can be used within the second()
            // method but not in the main() method
   ...
   }
}
```

Here we have an example of a variable being declared at the start of a block of statements. It shows a for loop where the index variable count, is declared within the loop initialisation. The variable count will only be in scope for the duration of the loop:

```
for (int count = 0; count < 10; count++)
   {
   // the count declared in the for loop is now in scope
   ...
   }
```

The following illustrates what happens if you declare a variable at the start of a method and then declare another variable with the same name inside a block within that method. While the program is executing the code within the inner block the first variable is hidden and cannot be accessed:

```
class FirstJavaApp
   {
   public static void main (String args[ ])
      {
      int count; //this variable is in scope at the moment
      ...
      for (int count = 0; count < 10; count++)
         {
         // the count declared in the for loop is now in scope
         // and the first count is hidden
         ...
         }
      // we are out of the for loop so the original count is
      // back in scope
      }
   }
```

The best thing to do to avoid this sort of situation is to make every variable name unique within a program.

Literals

The explicit values assigned to variables are called literals. Most of the time the literals you use will be simple values such as the number 28 or the character 'a'. We will now cover the most common representaions of literal values as well as some of the special options.

Integer literals

Integer literals can be expressed in decimal (base 10), hexadecimal (base 16), or octal (base 8) format. Decimal numbers have any combination of digits as long as the leading digit is not a 0. For example, 20 or 64. Octal numbers are denoted by a leading 0 followed by any combination of digits between 0 and 7 – for example, the decimal numbers 20 and 64 would be 024 and 0100 respectively in octal. Hexadecimal numbers consist of a leading 0x or 0X followed by any digits between 0 and 9 and the letters a to f or A to F to denote the digits from 10 to 15. The same decimal numbers, 20 and 64, would be 0x14 and 0x40 in hexadecimal.

Literals may be assigned to integer types `byte` and `short` if they are small enough, otherwise an `int` type will be assumed. If you want to force a small number to a `long` you can do so by appending a L or l to that number. For instance, 0L or 64l.

Floating-point literals

Floating-point literals, used to represent numbers with fractional parts, are usually presented in the standard format of a whole-number part, a decimal point and a fractional part. For example, 3.141 or 34.672. Scientific notation can also be used by including an exponent, 8.456E4 or 4.238e-5, for instance.

The standard floating-point literal is the double-precision type `double`. You can force a number to be a single-precision type `float` by using the suffix f or F, as in 34.672F or 4.238e-5f. (`Doubles` may also be given the optional suffix d or D.)

Character literals

A character literal can be expressed either as a character enclosed in single quotes – 't', '5' and '%' – or as an escape sequence enclosed in single quotes to represent any characters from the Unicode character set. The following table lists the various control characters that can be represented using the escape codes:

Table 6.3: *Control characters and escape codes*

Escape sequence	Designation	Description
\b	BS	Backspace
\t	HT	Horizontal tab
\n	NL (or LF)	Newline (or linefeed)
\f	FF	Form feed
\r	CR	Carriage return
\"	"	Double quote
\'	'	Single quote
\\	\	Backslash
\ddd	0ddd	Octal
\xdd	0xdd	Hexadecimal
\udddd	0xdddd	Unicode character

Boolean literals

The boolean type can have two literal values, true and false.

Keywords

The following list contains all the reserved keywords in Java that cannot be used as identifiers for variables, classes or methods.

abstract	boolean	break	byte
byvalue*	case	cast*	catch
char	class	const*	continue
default	do	double	else

extends	final	finally	float
for	future*	generic*	goto*
if	implements	import	inner*
instanceof	int	interface	long
native	new	operator*	outer*
package	private	protected	public
rest*	return	short	static
super	switch	synchronized	this
throw	throws	transient	try
var*	void	volatile	while

* keywords not used in Java 1.0 but reserved for future use.

Conversions

If you are performing binary operations on two numeric variables, eg. multiplying or adding two numbers, and the types are different, Java will automatically treat the result of the operation as the larger of the two types. For instance, if you are multiplying a `long` by an `int` the result will be treated as a `long`. Likewise, if you are multiplying a `double` by a `float` the result will be treated as a `double`. This applies to all numeric types. If you want to force a conversion from a larger type to a smaller one (eg. double to float, or long to int) you can *cast* it. Casting is accomplished by placing the target type in parenthesis before the variable name. For example:

```
long largeValue = 1760;
int smallValue;
smallValue = (int) largeValue;
```

will assign the value held in the `long` to the integer variable.

Note Java won't mind if you cast a number held in a `long` variable to an `int` if it is out of the range of the `int`. The result will be truncated to a number with a different value. If you use casting to convert from a floating-point number to an integer, the fractional part of the number will be lost. For instance,

```
float fractnumber = 6.6666;
int wholeNumber = (int) fractNumber;
```

and will result in the integer variable `wholeNumber` having the value 6.

Because boolean values can only be `true` or `false` you cannot cast between boolean and any numeric type.

If you are assigning a value of a variable from one numeric type to another and the target type is of a greater magnitude than Java will automatically convert it to the larger type.

This applies from a byte type to a short, from a short to an int, from an int to a long, from a long to a float and from a float to a double.

Constants

Although the word const is a reserved keyword in Java, it is not currently used for anything. You can, however, define constants by using the keywords static final. A constant defined in this way will be available to all the methods in the class. It is a convention of Java that CAPITAL letters are used for constants. The following piece of example illustrates the use of the keywords to define the constants PI and INTEREST_RATE:

```
class ConstantExamples
    {
    static final double PI = 3.1415;
    static final float INTEREST_RATE = 7.75;
    ...
    }
```

const =

const global

If you want a constant to be global, i.e. available to all classes in a program, you must use the keywords public static final. The full meaning of these modifier keywords will be explained in later chapters.

Expressions

Expressions specify calculations which will return a value. The result value is computed by combining values with operators. An *operator* specifies an operation to be carried out on one or more values or *operands*. The most common forms of expressions are arithmetic operations and tests for equality or inequality. The following are examples of expressions:

6 + 12   (6 and 12 are the operands, + is the operator)
-1   (The operator is minus, the operand is 1)
7 / 2   (7 and 2 are operands, / is the operator)

Variables and literals often form expressions:

```
x + 9
average / 2
```

Relational and boolean expressions return true or false as a result:

```
age == average
x && y
```

Operators

Java operators are almost all the same as those found in C. They can be split into arithmetic, assignment, incremental and decremental, relational and boolean.

Arithmetic operators

These standard arithmetic operators are available:

Addition	+
Subtraction	-
Multiplication	*
Division	/
Remainder (or modulus)	%

They all require two operands, with the exception of the subtraction operator which can also be used as a unary operator to negate a single operand. When the division operator is used with floating-point numbers, a floating-point result will be obtained. When used with integers, the result is an integer and any remainder is ignored.

For instance, 38 / 7 will give the result 5. To obtain the remainder, the modulus operator can be used. For example, 38 % 7 is 2.

Arithmetic between an integer and a floating-point number will give you a floating-point result.

Assignment operators

The standard assignment operator, which we have covered earlier, is =.

Shortcuts can be obtained for all of the binary arithmetic operators by combining each operator with the = operator in the following way:

```
x += 2       is equivalent to    x = x + 2
x -= 2            "              x = x - 2
```

```
x *= 2          "          x = x * 2
x /= 2          "          x = x / 2
x %= 2          "          x = x % 2
```

Incremental and decremental operators

The C and C++ incremental and decremental operators, ++ and --, are also available in Java. The ++ operator increments a variable by 1 and the -- operator decrements a variable by 1. For example, x++ results in the value of x being incremented by 1 and x-- results in x being decremented by 1.

These operators can be used as prefix or postfix operators. When you are just incrementing or decrementing a value, it doesn't matter which you use, prefix or postfix, because the value will be incremented or decremented accordingly. However, if you are assigning the result of an incremental or decremental operation to another variable, it becomes very important. For example, the following expression, using the incremental operator in prefix mode, will increment the value of y before assigning the result to the variable x:

```
x = ++y;
```

whereas the expression:

```
x = y++;
```

will assign the value of y to x and then increment y. This can obviously lead to confusing results if the user is not fully aware of the order in which events happen.

Relational operators

The following relational or comparison operators all return a boolean value, true or false:

Equal	==
Not equal	!=
Greater than	>
Less than	<
Greater than or equal to	>=
Less than or equal to	<=

Therefore, to test for, say, equality, you would use the expressions

```
i == 0 or count == 100
```

Note The equality operator == has always been a major source of bugs in C and C++ code due to programmers only using one equals sign, =. For example, if, in the test condition

(x == 10)

one of the equals sign is omitted so that it becomes

(x = 10)

the expression always evaluates to a non-zero result, which, in C and C++ is a true result. This cannot happen in Java because the numeric result cannot be converted into a boolean value when the code is compiled.

Boolean operators

It is possible to combine two expressions that produce boolean values as results using the boolean, or logical, operators: && for AND combinations, || for OR combinations, and ^ for the XOR operator.

Using the && operator with two operands will result in a true value if both operand expressions result in a true value. If either is false then the entire expression will be false. As in C, the left side of the expression is evaluated first, and, if the result is false, the whole expression will return false and the right side of the expression will not be evaluated.   *short circuit*

Combining two expressions with the || operator will result in a true value if either of the operands are true. As with the && operator, the left side of the expression is evaluated, and, if it is true then the entire expression will be true and the right operand will not be evaluated.

0 1
1 0 *^ returns true*

The XOR operator ^, will return true only if the two operand expressions are different – one must be true and the other false.

You can also use the NOT operator !, with a single argument to negate the value of the expression. For instance, if the variable hasPassed is true, then !hasPassed is false. If the expression is false then using ! will produce a true value.

Java also provides bitwise operators, which act upon individual bits in integers. The following all behave as they do in C and C++:

Bitwise AND   &
BitwiseOR |
BitwiseXOR   ^

Bitwise complement (XOR) ~
Left shift   <<
Right shift   >>

Java adds the zero fill right shift >>>, which fills the top bits with zero, ie. it treats the value being shifted as an unsigned integer, rather than extending the sign bit into the top bits. All of the above, with the exception of the bitwise complement, can be combined with the assignment operator =.

no Shortcurcuit

When the bitwise operators & and | are applied to integers, they behave as described above. However, if they are applied to boolean types, they behave in the same way as the logical AND and OR operators && and ||. The difference is that both sides of the expression are evaluated before the result of the whole expression is returned, even if the left operand has already determined the final result.

Operator precedence

The order in which operations are carried out is determined by the operator precedence, the higher the precedence of an operator, the earlier it will be carried out. For instance, the multiplication operator * takes precedence over the addition operator +. Therefore, in the expression

```
6 + 12 * 2
```

the multiplication would be carried out first, followed by the addition, yielding a result of 30. Parentheses can be used within an expression to overcome the priorities of operators:

```
(6 + 12) * 2
```

produces the result 36. The following list shows the hierarchy of operators in Java:

```
++--+ -  ~  !  (type)
*/ %
+-
<<>>>>>
<<=> >=
==!=
&
^

|
```

```
&&
||
?:
=+=-= *= /= %= &= |= ^= <<=>>=>>>=
```

Those operators on the same line are processed from left to right except for the operators on the top line which are right associative and are processed from right to left.

Summary

This chapter has formed an introduction to the fundamentals of the Java programming language.

We began by looking at the basic structure of a Java application: how all the functions and variables must be contained within one or more class definitions and that every Java application must contain a `main()` method.

We then went on to explain how Java implements the standard building blocks of all programming languages: statements, variables, literals, constants, expressions and operators. In the next chapter we will continue our look at the basics of Java by examining how you control the flow of a Java program.

7

Java Language Basics (Part 2)

Program Control Flow

Control flow in Java is based upon the usual conditional statements and loops found in most programming languages. C and C++ programmers in particular need only skim this chapter as the differences between control flow in Java and control flow in those two languages are minimal.

Conditional Statements

Conditional statements are used to give your program the ability to run some parts of the code but not others depending on the conditions you define. The decision making statements available to you in Java are almost identical to those found in C:

```
if
if...else
switch...case
```

The if statement

The if conditional statement allows you to run or not run a block of code based on the evaluation of a test expression. If the test expression is true, then the code in the statement (or block statement) following the if statement is run. If the test expression is false, the code is ignored.

The syntax of the if statement is

```
if (expression)
   statement; // if expression is true this statement
              // is executed
```

or, if you want to execute more than one statement if a a condition is true,

```
if (expression)
   {
   statement block  // if expression is true all the
   }                 // statements in this block are executed
```

Here are some examples of the if statement:

```
if (bankBalance <= 0)
   overdrawn = true;// single statement
if (examScore >= 50)
   {                      // block statement
   passedExam = true;
   System.out.println("Congratulations, you have passed.");
   }
```

The if...else statement

The else keyword can be added to the if conditional to allow another statement (or block statement) to be run if the test expression is false.

The syntax of the if...else statement is

```
if (expression)
   statement;// if expression is true this is executed
else
      statement;// if expression is false this is executed
```

As with the simple if statement, statement blocks can be used instead of either single statement or both.

Here are some examples:

```
if (length == width)
   System.out.println("This is a square");
else
   System.out.println("This is a rectangle");
```

```
if (examScore >= 50)
   {
   passedExam = true;
   System.out.println("Congratulations, you have passed.");
   }
else
   {
   passedExam = false;
   System.out.println("I'm afraid you have failed.");
   }
```

If you want to test a variable against a number of different values you can string a series of if...else statements together. For example:

```
if (key == 'A')
   System.out.println("American Express");
else if (key == 'M')
   System.out.println("Mastercard");
else if (key == 'V')
   System.out.println("Visa");
else
      System.out.println("Cash");
```

The expressions in the example above are evaluated in order; when any expression is found to be true the statement following that expression is executed and the chain of if statements is terminated. If none of the expressions are true the statement associated with the last else will be executed. You should be careful when using nested if statements like the example above, especially if you omit an else. When this happens an else is associated with the closest previous if which doesn't have an else itself. For example, in

```
if (numDirs > 0)
   if (numFiles == 0)
      System.out.println("There are no files present");
else
   System.out.println("There are no directories present");
```

the else actually goes with the second if, and an erroneous message will be displayed. You must use braces to force the proper association:

```
if (numDirs > 0)
   {
   if (numFiles == 0)
      System.out.println("There are no files present");
```

```
    }
  else
    System.out.println("There are no directories present");
```

If you are in any doubt as to which statements will be executed in a nest of if statements, always make the associations explicit by including braces.

The switch statement

If you want to test a variable against a number of different values you can use nested if statements. However, this can become extremely unwieldly if there are more than say, four tests, to perform. An alternative is provided by the switch statement. This has the following syntax:

```
switch (choice)
    {
    case value1:
      statement1;
      break;
    case value2:
      statement2;
      break;
    case value3:
      statement3;
      break;
    default:
      default statement;
    }
```

The value of the variable choice is compared with each of the case values. If a match is found the statement or statements following the case are executed. If no match is found then the statement(s) following the default label is executed. The break keyword must follow the statements otherwise execution will carry on with the statements associated with the next case. Note that braces are not required to encompass a block of statements. Here is an example of a switch statement:

```
switch (key)
    {
    case 'A':
      System.out.println("American Express");
      break;
    case 'M':
```

```
        System.out.println("Mastercard");
        break;
    case 'V':
        System.out.println("Visa");
        break;
    default:
        System.out.println("Cash");
    }
```

Although it can appear much neater than a nested if statement, the switch statement has a number of disadvantages. The test can only be carried out on the simplest primitive types: byte, short, int and char. Also, you can only test for equality, ie. you cannot use operators like < and >. One useful feature is that you can have a particular statement executed when the test matches a number of case values. For instance, in this example, the switch statement is testing for special characters. The key thing here is that, once a match has been found processing just drops through until the next break statement is encountered.

```
    switch (charValue)
        {
        case '\t':
        case '\r':
        case '\n':
            System.out.println("This is a white space character");
            break;
        case ',':
        case '.':
        case ';':
            System.out.println("This is a punctuation character");
            break;
        default:
            System.out.println("This is any other character");
        }
```

The default label is optional. Without a default label, if no matches occur, no action will take place within the switch statement.

The Conditional Operator

Although it is an expression, meaning that it returns a value, we have included the conditional operator in this section as it is a form of control flow. The syntax is:

```
expression1 ? expression2 : expression3
```

where `expression1` is evaluated and, if found to be true then `expression2` is evaluated and becomes the result of the whole conditional expression. If `expression1` is false, then `expression3` is evaluated and that becomes the value of the whole expression. For instance, in this example the expression will return the value of y if x is a positive number, or z if x is zero or negative:

```
(x > 0) ? y : z
```

The conditional operator is also sometimes known as the *ternary* operator because it has three terms.

Loop Statements

The other kind of structure used for controlling program flow is the loop. A loop lets you define a block of code that runs repeatedly until conditions you define allow it to stop. There are three kinds of commonly used loops:

- the `for` loop
- the `while` loop
- the `do...while` loop

The `for` loop

The `for` loop is used to repeat a statement or block of statements until a particular condition is met. It has the same syntax as the `for` loop in C or C++ but there are some small differences which we will mention shortly. This is the syntax:

```
for (expression1 ; expression2 ; expression3)
    statement;
```

or

```
for (expression1 ; expression2 ; expression3)
    {
    statement block
    }
```

The elements of a `for` loop are as follows:

1. The first expression initialises the index (or counter) variable of the loop. For instance, if you are using the `int` variable `i` as an index, the initialisation part could be `i = 0`.

    Note: in Java (unlike in C and C++), you can declare the index variable within the `for` loop and the variable will cease to exist once the loop has finished.

2. The second expression must be a boolean expression which returns a true or false result. The loop statement is executed while the test remains true. Once it becomes false, processing within the loop ends and program execution is carried on from the next statement after the loop. For example, if you used `i < 10` as the test part, the loop statement would be executed while the value of `i` was less than 10. (This is another area where Java differs from C and C++ – in those languages, an expression which returns zero will end the loop. In Java, a test expression must return a boolean value, true or false.) *not non or zero*

3. The third expression of the `for` loop changes the state of the index or counter. Usually, the change will involve incrementing the index so that it is closer to returning a false value and thus ending the loop.

One of the most common uses of the `for` loop is to manipulate the elements of an array. The following example loops through an integer array `numbers`, which has 10 elements, adding the contents of each element of the array to an accumulator variable, `sum`. (We will be covering arrays in a future chapter, but it is worth pointing out that, like C and C++, array elements in Java start with 0.

```
int sum = 0;
   for (i = 0; i < 10; i++)
      sum += numbers[i];
```

You can omit any of the three expressions in a `for` loop if you so desire, but you must include the semicolons. The likeliest use of this facility is the creation of an "infinite" loop, where execution has to be broken by means of a `break` statement (see below). For example,

```
for ( ; ; )// this loop will carry on forever
   {
   ...      // unless a break statement appears here (see later
   }        // on in this chapter)
```

The while loop

The while loop can be used virtually any time the for loop can be used. The while loop will enable a statement, or block of statements, to be executed while a particular condition remains true. This is the syntax:

```
while (expression)
    statement;
```

where the statement within the loop will be executed while *expression* is true. As usual, *statement* can be a single statement or a block of statements. The while loop can be directly equated with the for loop as shown in Table 6.4.

Table 6.4: *The equivalence of* while *and* for *loops*

while **loop**	for **loop**

expression1;
while (*expression2*)
    {
 	
        statement;
        expression3;
 	
    }
	for (*expression1* ; *expression2* ; *expression3*)
	        statement;

The same rules apply – you use *expression1* to initiliase a counter or index which will be incremented during the loop: for instance, x = 10. *expression2* will be evaluated before the loop is entered and if the result is true then the statement within the loop will be executed. (If *expression2* evaluates to false the loop will end).

Finally, the variable involved in the test *expression2* must be changed (eg. incremented or decremented) so that the expression is closer to returning false.

The following is an example of a while loop.

```
x = 10;
while (x > 0)
    {
    System.out.println("The value of x is greater than zero");
    x--;
    }
System.out.println("The value of x has reached zero");
```

The variable x, which is being used as the counter, is first initialised to 10. On each iteration of the loop the value of x is tested to see if it is greater then zero. While the value of x is positive, the statements inside the loop will be executed. The second line within the loop statement block decrements the value of x by one. It is obviously very important that there is a statement within the loop which alters the value of the variable used in the test expression so that it is closer to returning a false result when tested. Otherwise, the loop will continue executing indefinitely.

Once x reaches zero, the test expression returns `false`, the `while` loop ends and control drops through to the statement following the loop.

The usual Java rule regarding boolean values applies to the test expression. It must return either `true` or `false`. Therefore, you cannot use zero or non-zero numeric values as test expression results as you can in C.

The `do...while` **loop**

Both the `for` loop and the `while` loop test for a terminating condition before any statements inside the loop are executed. This means that, if the test expression returns false the first time it is evaluated, the body of the loop will never be entered. A different situation applies with the `do...while` loop – the test is not carried out until the bottom of each pass through the loop. This means that the body of the loop will always be executed at least once, even if the test expression returns false the first time through. Here is the syntax:

```
do
    statement
while (expression);
```

As usual, *statement* can either be a single statement or a block statement. Note the addition of a semicolon after the closing bracket of the test *expression*.

This loop is generally not used as frequently as the other two, due to there being at least one iteration. However, when that situation is required, the `do...while` loop is very useful. Here is an example:

```
do
    {
    System.out.println("This statement is within the loop");
    count--;
    }
while (count > 0);
```

If the value of the variable count is already equal or less than zero before the loop is executed the message within the body of the loop will still be displayed once, before the loop exits when the test expression returns false.

Breaking out of loops

Although goto is a reserved word in Java, it does not form part of the language. Most programmers would agree that this is not a great loss given the almost incomprehensible code that can be obtained through the injudicious use of goto statements. However, it is often convenient to have a means of jumping out of a loop before the loop has finished executing normally. Java provides two commands for this purpose – break and continue. These behave in the same manner as their counterparts in C and C++. Java goes a little further with the addition of the labelled break. This will be covered shortly.

The break statement is used to end execution of a loop before its terminating test condition becomes false. It can be used in any for, while or do loop, and, as you have already seen, it provides the means of terminating processing of a particular case in a switch statement. Here is an example:

```
for (i = 0; i < 10; i++)
    {
    if (numArray[i] == 0)
        break;
    }
```

This code example processes an integer array looking for the first element which equals zero. When it finds one the break statement is used to jump out of the loop. The variable i will contain the index of the required array element.

Note This will *not* work if you declare i inside the for loop: i will cease to exist as soon as the loop terminates so you will not be able to access its contents.

The break will transfer control out of one loop only. Therefore, if you have nested loops execution will resume in the next outer loop.

The continue statement halts execution of the current iteration of a loop – the program continues processing from the start of the next iteration. (The next iteration starts by re-evaluating the conditional expression.)

The following example processes an integer array, squaring the contents of each array element. However, if the value of the array element is zero or 1 the continue statement is used to skip the redundant process of squaring:

```
for (i = 0; i < 10; i++)
  {
  if (numArray[i] == 0 || numArray[i] == 1)
    continue;
  numArray[i] *= numArray[i];
  }
```

The labeled break statement is an additional feature specific to Java and not found in C and C++, which enables you to break completely out of all nested loops. To allow this you must precede the outermost loop out of which you want to break, with a *label* followed by a colon(:).

Here is an example of its use:

```
OutOfHere:            outside all loop
  for (i = 0; i < 10; i++)
    {
    for (j = 0; j < 10; j++)
    if (firstArray[i] == secondArray[j])
      break OutOfHere;
    }
    // break statement places us here
```

As you can see, the break statement must followed by the label that you specified at the start of the outer loop. This piece of code compares two arrays. When it finds a match between the two, the break is initiated and program execution resumes after the outermost loop. At this point the ith element of firstArray should equal the jth element of secondArray.

Summary

We continued our look at the fundamentals of Java programming by discussing how Java allows you to control the logical flow within your programs.

The *conditional statements* available are:

- if

- `if...else`
- `switch...case`

The *loop constructs* are:

- the `for` loop
- the `while` loop
- the `do...while` loop

All are very similar to their equivalents in C or C++. The main difference is that the test expressions must evaluate to true or false values – you cannot test for zero or non-zero values.

8

Classes and Objects in Java

Introduction

Although the main concepts of object-oriented programming are roughly the same in Java as they are in C++, there are some major differences in approach so C++ programmers should still pay careful attention to the contents of this chapter.

As mentioned in the earlier introductory chapter which talked about the fundamentals of object-oriented programming, *objects* are a combination of data (in the form of variables) and the functions or procedures that act upon that data. The variables (known as **instance variables** in Java) define the *state* of an object at any one time. The functions or procedures (known as **methods** in Java) provide the *behaviour* of the object.

A *class* can be thought of as the template of an object. A Java program is constructed from a number of class definitions which each determine the properties (or state) and available operations (or behaviour) for a number of objects. You create an object by creating an *instance* of a particular class. This is also known as *instantiating* a class. Therefore, an object and an instance of a class are one and the same thing.

A Java program always has to contain at least one class definition. When the program is run an instance of that class is created – a Java program itself therefore becomes an object.

Defining classes

The basic syntax of a class definition is:

```
class classname
    {
    ...  // class body
    }
```

All the variables and methods you wish to include in a class must be defined within the class definition, between the braces. You cannot define methods outside of a class definition as you can with C++.

If you wanted to create a class of rectangles you would start off with the basic definition:

```
class Rectangle
    {
    }
```

Although we haven't specified one for our Rectangle class, every class in Java has a superclass, ie. a class from which it will inherit all the methods and variables defined in that superclass. You can specify a superclass for your class using the keyword extends:

```
class ClassName extends SuperClassName
    {
    ...
    }
```

If you don't specify a superclass when defining your class (as we did for the Rectangle class), Java will assume the superclass to be the class Object. Therefore, our Rectangle class automatically inherits the methods and variables defined in the Object class. This is the highest class in the Java class hierarchy – all classes inherit from this one class. When a class is defined it becomes what is known as a subclass of the superclass. We will talk more about superclasses, subclasses and inheritance later.

By convention, class names in Java begin with a capital letter.

Defining Instance Variables

The data that defines the state of a class, ie. it's attributes, is held in the instance variables that are defined for a class. We will now define the attributes of our Rectangle class by including some instance variables:

```
class Rectangle
    {
    protected int width;        class attributes
    protected int height;
    }
```

The `protected` keyword is an access modifier which determines the access rights of a variable or a method. Making these variables `protected` means that they won't be visible outside of this class, or classes derived from this class. One of the main advantages of OOP is the ability to hide the internal data of an object so that it cannot be accessed directly from elsewhere in the program.

Outside agencies must access the instance variables only through the methods defined in the class. There are two other access modifiers – `public` and `private`. The `public` modifier allows access to the variable from outside of the class, whereas `private` means that the variable is only available to the class in which it is defined – even subclasses cannot use a variable declared as `private`. Instance variables are defined in a class to represent the attributes, or state, of an object. Each object instantiated from our Rectangle class will have the same attributes but each instance will have its own values stored in the instance variables. They might remain constant while the object is in existence or be changed at any time. Using the one class definition, we can create any number of Rectangle objects, each with its own width and height.

Defining Methods

Having created the instance variables which will determine the current state of a Rectangle object we will now add some methods to illustrate the behaviour of an object. The syntax for a method is:

```
accessModifier returnType methodName(parameters)
    {
    ...    // method body
    }
```

Again, we can specify an access modifier to determine the access rights allocated to the method. You can specify whether the method can be called from outside of the class (by using the `public` modifier) or whether it can only be accessed from within the class itself and is totally hidden from outside calls (by using the modifiers `private` or `protected`).

If the method is intended to return a value, the return type of that value must be included in the method definition. If it doesn't return a value, it must be declared as `void`. The method name must follow the usual rules for Java identifiers mentioned in the Java Language Basics chapter. Any parameters passed to the method take the form of a comma-delimited list inside the brackets.

Here is an example of a method for our Rectangle class which returns the area of the rectangle:

```
public int getArea()
    {
    int area;
    area = width * height;
    return area;
    }
```

The access modifier `public` has been used so that we can call this method from elsewhere in the program. As we want it to return a value for the area of a rectangle the return type has been defined as an `int`. There are no parameters being passed to the method.

Note that the variable `area` is a local variable and not an instance variable – it only has scope for the duration of the method. It is used to hold the result of the calculation before it is returned as the result of the whole method by using the `return` command. We have done this to make the internal working of the method as clear as possible – it would also be possible to define the method as follows:

```
public int getArea()
    {
    return (width * height);
    }
```

Method definitions must appear inside the class definition. The Rectangle class definition will therefore look like this:

```
class Rectangle
    {
    protected int width;
    protected int height;
```

```
public int getArea()
    {
    int area;
    area = width * height;
    return area;
    }
}
```

Because we don't want the instance variables to be read or set directly from outside of the class – which can't happen anyway as we have made them protected – we will now define some methods so that we can instruct the class itself to perform these functions:

```
public void setSize(int w, int h)
    {
    width = w;
    height = h;
    }
```

The setSize() method will change the current width and height of a Rectangle object to the values passed as the parameters w and h. The parameters of a method, within the parentheses, must be a set of variable declarations separated by commas:

```
(type arg1, type arg2, type arg3...)
```

When you call a method, the arguments that are passed to the method become local variables inside the method. If the arguments are primitive types, such as integers, they are passed by value only – any changes made to the value of the arguments inside the method will not be reflected outside the method.

```
public int getWidth()
    {
    return width;
    }
public int getHeight()
    {
    return height;
    }
```

The getWidth() and getHeight() methods will return the current values of those attributes.

Creating New Objects

Before discussing how methods are used in Java, we will first explain how an instance of a class, or, in other words, an object, is created. This is achieved by using the new operator.

First, we must declare an object variable:

```
Rectangle rect;
```

At the moment, all we have done is to declare an object variable, rect, which can refer to an object of type `Rectangle`. We cannot use it yet because the object itself has not been created. This is where the new operator comes in. The object is created as follows:

```
rect = new Rectangle();
```

The above declaration can also be combined into one command:

```
Rectangle rect = new Rectangle();
```

The new operator creates an instance of the class `Rectangle` and allocates the amount of memory it will require. Note that you must include the parentheses after the name of the class. When the parentheses are empty a basic version of the object is created. The parentheses must be be included because a special method called a constructor is actually being called when you create an object. Constructor methods are automatically called when a new object is created.

Different constructors can be called to initialise the object in different ways – they are differentiated by the number and type of parameters passed in the parentheses. As we haven't defined a constructor yet Java will call a default constructor which doesn't perform any special initialisations. We will cover constructors in a little more detail later on in the chapter.

It is important to be clear that the object variable rect, is not an object itself but merely a reference to an object. An object variable is an example of a reference data type, as opposed to a primitive data type like an integer. Whereas an integer variable holds an actual value, an object variable contains the reference to, or address, of an object. We could, for instance, create two instances of the Rectangle class:

```
Rectangle rect1 = new Rectangle();
Rectangle rect2 = new Rectangle();
```

We now have two Rectangle objects, referenced by the object variables rect1 and rect2. If we use the command,

```
rect2 = rect1;
```

we have not copied one object to another – both variables will now refer to the *same* object, ie. they both contain the same reference. We will explain how you can make a copy of an object later.

Accessing Instance Variables

Once you have used the new operator to create an instance of a class you can access the instance variables in that class by using dot notation. For instance, you could refer to the height of the Rectangle object rect, by using the expression rect.height. You can assign a value to the variable like this:

```
rect.height = 100;
```

and obtain the value of the instance variable by using it as you would any expression:

```
System.out.println("The height is " + rect.height);
```

(Of course, you would not want to access an object's instance variable from outside of that object as we have just done. That would break the rules of data encapsulation. You would call one of the object's methods to set or return the value of the radius for you.)

Using methods

Object methods are accessed in the same way. If you want to call an object method, you place a dot in between the name of the object variable and the method you wish to call. (You must, of course, include the parentheses after the name of the method, even if there are no parameters.) For example, we could use the setSize() and getHeight() methods that we defined earlier as follows:

```
rect.SetSize(100, 50);
```

sets the value of the width of the Rectangle rect to 100 and the height to 50. Similarly, the console display command that we used above could be rewritten as:

```
System.out.println("The height is " + rect.getHeight());
```

Constructors

We first mentioned constructors when we were discussing the creation of objects using the new operator. Whenever you use new to create an object a constructor method is called to initialise that object and its variables. Without a constructor defined for our Rectangle class, we have to explicitly set the values of the width and height after the object has been created by making a call to the setSize method:

```
Rectangle rect = new Rectangle();
rect.SetSize(100, 50);
```

We can define a constructor method which will take arguments as part of the object creation. Then, we can create a rectangle object with the following statement:

```
Rectangle rect = new Rectangle(100, 50);
```

A constructor method has the same name as the class itself. Therefore, if we want to define a constructor method which takes two integer values as arguments and sets the width and height of the rectangle accordingly we can define it as follows:

```
public Rectangle(int w, int h)
    {
    width = w;
    height = h;
    }
```

Notice that we didn't specify a return type. The constructor returns an instance of the class. It follows that you cannot use a return statement within a constructor.

Constructor Overloading

You are not restricted to having only one constructor method per class. Any number of constructors can be defined in a class, as long as the numbers and types of the parameters are different for each one. This is called method overloading and applies to all methods in Java, not just for constructors.

For instance, if you wanted to set a rectangle to a default size whenever one was created you could do so by declaring a constructor which didn't have any parameters at all but set the width and height of the rectangle to values defined in the method body. Suppose you always wanted newly created Rectangle objects to have a width of 20 and a height of 10 if you didn't explicitly include width and height parameters in the new statement. You would define a constructor like this:

```
public Rectangle()
    {
    width = 20;      default size
    height = 10;
    }
```

Now, whenever you create a Rectangle object with the statement

```
Rectangle rect = new Rectangle();
```

the width and height of the rectangle will be initialised to 20 and 10 respectively.

An example program

We will now create an example program which will illustrate the use of the Rectangle class. To make it slightly more interesting we will define two more methods – one to enable a rectangle object to draw itself – drawRect() – and one to display its current attributes, ie. its width and height – showDimensions(). We are not yet in a position to be able to show you how an object can be drawn in an applet, using graphics routines, so our draw method will just display simple ASCII characters on the console. Here is the drawRect() method:

```
public void drawRect()
    {
    for (int i = 0; i < width; i++)
       System.out.print("-");
    System.out.print("\n");
    for (int i = 0; i < height - 2; i++)
       {
       System.out.print("|");
       for (int j = 0; j < width - 2; j++)
          System.out.print(" ");
       System.out.print("|");      System.out.print('\h') ?
       }
    for (int i = 0; i < width; i++)
       System.out.print("-");
    System.out.println("\n");
    }
```

This is what the showDimensions() method looks like:

```
public void showDimensions()
    {
    System.out.println("The width is " + width);
    System.out.println("The height is " + height);
    }
```

We are now in a position to use our class in a Java program. Here is the complete definition of the Rectangle class:

Listing 8.1: *The Rectangle class*

```
class Rectangle
    {
    protected int width;
    protected int height;
    public Rectangle()
        {
        width = 20;
        height = 10;
        }
    public Rectangle(int w, int h)
        {
        width = w;
        height = h;
        }
    public int getArea()
        {
        int area;
        area = width * height;
        return area;
        }
    public void setSize(int w, int h)
        {
        width = w;
        height = h;
        }
    public int getWidth()
        {
        return width;
        }
    public int getHeight()
        {
        return height;
```

```
        }
    public void drawRect()
        {
        for (int i = 0; i < width; i++)
            System.out.print("-");
        System.out.print("\n");
        for (int i = 0; i < height - 2; i++)
            {
            System.out.print("|");
            for (int j = 0; j < width - 2; j++)
                System.out.print(" ");
            System.out.print("|\n");
            }
        for (int i = 0; i < width; i++)
            System.out.print("-");
        System.out.println("\n");
        }
    public void showDimensions()
        {
        System.out.println("The width is " + width);
        System.out.println("The height is " + height);
        }
    }
```

We now need to create a Java application that will make use of the Rectangle class. Here is the code for the application DoRectApp:

Listing 8.2: *The* DoRectApp *class*

```
class DoRectApp
    {
    public static void main (String args[ ])
        {
        Rectangle rect = new Rectangle();
        rect.drawRect();
        rect.showDimensions();
        }
    }
```

As we have mentioned before, you must include a main method in any Java applications that you write. In your text editor, enter the code for the Rectangle class and the code for the DoRectApp class and save it in a file called DoRectApp.java in your \Java\JavaApps directory. Also, remember that the name of the Java application source file must be the same as the class which contains the main method.

Compile the application using the command

```
javac DoRectApp.java
```

from the \Java\JavaApps directory and, providing you get no errors during the compilation, run the application with the command

```
java DoRectApp
```

You should see the following output:

Figure 8.1:
Output from the
DoRectApp *code*
(see Listing 8.1
and 8.2)

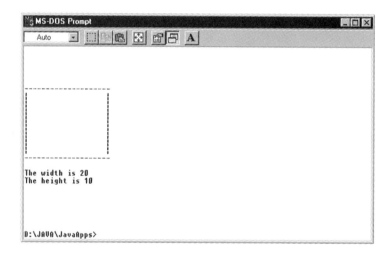

The finalize( ) Method

Other OO languages like C++ include destructor methods which are called when an object is deleted. They are most commonly used for reclaiming any memory used by the object. Java, however, has automatic garbage collection. It keeps track of all the objects used in a program and, when an object has no more references, it is tagged for removal and the memory used by the object is automatically reclaimed. You do not have to explicitly delete an object.

If you declare a finalize() method in your class it will be called just before the garbage collector removes the object from memory. You could, therefore, use the finalize() method to, say, close any files that your object has left open or free up other non-memory related resources.

However, this is not always a very good idea. The garbage collector runs as a low priority thread in the background and it is not possible to tell when an object might be cleared away – you cannot know when the garbage collector will call the `finalize()` method. It is therefore advisable to perform any required clearing up of resources (apart from memory) yourself when you are about to dispose of an object.

Class Variables and Methods

When you want to store information that all instances of a class can access you can use class variables.

Class variables are stored in the class itself and are global to the whole class and all of it's instances, unlike instance variables which relate only to each instance of the class. With instance variables, each instance of the class gets it's own copy of the variable and can change the value of that variable whenever it likes without affecting the same instance variable belonging to any other instance of the class. However, only one copy of a class variable exists for each class. Therefore, once it has been assigned a value, all of the objects created from the class see the same value. If it is changed, all of the objects created from that class will see the changed value.

Class variables are declared the same as instance variables but with the `static` keyword placed at the start of the declaration. For instance,

```
static int totalObjects;
```

Class variables are accessed using the usual dot notation. You can use either the instance or the class name on the left-hand side of the dot. To avoid unnecessary confusion between instance and class variables it is advisable to use the class name when referring to class variables.

We have already mentioned class variables in the Java Language Basics chapter when we spoke about constants. A class variable can be made a constant value by including the `final` keyword immediately after the `static` keyword. For example,

```
static final double PI = 3.1415;
```

Class methods, like class variables, are also global to the class in which they are defined. As with class variables they are defined by placing the

10, ...

static keyword in front of a method declaration. They are most commonly used for utility routines that a number of classes might want to utilise. If you are defining a number of general-purpose methods which don't relate to one particular class you can define them as class methods, grouping similar methods together in one class, and making them public so that they are available to other classes within your programs.

An example of this is the Math class that is provided with Java. The methods in the Math class can be used with any numeric values but no instances of the Math class are created at any time.

The Math class also includes a global declaration of PI that can be used by any class. It is declared in the same way as the example above except that the public keyword is used to make it available to any class. (It is also declared to a greater degree of accuracy!)

Inheritance

The ability for a class to inherit the attributes and behaviour of classes above it is one of the most important advantages of object-oriented programming. It means that you can make your new class a subclass of an existing class and have access to all of the features of that superclass as well as adding new functionality in the subclass.

You can call methods that have already been defined in the superclass and access the instance variables of that superclass. You can define new methods and variables in your subclass and you can also use method overriding to alter the behaviour of existing superclass methods. The next section will use a simple example to illustrate the concepts of inheritence and subclassing.

Subclassing

First, we will create a new class that we will use later as our superclass. We'll start off by creating a simple EmployeeRecord class which just contains Name and Job Title details:

Listing 8.3: *The EmployeeRecord class*

```
class EmployeeRecord
    {
    protected String surname;
    protected String forenames;
    protected String jobTitle;
```

```
// default constructor
public EmployeeRecord( )
   {
   surname = "";
   forenames = "";
   jobTitle = "";
   }

// second constructor for setting variables
public EmployeeRecord(surname, forenames, jobTitle)
   {
   this.surname = surname;
   this.forenames = forenames;
   this.jobTitle = jobTitle;
   }

// method to display current employee details
public showDetails( )
   {
   System.out.println("Employee Details");
   System.out.println("----------------");
   System.out.println("Surname    : " + surname);
   System.out.println("Forenames : " + forenames);
   System.out.println("Job Title : " + jobTitle);
   }
}
```

Two constructors have been defined, a default one which sets the values of the instance variables to empty strings, and another constructor which allows the name and job title details for the new employee to be passed as parameters when the object is first created. The showDetails() method displays the data held in the object.

The this keyword

The this keyword allows you to explicitly reference the instance variables and methods of the current object. this points to the current instance of the class and can be used whenever you want to access the variables or methods of that instance. The syntax is the same as when you are referring to a particular object, but instead of using the name of that object, you substitute the word this, and it will reference the current object.

In the above example we have used this to refer to the instance variables of the object being created. It allows us to differentiate between the instance variables and the arguments passed as parameters in the constructor method. In the past we have been able to omit the this keyword because there has been no ambiguity regarding the variables we have been working with. If there are no variables with the same name as the instance variables in the current scope, this can be omitted. Because this refers to the current instance, you would normally only use it inside the class definition to refer to variables and methods in that class. It cannot be used with class methods or variables because they don't relate to any particular instance of the class.

We could now use the EmployeeRecord class to set up some employees. The records can be created as follows:

```
EmployeeRecord Smith =
   new EmployeeRecord("Smith", "Will", "Pilot");
EmployeeRecord Goldblum =
   new EmployeeRecord("Goldblum", "Jeff", "Software Engineer");
```

The showDetails() method can now be used to display each employee's data on the screen:

```
Smith.showDetails( );
Goldblum.showDetails( );
```

This will result in the following output:

```
Employee Details
----------------
Surname   : Smith
Forenames : Will
Job Title : Pilot

Employee Details
----------------
Surname   : Goldblum
Forenames : Jeff
Job Title : Software Engineer
```

Suppose we now want to increase the functionality of the employee record by adding fields relating to the employee's salary. We can define a SalaryRecord class as a subclass of the EmployeeRecord class. This is also known as deriving a subclass from an existing class. The EmployeeRecord class will now be a superclass. In Java, as we saw earlier in this chapter, you use the extends keyword for this purpose. For example, here is our definition of the SalaryRecord class:

Listing 8.4: *The*
SalaryRecord
class, derived from
EmployeeRecord

```
class SalaryRecord extends EmployeeRecord
  {
  protected double salary;
  protected Date nextRaiseDue;
    // default constructor
  public SalaryRecord( )
    {
    super( );
    salary = 0.00;
    nextRaiseDue = 01/04/97;
    }
    // second constructor
  public SalaryRecord(surname, forenames, jobTitle, salary)
    {
    super(surname, forenames, jobTitle);
    this.salary = salary;
    this.nextRaiseDue = 01/04/97;
    }
    // method for setting the salary data
  public changeSalary(double newSalary)
    {
    this.salary = newSalary;
    }
  }
```

We have added two extra fields to the new class, salary and nextRaiseDue. But, as the SalaryRecord class has been derived from the EmployeeRecord class, it will also contain the instance variables defined in the EmployeeRecord class – surname, forenames and jobTitle.

Again, two constructors have been defined. The default constructor merely initialises the data – the salary is set to 0.00 and the nextRaiseDue date has been given the default date, 01/04/96. Notice that we don't have to explicitly set all the variables in the class – we can use the constructor from the EmployeeRecord superclass to set the values of the variables defined in EmployeeRecord by calling the method super().

Alternatively, the second constructor can be used to set the field data by including the values as parameters when the object is created. This time the second constructor in the `EmployeeRecord` class is called because the parameters `surname`, `forenames` and `jobTitle` have been included (you obviously have to make sure that the type and number of variables you pass to a superclass constructor match the signature of the constructor defined in that class).

A method to set the date of the next salary raise has also been defined. This method only exists in the `SalaryRecord` so cannot be called by an `EmployeeRecord` object.

The `SalaryRecord` class has also inherited (and can therefore make use of) the `showDetails()` method. However, there is a problem. When called by a `SalaryRecord` object, the method will only display the name and job title details. To be able to display all the details contained within the Salary Record, we need to redefine the `showDetails()` method. As long as the method we define has the same signature as the `showDetails()` method in the `EmployeeRecord` class, it will override that method. Method overriding is used when you want to replace a method that is inherited from the superclass. Here is the definition of our new `showDetails()` method:

```
// method to display current salary details
public showDetails( )
    {
    super.showDetails( );
    System.out.println("Salary    : " + salary);
    System.out.println("Next raise: " + nextRaiseDue);
    }
```

[handwritten annotation: override]

Notice that we have again made use of the ability to call the original method in the superclass so that we don't have to recode that part of the method. The call to `super.showDetails()` results in the employee data being displayed as before. The salary and raise date information will then be displayed. Here is an example using the `SalaryRecord` class:

```
SalaryRecord Pullman = new SalaryRecord("Pullman", "Bill",
    "President", 100000.00);
Pullman.showDetails( );
```

This will result in the following output:

```
Employee Details
----------------
Surname   : Pullman
Forenames : Bill
```

```
Job Title : President
Salary    : 100000.00
Next raise: 01/04/97
```

Which Method?

How does Java determine which method it should execute in a class hierarchy?

As mentioned above, objects have access to any methods declared in their class and their superclasses. When you call a method from a particular object, Java will first check to see if the method is defined within that object's class. If it can't find the method within the class definition, it starts to work it's way up the class hierarchy until it finds the method definition.

The search for a method definition always starts in the subclass and works upward through the hierarchy. If a method is defined with the same signature (ie. the same method name, with the same type and number of arguments), as one further up the class hierarchy, the method found first will be the one that is executed.

Packages

Java provides a means for grouping classes together in an organised way. The term for one of these collections of classes is a *package*. A number of class libraries come ready-made as part of the Java Developer's Kit. These are contained within the java package. The classes in the java package are guaranteed to be available in any implementation of Java. The java package itself is split into eight other packages. Here is an short overview of those packages.

- **java.lang** This is the main Java package containing, amongst other things, the Object class, from which all other classes are derived, type wrapper classes, the String class, classes for managing threads and the Math class. This is the only package which is automatically imported by the compiler and is thus always available. The other packages must be explicitly imported by you before they can be used.

- **java.applet** This package provides the Applet class that must be subclassed to create a Java applet. It also contains a class that allows you to find out imformation about the browser that is being used to run your applets.

- **java.awt** This contains the Java *Abstract Window Toolkit*, a collection of classes which allow you to create a visual user interface for your applets. It provides standard graphics capabilities such as fonts, colours and line drawing as well as GUI elements like windows, buttons and menus.

- **java.awt.image** This is a sub-package of the main AWT package and provides image processing classes.

- **java.awt.peer** This is another sub-package of the java.awt package and contains the interface definitions which map the Java AWT components to the underlying platform components.

- **java.io** This is the Java I/O package which provides classes for handling input and output streams for reading and writing data to files and other I/O sources.

- **java.net** The Java networking package contains classes relating to socket connections, URLs and datagrams.

- **java.util** This package contains the utility classes allowing you to manipulate data structures such as stacks and hash tables, and a class for manipulating dates.

To use the classes that are defined within a package you must use the import statement to import that class. The import statement or statements must always be the first statement, or statements, in your program.

For instance, if we wanted to use the Java Button class we would use the following statement at the beginning of our program:

```
import java.awt.Button;
```

You can use all the classes contained within a package by using the * wildcard symbol. This statement will bring in all the classes defined within the java.awt package:

```
import java.awt.*;
```

Interfaces

An interface is very similar to a class in that it is defined as a collection of methods and constant values. However, there is one important difference – the methods within an interface are not implemented. That is, there is no code to define what each method does. These are known as *abstract* methods. An interface is used to define the behaviour of a class that *implements* it. The methods defined within an interface provide a way of specifying which methods a class should be using but leaves the actual implementation of the methods up to the class involved.

An example of an interface which you will meet later on, in the chapters on animation and on multithreading, is the Runnable interface. To use a thread you would normally derive a class from the Thread class. However, as you will shortly see in the chapter on applet basics, to create an applet you must derive from the Applet class. This presents a problem when you want to include threads in an applet. There is no multiple inheritance in Java so you cannot derive from more than one parent class. Because you cannot derive from both the Applet class and the Thread class you have to use an interface.

Java provides the Runnable interface for this purpose. Runnable only contains one method definition – for the run() method (which should contain the code that will be run in a thread) – but the code that determines what the run() method will do is not defined within Runnable, you must write, or implement, the code within your program.

The syntax for implementing an interface in a class is as follows:

```
public class SubClass extends ParentClass implements Interface
    {
    ...
    }
```

Although interfaces are a way around the limitations of single inheritance, they are not a complete answer. You cannot, for instance, inherit variables or method implementations from an interface as you can with multiple inheritance.

Summary

We will be covering more aspects of inheritance in future chapters when we start subclassing from the classes that form part of the Java class library. This chapter discussed the creation, destruction and use of classes within Java.

You can think of a class as the template of an object, and that a Java program is constructed from a number of class definitions with each determining the properties (or state) and available operations (the behaviour) for a number of objects. A class is created by creating what is known as an instance of that class – or instantiating a class as it is also known.

When creating a class you must define all the variables and methods within the class definition. You cannot define methods outside of a class as you can with the C++ programming language.

The data that defines the state of a class (namely its attributes) is held within its instance variables which are held in the definition of the class.

Although other OO-based languages use a destructor method to delete an object when it is of no further use Java works differently. It uses a garbage collection utility to clean up after itself. It keeps track of all objects used within a Java program and when there are no longer any references to it will tag it for removal and give the memory used by the object back to the system. If you declare a `finalize()` method in your class it will be called just before the garbage collector removes the object from memory.

Java organises the classes it includes in a series of class libraries called packages. To use a class from a particular package you must use the import statement at the beginning of your program. Interfaces are classes that can be used to define the behaviour of a class that implements them without actually specifying the code that carries out the actions required.

9

Strings and Arrays

Strings

Strings in Java are actually objects, created as instances of the class `String`. In C and C++, they are arrays of characters which can be manipulated the same way as any other array. This is not the case in Java. The `String` class includes methods which allow you to concatenate, compare and copy strings far more easily than you can in C or C++. However, Java complicates matters by defining two string classes – `String` and `StringBuffer`. The former is used for strings that are not changed at all, ie. they are constants – once you have created an object of type `String`, you cannot change its contents. The latter, `String-Buffer`, is used for strings that will be changed during their lifecycle.

Constant

String Literals

A string literal is a sequence of characters inside double quotes. For instance, all of the following are examples of string literals:

```
"This is a string literal."
"The quality of mercy is not strained."
"1"
```

The last example might look like a integer literal but the fact that it is surrounded by double quotes means that it is a string. You can define an empty string by just using two double quotes together:

```
""
```

Character escape codes such as Tab and Newline can be included in strings:

```
"There is a tab \t character right here."
"This string will \n occupy two lines."
```

Unicode characters can also be used if you want to place special characters like the copyright symbol (©) in a string. If you want to include quotation marks within a string you must prefix them with a backslash:

```
"The line \"The quality of mercy is not strained\" comes from
The Merchant of Venice by William Shakespeare."
```

Creating Strings

The easiest way to create a String object is to declare a variable and assign it a string literal. For example,

```
String s = "This is a string";
```

or

```
String c = "Yet another example of a string in use";
```

Strings, being objects, can also be created like any other object in Java by using the new operator:

```
String s;
s = new String("Hello, I must be going.");
```

or

```
String s = new String("foo bar");
```

Strings can be created from character arrays as well. If you had defined a character array, charData:

```
char charData[] = {'f', 'o', 'o', ' ', 'b', 'a', 'r'};
```

you can create a String object by passing the array as an argument of the String constructor:

```
String s = new String(charData);
```

You can even make a string from part of a character array. The syntax is as follows:

```
String stringName = new(value[], offset, count);
```

where `value` is a character array, `offset` is an integer indicating where the subarray should begin, and `count` is an integer indicating how many characters should be used. Therefore, you could create a `String` object with the value "bar" by using the following command:

```
String s = new String(charData, 4, 3);
```

(Remember, you start counting the offset in an array from 0, not 1.)

String Concatenation

String concatentation in C tends to be a laborious task, taking a line of code to add each new string. Java has the same advantage as languages like Visual Basic which allow you to use the addition operator, + , to concatenate two strings. The following code example produces a single string:

```
"The quality of " + "mercy is " + "not strained."
```

You have already seen examples of another feature of Java programming regarding the concatentation of strings. In the programming examples in the last chapter on classes and objects we used the statement: *concatenation*

```
System.out.println("The height is " + rect.height);
```

The more astute among you might have noticed that we are adding an integer value to a string in this example. Java will automatically convert the integer value to a string before it concatenates it with the first string. In fact, Java will convert the value of any object to a string when you are concatenating it with another string.

Java combines strings together exactly as they are given. So, if you were to use the following command,

```
String s = "Dimming" + "of the" + "day";
```

you would get the string,

```
"Dimmingof theday"
```

You must make sure that you include spaces where required.

String Comparisons

Although it is possible to use the + operator to concatenate two strings, you cannot use the equality operator, ==, to test whether two strings are identical. Strings are objects so a String variable is actually a reference to an object. Therefore, if you use the == operator to find out if two strings are equal, you will actually be comparing the addresses, or locations, where those strings are stored.

Java provides a method to check whether two strings are equal – the `equals()` method. If you wanted to compare the strings `str1` and `str2`, you would use the following command:

str1 = "Broad"

Str2 = "bad"

```
str1.equals(str2)
```
or compareTo

If the strings are equal, `true` will be returned, if they are not, then `false` will be returned.

You can also use this method with string literals. For instance, if you wanted to test whether the string `name` contained John, you could use the following:

```
name.equals("John")
```

For C programmers who are used to using the `strcmp` function to compare strings, Java thoughtfully provides an exact equivalent – `compareTo()`. This is another method within the String class and is called in the same way as the equals method:

```
str1.compareTo(str2)
```

Instead of returning true or false, `compareTo()` returns a number greater than zero if the string `str2` is greater than `str1`, zero if they are equal, and a number less than zero if `str2` is less than `str1`.

Substrings

The substring method enables you to extract a substring from a larger string. For example, if you had declared a string quotation as follows:

0 1 2 3 4 5 6 7 8 9 10 11

```
String quotation = "The quality of mercy is not strained";
```
first word   *first don't want*
the command,   *to copy*

```
String part = quotation.substring(4, 11);
```

would create another string, `season`, containing the string "quality". The first argument of the `substring()` method is the offset into the first string where you want the copy to start and the second argument is the first position in the string that you do not want to copy. Here is another example:

```
String duo = "Simon and Garfunkel";
String solo;
solo = duo.substring(0, 5);
```

The string, solo, will now equal Simon.

The substring() method is overloaded such that, when you only supply one argument, the resulting substring will contain those characters starting from the offset provided as an argument, to the end of the string. So, using the same string duo, the following statement would result in solo being equal to "Garfunkel":

```
String solo = duo.substring(10);
```

Other String Methods

Here are some of the other methods defined for the String class:

- public int length( )

  Returns the number of characters in the string.

  Example:

  ```
  String s = "Goodbye";
  numChars = s.length;// numChars is 7
  ```

- public char charAt(int index)

  Returns the character at the position index in the string.

  Example:

  ```
  String s = "Goodbye";
  firstChar = s.charAt(0);// firstChar = 'G'
  ```

- public boolean regionMatches(int toffset, String other, int ooffset, int len)

  Returns true if a region of this string matches a region in the specified string. toffset is the position in this string to start looking, other is the other String, ooffset is the starting position in the other String and len is the number of characters to compare.

  Example:

  ```
  String s = "Forever Young";
  isMatch = s.regionMatches(8, "Neil Young", 5, 5); // true
  ```

■ public boolean startsWith(String prefix)

Determines whether the String starts with the specified prefix.

Example:

```
String s = "Goodbye";
start = s.startsWith("Good");// true
```

■ public boolean endsWith(String suffix)

Determines whether the String ends with the specified suffix.

Example:

```
String s = "Goodbye";
end = s.endsWith("night");// false
```

■ public int indexOf(int ch)

Searches for the first occurence of the character ch within the String. Returns the index if the character is found, -1 if the character is not found.

Example:

```
String s = "Goodbye";
index = s.indexOf('d');// index is 3
```

■ public int lastIndexOf(int ch)

Searches for the last occurence of the character ch within the String. The String is searched backwards starting from the last character in the String. Returns the index if the character is found, -1 if the character is not found.

Example:

```
String s = "Goodbye";
index = s.lastIndexOf('y');// index is 5
```

■ public String concat(String str)

Concatenates the specified String str to the end of this String.

Example:

```
String s = "Hello";
String newString = s.concat(", how are you?");
```

■ public String toLowerCase( )

Converts all the characters in the String to lower case.

Example:
```
String s = "GOODBYE";
String s2 = s.toLowerCase(); // s2 is "goodbye"
```

- `public String toUpperCase( )`

    upper

    Converts all the characters in the String to ~~lower~~ case.

    Example:
    ```
    String s = "goodbye";
    String s2 = s.toUpperCase(); // s2 is "GOODBYE"
    ```

- `public String trim( )`

    Removes leading and trailing whitespace from the String.

    Example:
    ```
    String s = " Good Morning   ";
    s.trim() // s is now "Good Morning"
    ```

- `public char[ ] toCharArray( )`

    Converts the String to a character array. This creates a new array.

    Example:
    ```
    String s = "Hello";
    charArray = s.toCharArray // charArray is {'H', 'e', 'l', 'l', 'o'}
    ```

- `public static String valueOf(type variable)`

    Returns a String object that represents whatever variable is passed to it. The variable can be any primitive type or object. This is a class method so it is not invoked with a particular instance of a String.

    Example:
    ```
    int number = 1000;
    String s = String.valueOf(number);// s is "1000"
    ```

There are numerous variations of the above methods. Consult the API reference to find out what other methods are defined.

The StringBuffer class

The `StringBuffer` class is used for strings that you know you will change during their lifetime. Because Java Strings cannot be amended once created, the only way you can append characters to an existing string is to use concatenation. This means that Java has to create a new String each time.

The StringBuffer class allows you to create what is, essentially, an expanding string buffer. This can either have an initial size or be empty to start of with and increase in size as characters, or indeed any type of object, is appended to it. Once you have finished inserting or appending characters to a StringBuffer, you can convert it to a String using toString(), and then make use of the String class methods.

Some of the methods available for the StringBuffer class are the same as those in the String class. For instance, the constructors allow you to create a StringBuffer from an existing String or from an array of characters or as an empty string.

Here are some of the StringBuffer methods not available to the String class.

- public synchronized StringBuffer append(type variable)

    Appends the variable, which can be any primitive type or object, to the end of the StringBuffer.

    Examples:

    ```
    StringBuffer buf = new StringBuffer("Good Morning");
    buf.append(", Vietnam.");

    boolean result = false;
    StringBuffer buf = new StringBuffer("The result is ");
    buf.append(true);
    // buf is "The result is false"

    int intAmount = 100;
    StringBuffer buf = new StringBuffer("The value is ");
    buf.append(intAmount);
    // buf is "The value is 100"
    ```

- public synchronized StringBuffer insert(int offset, type variable)

    Inserts the variable, which can be any primitive type or object, to the StringBuffer at the offset specified by offset.

    Example:

    ```
    StringBuffer buf = new StringBuffer("Good Vietnam.");
    buf.insert(5, "Morning, ");
    ```

- `public int length( )`

  Returns the length of the string in the buffer, ie. the actual character count.

  Example: *create a Buffer with size=1000*

  ```
  StringBuffer buf = new StringBuffer(1000);
  buf.append("Good Morning");
  amountUsed = buf.length;// amountUsed = 12
  ```

- `public int capacity( )`

  Returns the current capacity of the String buffer, ie. the amount of space available for new characters.

  Example:

  ```
  StringBuffer buf = new StringBuffer(1000);
  buf.append("Good Morning");
  amountLeft = buf.capacity;// amountLeft = 992
  ```

Arrays

Java arrays are, like strings, objects. They can contain any type of value, either primitive types or objects, as long as the same type is stored in a single array. You can therefore have arrays of integers, floating-point numbers or Strings but you can't have an array which mixes, say, integers and floats. Once an array has been created, you cannot change its size. As with other objects, you must first declare an array variable. You can then use the new operator to create a new array object and assign it to the variable.

Declaring Arrays

There are two different methods for declaring arrays. The first method is to declare the type of object that the array will hold, followed by the array name, followed by empty brackets:

```
type ArrayName[];
```

Here are some example array declarations:

```
int numArray[];// array of integers
String names[];// array of strings
double salaries[];// array of doubles
```

As you can see, the size of an array is not fixed when it is declared. That happens when you actually create the array.

The above method of declaring arrays will seem quite familiar to most programmers. Another method that Java provides is to place the empty brackets after the type instead of after the array name. For instance, the above examples would appear like this:

```
int[] numArray;
String[] names;
double[] salaries;
```

The advantage of this method is that it is more obvious that int[] is an array of ints. Some programmers think it is more readable. A disadvantage is that, if you are going to continue programming in, say, C, you are more likely to make errors when making declarations in both languages as you will be using two different styles.

Creating Arrays

Once you have declared your array variable you can create an array object and assign it to the variable. Having seen how other objects are created, the syntax will seem quite familiar. You can separate the declaration and creation or combine the two in one statement. These two examples both create instances of a String array containing 10 elements:

```
String stringArray[];
stringArray = new String[10];
String stringArray[] = new String[10];
```

When you create an array object you must always specify the number of elements that array will hold. All the elements in an array object are initialised when you use new. Numeric arrays are set to 0, boolean arrays to false, character arrays to '\0' and object arrays to null.

Another way of creating arrays is to explicitly define the array elements, separated by commas, within parentheses. For example, here is a declaration of an array of strings:

```
String capitals[] = { "Paris", "London", "Berlin", "Rome", "Prague", "Madrid" };
```

This will create an array of String objects, capitals, with six elements.

Manipulating Arrays

Array elements are accessed by specifying the name of the array followed by an integer, enclosed within brackets (known as a subscript), to denote the element of the array. For instance, to set the first three elements of a String array you would use the following:

```
String countries[] = new String[10];
countries[0] = "France";
countries[1] = "Britain";
countries[2] = "Germany";
```

Notice that the elements are numbered from zero, as they are in C and C++. So, an array of ten elements would be numbered from 0 to 9.

Java has checks to make sure that the bounds of an array are not broken. This is one of the most common programming errors. It occurs when you create an array containing, say, 10 elements which will therefore be accessed using the subscripts 0 to 9. The mistake is to try to assign a value to the array element with the subscript 10, which is outside the limits of the array.

For example:

```
int numArray[] = new int[10];
int numArray[1] = 2;
int numArray[2] = 4;
int numArray[3] = 6;
int numArray[4] = 8;
int numArray[5] = 10;
int numArray[6] = 12;
int numArray[7] = 14;
int numArray[8] = 16;
int numArray[9] = 18;
int numArray[10] = 20;
```

This error, where the subscripts run from 1 to 10, instead of from 0 to 9, will be picked up by the compiler because the array element that is outside the boundaries of the array, 10, is being assigned a value before the source is compiled. If the array subscripts are calculated at run-time, most probably in a loop, then the java interpreter will throw an exception. (Exception handling allows your program to recover from errors in an orderly fashion and will be explained fully in a later chapter.)

You can prevent this sort of error from occurring by using the array instance variable, length. The length variable returns the number of elements in that array. In this example a loop is used to set the elements of an integer array to the square of the subscript. The length variable is used to calculate the upper limit of the array:

```
int numArray[] = new int[10];
for (i = 0; i < numArray.length; i++)// numArray.length returns 10
    numArray[i] = i * 1;
```

Multidimensional Arrays

Multidimensional arrays are created in Java by declaring arrays of arrays. The following statement declares and creates a 10 by 10 array of integers:

```
int multiArray[][] = new int[10][10];
```

The elements of a multidimensional array are accessed they same way as they are in C, by specifying the subscript of each array. For example:

```
multiArray[0][0] = 1;
multiArray[0][1] = 2;
multiArray[0][2] = 3;
...
multiArray[9][8] = 99;
multiArray[9][9] = 100;
```

Summary

Java strings are objects, created as instances of the String class. Java provides many useful methods in the String class that allow you to easily perform tasks such as string concatentation, string comparisons and string copying. A second class, StringBuffer, can be used for strings that you know will expand in size during their lifetime.

Arrays are also objects in Java programming. They can be of any type: either primitive types, such as integers or characters, or objects, such as strings. All the elements of one array must be of the same type, however. Multidimensional arrays may be created by declaring arrays of arrays.

Java Applet Basics

Our First Java Applet revisited

In the Getting Started chapter we presented an extremely simple Java applet for you to type in and compile, mainly to make sure that the Java compiler was correctly installed and set up. We will now begin our look at the basics of Java applets by taking another look at that applet. Here is the code again:

Listing 10.1: *A simple applet to display a line of text on a Web page*

```
import java.awt.Graphics;
public class FirstJavaApplet extends java.applet.Applet
    {
    public void paint(Graphics g)
        {
        g.drawString("My First Java Applet", 20, 25);
        }
    }
```

Lets go through the program line by line. The first statement imports the classes within the `java.awt.Graphics` package so that they are available to the class or classes that we define in our program. The `import` statement must always be the first statement(s) in a Java program.

The next line derives the class `FirstJavaApplet` from the `Applet` class in the `java.applet` package. The main applet class of all Java applets must be created as a subclass of the `Applet` class. It must also be declared public. Other classes in the applet do not have to be public.

The Applet class provides all the functionality required for an applet to run in a browser. It contains the methods which handle the life-cycle of an applet – initialisation, starting, stopping and destroying – and can also be used for loading images and audio files. The Applet class is itself a subclass of the AWT Component class and therefore has access to all of the various graphics capabilities of AWT and its event handling abilities.

Applets do not require a main() method like Java applications. When an applet is loaded an instance of the initial class is created – the applet becomes an object to which all system messages (eg. mouse clicks, keystrikes) are sent.

The only method defined within our FirstJavaApplet class is the paint() method. The paint() method is the means by which all drawing that the applet performs is actually accomplished. Anything that appears on the screen – text, lines, images – have to be drawn there by the paint() method. The paint() method can be called numerous times during the life of an applet. It is called automatically when the applet first starts running, when it is covered by something else on the screen and then uncovered again or when the browser window is moved, or minimised and maximised. It can be called a number of times if you are displaying animations.

The paint() method is actually defined in the AWT Component class. By placing a version in our applet we are overriding the original method so that we can perform whatever drawing on the screen we like. Notice that paint() receives an object of type Graphics as an argument. The Graphics object contains various settings which describe the current graphics state. This includes the current font and colour for instance. (Windows programmers can look upon the Graphics object as being similar to the device context.) Any drawing that you perform in Java must be through an instance of the Graphics class.

There is only one statement in the paint() method:

```
g.drawString("My First Java Applet", 20, 25);
```

drawString() is a method defined in the Graphics class and, as you may have guessed, draws the string "My First Java Applet". The string will be drawn starting at the x coordinate, 20, and the y coordinate, 25. The x and y coordinates specify the lower left-hand corner of the text. In Java, the origin of the coordinate system is at the top left-hand corner of the applet's bounding box, so positive values of x move to the right and positive values of y move downwards.

Figure 10.1 shows how the coordinates are applied in the above example.

Figure 10.1:

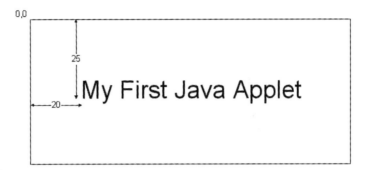

HTML and Applets

Here is the HTML code that we presented in the Getting Started chapter. We will not be covering any of the standard HTML tags that are present on this page – we leave that to the many books already available on the subject. What we will cover is the APPLET tag – the means by which Java applets are included on WWW pages.

```
<HTML>
<HEAD>
<TITLE>Java applet test page</TITLE>
</HEAD>
<BODY>
<H1>A test page for my Java applet<BR>
</H1>
<P>
This is the output from a Java applet:<BR>
<BR>
<APPLET CODE="FirstJavaApplet.class" CODEBASE="classes" WIDTH=150
HEIGHT=50>
</APPLET>
</BODY>
</HTML>
```

An applet is positioned on an HTML page using the <APPLET> tag. In the example above the following piece of code determines how and where the applet will appear on the page:

```
<APPLET CODE="FirstJavaApplet.class" CODEBASE="classes"
WIDTH=150 HEIGHT=50></APPLET>
```

Included in the above `APPLET` tag are all the attributes that you will always require when placing an applet on a web page.

The `CODE` attribute determines the name of the applet class you want to use. The browser (as long as it is Java cabable) will look for a Java `.class` file of this name. The `.class` extension can be omitted if you wish.

The `CODEBASE` attribute allows you to specify the URL where your Java class files are located. (It is not strictly necessary to include this attribute – if you omit it, the browser will look in the directory where the HTML file is located. It is, however, a good idea to keep your Java class files in a separate directory so the use of the `CODEBASE` attribute is recommended.)

In the example above, a relative URL has been used and the browser will expect to find the class file in the directory `classes`, under the current directory. If you have placed your HTML page in a directory called `\htmldocs`, the browser will look for the Java class file, `FirstJavaApplet.class`, in the directory `\htmldocs\classes`.

You can also specify an absolute URL as the `CODEBASE` attribute. For instance, if you specify `CODEBASE` as follows:

```
CODEBASE=" file:///C|/javadev\classes"
```

the browser will look for the class file in the `c:\javadev\classes` directory.

The `WIDTH` and `HEIGHT` attributes determine the bounding region of the applet. Like the `CODE` attribute, you must always specify these attributes. The dimensions are measured in pixels, so, in the above example, the width allocated for the applet will be 150 pixels and the height will be 50 pixels. You need to bear in mind the different screen resolutions that internet users will be utilising. What might seem a good size for your applet on a 640 × 480 screen might appear tiny on a 1024 × 768 screen. You will have to experiment with these settings to arrive at an acceptable compromise.

The `</APPLET>` tag indicated the end of the `APPLET` attributes. If you include text within the `<APPLET>` and `</APPLET>` tags, that text will be displayed on the viewed page instead of the Java applet by browsers that do not support Java. For instance, the following code:

```
<APPLET CODE="FirstJavaApplet" CODEBASE="classes"
WIDTH=150 HEIGHT=50
A Java applet will appear here if
you had a Java-capable browser. </APPLET>
```

would result in the text:

```
A Java applet will appear here if
you had a Java-capable browser.
```

being displayed on the page in a non Java-aware browser. Java-aware browsers will simply ignore the text. It is worth pointing out that if you turn the Java capability off in your Java-aware browser, it will not only fail to run the applet, but will also not display the substitute text either.

Enhancing an applet

We will now start to make our simple applet a little more interesting by showing you how you can specify a particular font, size and colour for the text displayed by the applet. Here is the code for our SimpleText applet:

Listing 10.2:
SimpleText *applet*
(see Figure 10.2)

```
import java.awt.Graphics;
import java.awt.Font;
import java.awt.Color;
public class SimpleText extends java.applet.Applet
    {
    Font f = new Font("Helvetica", Font.BOLD, 20);
    public void paint(Graphics g)
        {
        g.setFont(f);
        g.setColor(Color.blue);
        g.drawString("Some simple text", 10, 25);
        }
    }
```

Figure 10.2 shows what the SimpleText applet should display in your HTML page. There are now three import statements at the start of the source file. We already know that the java.awt.Graphics package is required for the Graphics class. The other two packages that are being imported, java.awt.Font and java.awt.Color, make available the Font and Color classes that we will utilise in this applet.

Figure 10.2: *The*
output from the
SimpleText *applet*
(see Listing 10.2)

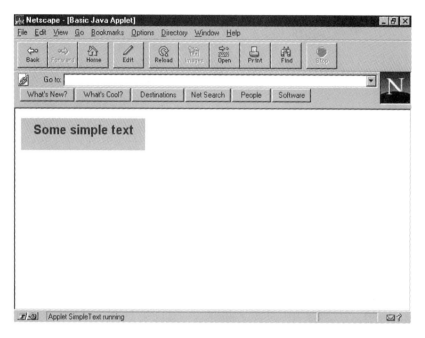

We are again deriving our applet class from the `java.applet.Applet`
class but this time the class is called `SimpleText`. This means of course,
that the source file for this applet must be named `SimpleText.java`.

In our `FirstJavaApplet` applet we didn't specify the font that we
wanted to use when drawing the text so Java displayed the text in a
default font. This time we will specify the font we want to use. The next
line in the source file,

```
Font f = new Font("Helvetica", Font.BOLD, 20);
```

creates an instance of the Font class and assigns it to the variable f.

We could have split this statement over two lines to make it clear that
we are declaring an instance variable, f, and then assigning it a Font
object:

```
Font f;
f = new Font("Helvetica", Font.BOLD, 20);
```

The Font constructor takes three arguments – the name of the font, its
style and the size. A font is identified by the font family name – in this
case "Helvetica". The style of the font is represented by three constants, defined in the Font class – PLAIN, BOLD or ITALIC. (The BOLD and

ITALIC styles can also be combined if you want the text to have both attributes.) The size of the font is measured in points and can vary from 8 points up to 72 points. We will be covering fonts in much greater detail in the next chapter. For the moment, we have now created a Font object which has the following attributes: the font is Helvetica, the style is bold and the size is 20 points.

Having created the font as we want to display it, we now override the paint() method to actually display the text. The first thing is to inform the graphics object that has been passed to the paint() method that we want to change the default font. This is done using the setFont() method of the Graphics class. The line

```
g.setFont(f);
```

tells the instance of the Graphics class, g, to set the default font to the one held in the instance variable, f. Any text displayed from now on will be displayed in Helvetica, with a bold style, at 20 point.

The next line changes the default colour of the graphics object:

```
g.setColor(Color.blue);
```

The setColor() method passes an instance of the Color class to the graphics object. A Color object is used in Java to represent any colour. Java uses a 24-bit colour model, made up of three byte values, representing a red, a green and a blue value (known as RGB values). Each value can be in the range 0 to 255 and the combination of these three values determines the actual colour.

For instance, the colour blue is made up of the three values, 0, 0, 255 (red = 0, green = 0, blue = 255). White and black have the RGB values of 255, 255, 255 and 0, 0, 0 respectively. Different shades can be created by combining different values of red, green and blue. A number of standard Color objects have been defined as class variables to make it slightly easier for you to set a colour – the Color.blue object that we have used above is one – but you can also create your own colour objects. We will cover colour is much more detail in the next chapter.

The last line:

```
g.drawString("Some simple text", 10, 25);
```

which we have seen before, displays the text string, "Some simple text", in the HTML document.

Passing parameters from HTML

Parameters can be passed to a Java applet from the HTML file that calls it by using the <PARAM> tag. The <PARAM> tag is placed inside the confines of the <APPLET> tag that you are familiar with. Here is an example:

```
<APPLET CODE="FirstJavaApplet" CODEBASE="classes"
WIDTH=150 HEIGHT=50>
<PARAM NAME=text VALUE="Some simple text">
A Java applet will appear here if
you had a Java-capable browser.</APPLET>
```

As you can see the <PARAM> tag has two attributes – NAME and VALUE. The NAME attribute is used by the applet to identify the parameter that is being passed and the VALUE is, funnily enough, the actual value of that parameter. In the example above text is the name of the parameter and "Some simple text" is the value.

The name can be anything you choose as long as you use the same name inside the applet code. You can include as many <PARAM> tags as you like within the <APPLET> tag. For instance, this example passes the name of the font to the applet as well as the text that you want to display:

```
<APPLET CODE="FirstJavaApplet" CODEBASE="classes"
WIDTH=150 HEIGHT=50>
<PARAM NAME=text VALUE="Some simple text">
<PARAM NAME=font VALUE="Helvetica">
A Java applet will appear here if
you had a Java-capable browser.</APPLET>
```

Inside the applet you have to include some code that will obtain the value passed for each parameter. The getParameter() method is used for this purpose. All parameters passed to an applet are passed as strings – even numeric values. (This means that you have to do the conversion yourself – from a string to say, an integer, if you are passing a numeric value to your applet.

Here are the statements to obtain the values of the two parameters included in the HTML code above:

```
String text = getParameter("text");
String fontName = getParameter("font");
```

As you can see, you use a string representing the NAME attribute, as specified by the <PARAM> tag, as the argument for the getParameter() call.

A string containing the VALUE is returned. It is important to note that the name used in the <PARAM> tag and the name used in the getParameter() call must match exactly. The name is case-sensitive, so text is different from Text, for example, and font is different from FONT.

The parameters are passed to the applet when it is first loaded. We therefore have to make the calls to getParameter() at that time. How do we do this? We obviously cannot locate the getParameter() calls in the paint() method as that can be called numerous times during the lifetime of the applet. The answer is that we override another method – the init() method. When an applet is first loaded the init() method is called.

The method is only called once and can be used to perform any initialisation that the applet requires. This might include setting up resources that will be used during the lifetime of the applet, such as fonts, or, indeed, the obtaining of parameters passed from the HTML file.

Note The init() method will also be called anytime the applet is reloaded. It is not always necessary to override this method but if you do have to initialise any resources, this is the obvious place to do it.

Here is an example of the use of the init() method to obtain the two parameters we have already mentioned (assume that text and fontName have been declared as strings):

```
public void init()
    {
    text = getParameter("text");
    if (text == null)
        text = "No text parameter provided!";
    fontName = getParameter("font");
    if (fontName == null)
        fontName = "Helvetica";
    }
```

If a parameter has not been specified in the HTML file, or the NAME attribute of the parameter has been entered incorrectly, the getParameter() call will return a null value. It is therefore advisable to always test the returned string for null and, if true, set a default value as shown in the above example.

We will now provide an amended version of the SimpleText applet which makes use of the getParameter() method to set the font, the size and the text to be displayed to values passed to it from the HTML file.

First of all, here is the HTML document with the required <PARAM> tags added:

```
<HTML>
<HEAD>
<TITLE>Java applet test page</TITLE>
</HEAD>
<BODY>
<H1>A test page for my Java applet<BR>
</H1>
<P>
This is the output from a Java applet:<BR>
<BR>
<APPLET CODE="FirstJavaApplet.class" CODEBASE="classes" WIDTH=150
HEIGHT=50>
    <PARAM NAME=text VALUE="Some simple text">
    <PARAM NAME=font VALUE="Helvetica">
    <PARAM NAME=size VALUE="20">
A Java applet will appear here if you had a Java-capable browser
</APPLET>
</BODY>
</HTML>
```

Here is the new SimpleText applet:

Listing 10.3:
Example showing how parameters may be obtained from the HTML file

```
import java.awt.Graphics;
import java.awt.Font;
import java.awt.Color;

public class SimpleText2 extends java.applet.Applet
    {
    Font f;
    String text;
    String fontName;
    int fontSize;

    public void init()
        {
        text = getParameter("text");
        if (text == null)
            text = "No text parameter provided!";
        fontName = getParameter("font");
        if (fontName == null)
```

```
        fontName = "Helvetica";
    String strSize = getParameter("size");
    if (strSize == null)
        fontSize = 18;
    else
        fontSize = Integer.parseInt(strSize);
    f = new Font(fontName, font.BOLD, fontSize);
    }
public void paint(Graphics g)
    {
    g.setFont(f);
    g.setColor(Color.blue);
    g.drawString(text, 10, 25);
    }
}
```

Here is an explanation of the section that obtains the font size:

```
String strSize = getParameter("size");
if (strSize == null)
    fontSize = 18;
else
    fontSize = Integer.parseInt(strSize);
```

First, we call the getParameter() method with the size name specified and assign it to a temporary string that will only exist for the duration of the init() method. We then test for a null value in case the parameter has not been included in the HTML document and, if it is null, set the fontSize integer variable to 18. If a proper string value has been returned we use the parseInt() method of the Integer class to convert the string to a numeric type. The only other changes to the original SimpleText applet are the statement setting the font,

```
f = new Font(fontName, font.BOLD, fontSize);
```

and the drawString method,

```
g.drawString(text, 10, 25);
```

where we have substituted the original string and integer literals with the variables that we got from the getParameter method.

The output from this applet should be the same as it was before. You can of course experiment by using different values for the HTML parameters. (You might have to alter the bounds of the applet if you are specifying very large font sizes!)

The Applet Lifecycle

We will conclude this introductory chapter on applets with a short discussion about the lifecycle of a typical applet. You can override four methods to control the lifecycle of an applet. The first one, init(), has already been mentioned but we will include it again for completeness. These are the four methods and each is discussed below.

init()

This method is called when the applet is first loaded. It can be used to perform any initialisation that the applet requires. This might include setting up resources that will be used during the lifetime of the applet, such as fonts, or obtaining parameters passed from the HTML file. The init() method will also be called if the applet is reloaded for any reason. It is not always necessary to override this method but if you do have to initialise any resources, this is the obvious place to do it.

start()

and reload

The start() method is called after the init() method when the applet is first loaded. If the user leaves the page containing your applet and then returns to it the start() method will again be called. Therefore, the start() method can be called a number of times during the lifetime of the applet – every time the page on which your applet resides becomes the current page. You should therefore never put code in the start() method that you only want to be called once – the init() method should be used for that. The usual reason for overriding the start() method is to start or restart a thread that might be controlling say, an animation. We will provide examples of this when we discuss threads in a later chapter.

restart a thread

stop()

The stop() method partners the start() method. It is called whenever the user leaves the page containing your applet. Thus, like the start() method, it can be called numerous times during the applet's lifetime. It should be used to stop any threads that you don't want left running while the applet is not visible (which might be using valuable system resources). Again, animation is an obvious example that we will be covering later.

stop thread

destroy()

When the applet is being shut down the destroy() method is called. This will normally be when the user exits the browser. You should only use this method for releasing any resources, such as threads, that your applet has created. Here is a simple program, called LifeCycle.java, which illustrates the way these methods behave. We are overriding each of the four methods mentioned above so that, each time they are automatically called, they will display a relevant message. When you first load the page with the applet on it, you should see the first, init() method being called, followed by the start() method. Try leaving the page on which the applet resides and returning to it a few times and watch the behaviour of the stop() and start() methods.

Listing 10.4:
Example illustrating the lifecycle of an applet

```java
import java.awt.*;
import java.applet.Applet;

public class LifeCycle extends Applet
    {
    StringBuffer text;
    public void init()
        {
        text = new StringBuffer();
        text.append("Initialised...");
        }
    public void start()
        {
        text.append("Started...");
        }
    public void stop()
        {
        text.append("Stopped...");
        }
    public void destroy()
        {
        text.append("Destroyed...");
        }
    public void paint(Graphics g)
        {
        g.drawString(text.toString(), 0, 25);
        }
    }
```

Here is the <APPLET> tag that you should use in the HTML file:

```
<APPLET CODE="LifeCycle" WIDTH=400 HEIGHT=50></APPLET>
```

This is a fairly straightforward program so we have taken the opportunity to introduce some new points. First of all, the import statements are slightly different. By using an asterisk after the second period in the first import statement we are telling the compiler to import all the classes included in the java.awt package. This means that, instead of having three import statements as we did earlier,

```
import java.awt.Graphics;
import java.awt.Font;
import java.awt.Color;
```

we only need the one,

```
import java.awt.*;
```

There is no disadvantage in terms of code size or compile time so there is no reason why you should not do this. The only time you are prevented from doing so is if two packages contain classes with the same name. Also, you can only use the * with single packages. You cannot, for instance, use import java.* to import all the java packages in one go. Up until now we have explicitly specified that we are deriving our applet class from the java.applet.Applet class. By including the import statement,

```
import java.applet.Applet;
```

we have now imported the java.applet.Applet class so we only need to use the name of the Applet class in the first line of the class definition,

```
public class LifeCycle extends Applet
    {
    ...
    }
```

We are also making use of the StringBuffer class to create an instance variable, buffer, to which we can append our string messages as the methods are called. The toString() method is used as one of the parameters to the g.drawString() command to convert the StringBuffer to a normal string for display.

Summary

This chapter has presented the basics of writing Java applets. During the next few chapters we will build upon this foundation and gradually introduce lots of more advanced features that can be included in your applets.

A very simple Java applet was dissected to explain how an applet must be constructed. An applet is, in fact, a class derived from the Java Component class. When you run an applet the class is instantiated to create an Applet object. The `paint()` method inherited from the Component class is overridden to actually carry out any drawing that we require in the applet. The font used for any text to be displayed and the colour in which it is drawn is set in the Graphics object that is passed to the `paint()` method.

An applet is run from an HTML document by including the name of the applet class file within the bounds of the HTML `<APPLET>` tag. Parameters entered in the HTML code may be passed to the applet to make the program more adaptable.

The chapter concluded by taking a look at the lifecycle of an applet – concentrating on the `init()`, `start()`, `stop()` and `destroy()` methods.

Drawing Text in Java

Introduction

This chapter will cover the standard font types and font styles that are available to you under Java: Helvetica, TimesRoman, **bold**, *italic*, ***bold italic*** and so on. It will discuss the drawing of text to a screen and how to locate it using the coordinate system.

We will look at the various methods that can be employed to interrogate a font for information – such as getName() – and go on to look at the physical construction of a font, such as its height and leading. This will be followed by the various methods used to define the size and shape of a font. We will also look at how colours are used in Java by discussing the Color class.

Fonts

Standard Fonts in Java

Java defines a number of fonts which should always be available on whatever platform is being used:

Helvetica
TimesRoman
Courier
Dialog
DialogInput
Σψμβολ (this is the Symbol font)

The first five should always be available but the presence of Symbol cannot always be expected. It is not, for instance, available under the X Windows System on Unix. The fonts are implemented differently on each platform. For example, Table 11.1 shows the equivalent fonts under Windows 95 or Windows NT.

Table 11.1: *Equivalent fonts*

Standard Java	Windows
Helvetica	Arial
TimesRoman	Times New Roman
Courier	Courier New
Dialog	MS Sans Serif
DialogInput	MS Sans Serif
Symbol	WingDings

If the font you have used in your program is not found on a user's machine, Java will use a default font. Under Windows this will usually be **Arial**. There is a way of obtaining a list of the fonts that are available on whatever machine is running your applet, the `getFontList()` method in the `java.awt.Toolkit` class, but it is probably easiest to stick to the three main fonts: **Helvetica**, TimesRoman and `Courier`. These are almost certain to be available to you.

Font Styles

We have already mentioned the different font styles: plain, bold, italic and bold-italic. As you saw in the last chapter, the font style is applied when a font is created using the new operator. For example,

```
Font f = new Font("Helvetica", Font.BOLD, 20);
```

In this instance the font, f, has been created with a style of bold. The other styles are applied by using the relevant argument as the second parameter: `Font.PLAIN`, `Font.BOLD` or `Font.ITALIC`. As the style is actually implemented as an integer constant, you can combine two styles if you want. If you want a bold, italic style you simply include both style constants with a + operator:

```
Font f = new Font("Helvetica", Font.BOLD + Font.ITALIC, 20);
```

Drawing Strings

The drawString() method should be familiar to you by now. We have used it in various examples. Here is the syntax:

```
g.drawString(textString, x-coordinate, y-coordinate);
```

where textString is a String object and x-coordinate and y-coordinate are integers specifying the horizontal and vertical location of the start of the text. Here is an example program which uses drawString() to display the three main fonts in their different styles:

Listing 11.1:
Example to display the three main fonts (see Figure 11.1)

```
import java.awt.*;
import java.applet.Applet;
public class DisplayFonts extends Applet
    {
    private Font helv;
    private Font helvBold;
    private Font helvItal;
    private Font helvBI;
    private Font cour;
    private Font courBold;
    private Font courItal;
    private Font courBI;
    private Font times;
    private Font timesBold;
    private Font timesItal;
    private Font timesBI;
    public void init()
        {
        helv = new Font("Helvetica", Font.PLAIN, 14);
        helvBold = new Font("Helvetica", Font.BOLD, 14);
        helvItal = new Font("Helvetica", Font.ITALIC, 14);
        helvBI = new Font("Helvetica", Font.BOLD + Font.ITALIC, 14);
        cour = new Font("Courier", Font. PLAIN, 14);
        courBold = new Font("Courier", Font.BOLD, 14);
        courItal = new Font("Courier", Font.ITALIC, 14);
        courBI = new Font("Courier", Font.BOLD + Font.ITALIC, 14);
        times = new Font("TimesRoman", Font. PLAIN, 14);
        timesBold = new Font("TimesRoman", Font.BOLD, 14);
        timesItal = new Font("TimesRoman", Font.ITALIC, 14);
        timesBI = new Font("TimesRoman", Font.BOLD + Font.ITALIC, 14);
        }
    public void paint(Graphics g)
        {
```

```
    g.setFont(helv);
    g.drawString("This is plain Helvetica", 10, 20);
    g.setFont(helvBold);
    g.drawString("This is bold Helvetica", 10, 40);
    g.setFont(helvItal);
    g.drawString("This is italic Helvetica", 10, 60);
    g.setFont(helvBI);
    g.drawString("This is bold italic Helvetica", 10, 80);
    g.setFont(cour);
    g.drawString("This is plain Courier", 10, 100);
    g.setFont(courBold);
    g.drawString("This is bold Courier", 10, 120);
    g.setFont(courItal);
    g.drawString("This is italic Courier", 10, 140);
    g.setFont(courBI);
    g.drawString("This is bold italic Courier", 10, 160);
    g.setFont(times);
    g.drawString("This is plain TimesRoman", 10, 180);
    g.setFont(timesBold);
    g.drawString("This is bold TimesRoman", 10, 200);
    g.setFont(timesItal);
    g.drawString("This is italic TimesRoman", 10, 220);
    g.setFont(timesBI);
    g.drawString("This is bold italic TimesRoman", 10, 240);
    }
}
```

Figure 11.1: *The* `DisplayFonts` *applet (see Listing 11.1)*

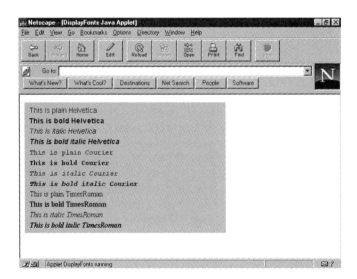

Figure 11.1 shows the output from the DisplayFonts applet.

Getting Information about Fonts

There are a number of methods for obtaining information about the current font. The following methods are available in the Font class.

- `public String getName()` returns the name of the current font (as set by the previous call to `setFont()`) . *such as, helv*
- `public int getStyle()` returns the current style of the font. The style, as mentioned before, is an integer constant. The values returned by this method are as follows:

  0 = plain, 1 = bold, 2 = italic, 3 = bold italic.

- `public int getSize()` returns the point size of the font as an integer value.
- `public boolean isPlain()` returns a true value if the font style is plain.
- `public boolean isBold()` returns a true value if the font style is bold.
- `public boolean isItalic()` returns a true value if the font style is italic.

The above methods return standard information about the font which, while useful in some circumstances, you will probably not use that often. To obtain information about the font that you will require in order to, for instance, correctly position text on the screen, you will need to make use of the data provided by the FontMetrics class. However, before looking at the FontMetrics class in detail we will first cover some typesetting terminology that you need to know.

Typesetting terms

To be able to use fonts properly in Java, you need to be aware of the meaning of some typesetting terms. There are a number of methods available to you in Java for manipulating fonts and they tend to relate directly to the terms we are about to discuss.

We have mentioned before that the x and y coordinates that you supply as arguments to the drawString() method specify the position of the lower left-hand corner of the text string. In fact, the y coordinate specifies the baseline of the text. The baseline is the invisible line that most characters rest on.

It is the lower edge of all uppercase characters and most lowercase characters like a, b and c. However, characters that have "tails" like g and y actually extend below the baseline. The "tail" part is known as the descender and the distance from the baseline to the bottom of a descender is known as the descent.

The highest part of all uppercase characters and some lowercase characters like d, k and t is known as the ascender. The distance from the baseline to the top of an ascender is known as the ascent.

The other terms relating to fonts that you will need are leading and height. Leading (pronounced "ledding") is the distance between the descent of one line and the ascent of the next line below. That is, it is the distance between the lowest point of say, a g, and the top of a d on the line below. The height of a font is the distance between two baselines. It is therefore the same as the *descent+leading+ascent*.

The following diagram illustrates the terms that we have just covered.

Figure 11.2: *Some terms from typography*

Certain characters do not fall into the above categories. If an uppercase character has an accent or diacritic, such as Ä, the topmost point of the characters will extend beyond the normal ascent. The largest height of this sort of character within a font is known as the maximum ascent.

The FontMetrics Class

The FontMetrics class enables you to obtain information about a font regarding the width and height of characters. This information is a necessity if you want to correctly position text in your programs.

To gain access to the information, you first have to create a FontMetrics object based on the current font. This is done using the `getFont-Metrics()` method (part of the Graphics class). Here is an example:

```
Font f = new Font("Helvetica", Font.PLAIN, 18);
FontMetrics fm = getFontMetrics(f);
```

Having created a FontMetrics object, you can use the object to call the FontMetrics methods. First, we will take a look at the methods available as part of the FontMetrics class. We will then show you how these methods are used in an example program.

The following methods are available in the FontMetrics class.

- `public int getLeading()` returns the standard leading, or line spacing, for the font – the amount of space that is reserved between the descent of one line of text and the ascent of the following line.

- `public int getAscent()` returns the ascent of the font – the distance from the baseline to the top of the characters.

- `public int getDescent()` returns the descent of the font – the distance from the baseline to the bottom of characters that have descenders, such as g and y.

- `public int getHeight()` returns the total height of the font – the distance between the baselines of two adjacent lines of text. It is the sum of the leading, the ascent and the descent.

- `public int getMaxAscent()` returns the maximum ascent of all characters in this font. No character will extend further than this value above the baseline.

- `public int getMaxDescent()` returns the maximum descent of all characters in this font. No character will extend further than this value below the baseline.

- `public int charWidth(int ch)` returns the width of the specified character, `ch`, in this font.

- `public int stringWidth(String str)` returns the width of the specified string, `str`, in this font.

One of the problems associated with drawing text in Java is that, if you want to mix the fonts used in a line of text, you have to work out for yourself where a string displayed in one font will end so that you can correctly place the beginning of the next string if it is displayed in a different font.

Java doesn't remember the current writing position for text. This example program will illustrate the difficulties involved with positioning text and how the FontMetrics class can help. The program will display two lines of text in the four different styles of the Times Roman font – plain, bold, italic and bold-italic. The text will be centered within the applet area.

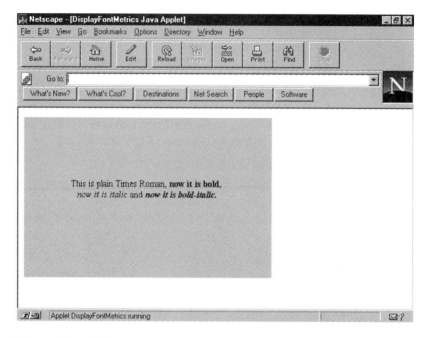

Here is the code listing:

Listing 11.2:
Example
showing how the
FontMetrics
class can be used
(see Figure 11.3)

```java
import java.awt.*;
import java.applet.Applet;
public class DisplayFontMetrics extends Applet
    {
    private Font times;
    private Font timesBold;
    private Font timesItal;
    private Font timesBI;
    private FontMetrics fmTimes;
    private FontMetrics fmTimesBold;
    private FontMetrics fmTimesItal;
    private FontMetrics fmTimesBI;
    public void init()
        {
        times = new Font("TimesRoman", Font. PLAIN, 14);
        timesBold = new Font("TimesRoman", Font.BOLD, 14);
        timesItal = new Font("TimesRoman", Font.ITALIC, 14);
        timesBI = new Font("TimesRoman", Font.BOLD + Font.ITALIC, 14);
        fmTimes = getFontMetrics(times);
```

```
            fmTimesBold = getFontMetrics(timesBold);
            fmTimesItal = getFontMetrics(timesItal);
            fmTimesBI = getFontMetrics(timesBI);
            }

        public void paint(Graphics g)
            {
            String str1 = "This is plain Times Roman, ";
            String str2 = "now it is bold, ";
            String str3 = "now it is italic ";
            String str4 = "and ";
            String str5 = "now it is bold-italic.";
            int wStr1 = fmTimes.stringWidth(str1);
            int wStr2 = fmTimesBold.stringWidth(str2);
            int wStr3 = fmTimesItal.stringWidth(str3);
            int wStr4 = fmTimes.stringWidth(str4);
            int wStr5 = fmTimesBI.stringWidth(str5);
            int yPos = (this.size().height - (fmTimes.getHeight()*2)) / 2;
            int xPos = (this.size().width - (wStr1 + wStr2)) / 2;
            g.setFont(times);
            g.drawString(str1, xPos, yPos);
            xPos += fmTimes.stringWidth(str1);
            g.setFont(timesBold);
            g.drawString(str2, xPos, yPos);
            xPos = (this.size().width - (wStr3 + wStr4 + wStr5)) / 2;
            yPos += fmTimes.getHeight();
            g.setFont(timesItal);
            g.drawString(str3, xPos, yPos);
            xPos += fmTimesItal.stringWidth(str3);
            g.setFont(times);
            g.drawString(str4, xPos, yPos);
            xPos += fmTimes.stringWidth(str4);
            g.setFont(timesBI);
            g.drawString(str5, xPos, yPos);
            }
        }
```

The init() method first creates the font objects for the four different styles of the Times Roman font. The next four lines create FontMetrics objects for each of the fonts using the getFontMetrics() method.

Note   It is more efficient to create the font and font metrics objects as part of the initialisation rather than in the paint() method. The paint() method is called a number of times during the lifetime of an applet and creating and destroying font objects each time adds to the system over-heads. Efficiency is improved by creating the objects once, in the init() method.

In the paint() method we create the five strings that will make up the text to be displayed. The stringWidth() method of the FontMetrics class is then called to calculate the length, in pixels, of each string and assign it to a local variable. Notice that we make the stringWidth() call using the relevant FontMetric object in each case. For instance, the fmTimes object is used to obtain the length of the first string which will be displayed in a plain Times Roman font:

```
int wStr1 = fmTimes.stringWidth(str1);
```

and the fmTimesBold object is used for the second string, which is in a bold typeface:

```
int wStr2 = fmTimesBold.stringWidth(str2);
```

The next two lines calculate the coordinates for the starting position of the first line of text:

```
int yPos = (this.size().height - (fmTimes.getHeight()*2)) / 2;
int xPos = (this.size().width - (wStr1 + wStr2)) / 2;
```

The size() method returns the current size of a component. In this case we use the this keyword to find the size if the applet. The size() method returns a dimension object which has two integer instance variables, width and height.

To calculate the y coordinate we first use the FontMetrics getHeight() method to obtain the total height of the text, multiply it by two as we are displaying two lines of text, subtract it from the height of the applet area and then divide the result by two to centre the text. The x coordinate is calculated by adding the widths of the two strings forming the first line, subtracting the toal from the width of the applet and then dividing by two. The next five statements draw the first line of text:

```
g.setFont(times);
g.drawString(str1, xPos, yPos);
xPos += fmTimes.stringWidth(str1);
g.setFont(timesBold);
g.drawString(str2, xPos, yPos);
```

Notice that once we have drawn the first string, we have to recalculate the starting x coordinate for the second string (in a bold font) by adding the length of the first string to the original starting position. Once this has been obtained we change the current font to bold and draw the next string.

Next, we calculate the x and y cordinates for the second line of text:

```
xPos = (this.size().width - (wStr3 + wStr4 + wStr5)) / 2;
yPos += fmTimes.getHeight();
```

Finally, the second line of text is drawn:

```
g.setFont(timesItal);
g.drawString(str3, xPos, yPos);
xPos += fmTimesItal.stringWidth(str3);
g.setFont(times);
g.drawString(str4, xPos, yPos);
xPos += fmTimes.stringWidth(str4);
g.setFont(timesBI);
g.drawString(str5, xPos, yPos);
```

Once a string has been displayed, we recalculate the x position by adding the length of that string to the previous x coordinate.

When calling the getFontMetrics() method, we have passed the name of the font as a parameter. It is also possible to omit the font as an argument to the getTextMetrics() method – if this is the case the font metrics for the current font will be returned. However, you must use the current graphics object in the call.

For instance:

```
g.setFont(times);
FontMetrics fmTimes = g.getFontMetrics();
```

Colour

Colours in Java are represented by the Color class where an object of type Color is a combination of RGB values. An instance of the Color class has a red, a green and a blue component with a value between 0 and 255. These three byte values combine to form a 24-bit colour representation. White is 255, 255, 255 and black is 0, 0, 0 – millions of other colours can be represented by all the possible combinations of the three values between these two extremes.

On platforms that don't support 24-bit colour, Java will map the colour to the closest value. You must therefore bear in mind that most users are probably going to be restricted to 256 colours when you are designing your programs.

A number of standard colours are implemented as static variables in the Color class. For instance, Color.green is made up of a value of 0 for the red component, 255 for the green component and 0 again for the blue, ie. 0, 255, 0. Color.red is 255, 0, 0 and Color.blue is 0, 0, 255. Here is the complete list of the defined variables:

Table 11.2: *Colours and their RGB values*

Name	RGB value	Name	RGB value
Color.red	255, 0, 0	Color.cyan	0, 255, 255
Color.green	0, 255, 0	Color.orange	255, 200, 0
Color.blue	0, 0, 255	Color.pink	255, 175, 175
Color.black	0, 0, 0	Color.gray	128, 128, 128
Color.white	255, 255, 255	Color.darkGray	64, 64, 64
Color.yellow	255, 255, 0	Color.lightGray	192, 192, 192
Color.magenta	255, 0, 255		

You can also create your own colours by creating a Color object with the required red, green and blue values. For instance, to create a dark red colour you would create a new color object like this:

```
Color darkRed = new Color (128, 0, 0);
```

Colours can also be created using three floating point values between 0.0 and 1.0. For example, this is a dark green colour:

```
Color darkGreen = new Color (0.0f, 0.3f, 0.0f);
```

You set the current colour in Java the same way as you set the current font, by using the Graphics class method, setColor(). These statements will set the current font to Helvetica and the current colour to blue:

```
Font helv = new Font("Helvetica", Font.PLAIN, 14);
g.setFont(helv);
g.setColor(Color.blue);
```

All text displayed from this point will be in the Helvetica font in the colour blue.

The Color class also contains two methods for making colours brighter or darker. They are called, amazingly, brighter() and darker(). They work by increasing or decreasing each element of a colour by a set factor.

This example program illustrates the use of colour with text:

Listing 11.3:
Example showing how colours are displayed (see Figure 11.4)

```java
import java.awt.*;
import java.applet.Applet;
public class Colours extends Applet
    {
    private Font timesBold;
    public void init()
        {
        timesBold = new Font("TimesRoman", Font.BOLD, 14);
        }
    public void paint(Graphics g)
        {
        g.setFont(timesBold);
        int fontHeight = g.getFontMetrics().getHeight();
        g.setColor(Color.red);
        g.drawString("This is red", 10, fontHeight);
        g.setColor(Color.green);
        g.drawString("This is green", 10, fontHeight*2);
        g.setColor(Color.blue);
        g.drawString("This is blue", 10, fontHeight*3);
        g.setColor(Color.black);
        g.drawString("This is black", 10, fontHeight*4);
        g.setColor(Color.white);
        g.drawString("This is white", 10, fontHeight*5);
        g.setColor(Color.yellow);
        g.drawString("This is yellow", 10, fontHeight*6);
        g.setColor(Color.magenta);
        g.drawString("This is magenta", 10, fontHeight*7);
        g.setColor(Color.cyan);
        g.drawString("This is cyan", 10, fontHeight*8);
        g.setColor(Color.darkGray);
        g.drawString("This is darkGray", 10, fontHeight*9);
        Color darkRed = new Color(128, 0, 0);
        g.setColor(darkRed);
```

```
                    g.drawString("This is dark red", 10, fontHeight*10);
                    Color darkerRed = darkRed.darker();
                    g.setColor(darkerRed);
                    g.drawString("This is a darker red", 10, fontHeight*11);
                    Color brighterRed = darkRed.brighter();
                    g.setColor(brighterRed);
                    g.drawString("This is a brighter red", 10, fontHeight*12);
                    Color darkGreen = new Color(0.0f, 0.3f, 0.0f);
                    g.setColor(darkGreen);
                    g.drawString("This is darker green", 10, fontHeight*13);
                    }
            }
```

Figure 11.4: *The* Colours *applet (see Listing 11.3)*

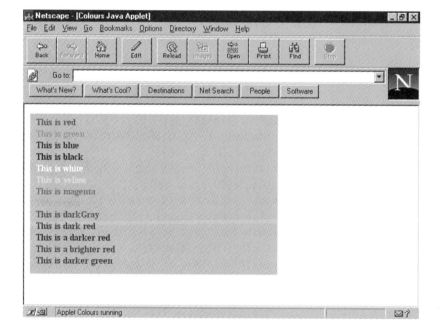

Summary

In short, the five fonts that you can guarantee to always be there no matter which computer platform you deploy an application on are: Helvetica, TimesRoman. Courier, Dialog and DialogInput. You may or may not be able to get hold of the Symbol font.

Fonts have several different styles: bold, italic, bold italic and plain. There are several methods that can be employed to affect a font's style. Also, there are several methods at your disposal that will determine a font's characteristics, such as `getStyle()` and `getSize()`.

In order to manage fonts inside Java properly you will need to be aware of the physical elements that make up the construction of a font: height, leading, width, ascent, descent and so on.

When changing the colour of a font (do not forget that when programming it is COLOR you will use and not COLOUR) you will be working with RGB values (Red, Green and Blue) and these three bytes values will combine to give a 24-bit colour representation.

12

Graphics

Introduction

The Graphics class provides methods for drawing a variety of graphical shapes – lines, rectangles, ovals, circles, arcs and polygons. As mentioned before, any drawing that you perform in Java must be through an instance of the Graphics class. All of the methods in the Graphics class use the Java coordinate system – x and y values that define a point on the screen within the applet. The origin (0, 0) lies at the upper left-hand corner of the screen with the x values for the horizontal coordinate increasing to the right and the y value defining the vertical coordinate increasing downwards. There are no negative values – all graphics coordinates must be positive. The graphics methods in Java are very limited in scope. For instance, all drawing is carried out using a line thickness of one pixel. If you want thicker lines you must write your own methods. We include some examples of how to do this later on in the chapter. There is also no provision for different pens such as you get in Windows for drawing dashed or dotted lines. All shapes, in outline form or filled, are drawn in the colour that is current for the Graphics object.

Drawing Lines

The drawLine() method allows you to draw a straight line from one point on the screen to another. The method requires four arguments – the x and y coordinates of the starting point and the x and y coordinates of the end point. Here is the syntax:

```
g.drawLine(xStart, yStart, xEnd, yEnd);
```

This simple example program draws a noughts and crosses game:

```java
import java.awt.*;
import java.applet.Applet;
public class NoughtsAndCrosses extends Applet
    {
    public void paint(Graphics g)
        {
        g.drawLine(50, 100, 200, 100);
        g.drawLine(50, 150, 200, 150);
        g.drawLine(100, 50, 100, 200);
        g.drawLine(150, 50, 150, 200);
        }
    }
```

Figure 12.1: *The
NoughtsAnd-
Crosses applet
(see Listing 12.1)*

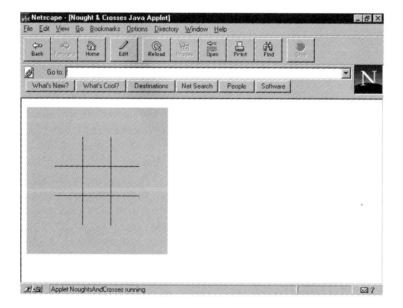

Drawing Rectangles

Three different types of rectangle can be drawn using the drawing
methods – ordinary rectangles, rectangles with rounded corners, and
three-dimensional rectangles which have a shaded border. The first
two types can be drawn either in outline form or filled with a colour.
The 3D rectangle can be either raised or indented.

Ordinary Rectangles

Ordinary rectangles are drawn with the drawRect() and fillRect() methods. The drawRect() method draws a rectangle in outline form, and fillRect() draws a filled-in rectangle. Here is the syntax for both:

```
g.drawRect(xStart, yStart, width, height);
g.fillRect(xStart, yStart, width, height);
```

Four arguments are required for each – the x and y coordinates of the upper left-hand corner and the width and height values of the rectangle. For instance, the following paint() method will draw two rectangles with a width of 150 pixels and a height of 200 pixels side by side, the left one in outline form and the right filled with the colour blue.

Listing 12.2:
Drawing plain rectangles (see Figure 12.2)

```
import java.awt.*;
import java.applet.Applet;
public class PlainRectangles extends Applet
    {
    public void paint(Graphics g)
        {
        g.drawRect(20, 20, 150, 200);
        g.setColor(Color.blue);
        g.fillRect(200, 20, 150, 200);
        }
    }
```

Figure 12.2: *The* PlainRectangles *applet list (see Listing 12.2)*

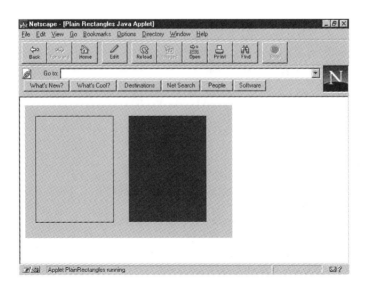

The following program draws two sets of ever-decreasing rectangles – one in outline form and one filled alternately in black and white:

Listing 12.3: *Ever decreasing rectangles (see Figure 12.3)*

```java
import java.awt.*;
import java.applet.Applet;
public class Rectangles extends Applet
    {
    public void paint(Graphics g)
        {
        int left = 5;
        int top = 5;
        int width = (this.size().width) / 2 - 10;
        int height = this.size().height - 10;
        drawRects(g, left, top, width, height);
        left = width + 15;
        drawFilledRects(g, left, top, width, height);
        }
    public void drawRects(Graphics g, int l, int t, int w, int h)
        {
        while (h > 0)
            {
            g.drawRect(l, t, w, h);
            l += 10;
            t += 10;
            w -= 20;
            h -= 20;
            }
        }
    public void drawFilledRects(Graphics g, int l, int t, int w, int h)
        {
        g.setColor(Color.black);
        while (h > 0)
            {
            g.fillRect(l, t, w, h);
            l += 10;
            t += 10;
            w -= 20;
            h -= 20;
            if (g.getColor() == Color.white)
                g.setColor(Color.black);
            else
                g.setColor(Color.white);
            }
        }
    }
```

Figure 12.3: *The Rectangles applet (see Listing 12.3)*

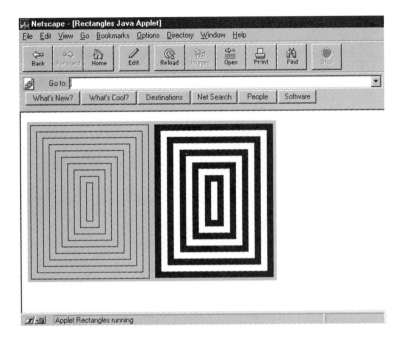

The paint() method controls the drawing of the two sets of rectangles. The x and y coordinates of the upper left corner are set first of all:

```
int left = 5;
int top = 5;
```

The program then uses the size() method to obtain the width and height of the applet. We use this information to calculate the width and height of the rectangles:

```
int width = (this.size().width) / 2 - 10;
int height = this.size().height - 10;
```

The first set of rectangles, in outline form, is drawn by the method drawRects(). The Graphics object g is passed as the first argument:

```
drawRects(g, left, top, width, height);
```

After drawing the first set of rectangles the left variable is recalculated to correctly position the filled rectangles. The drawFilledRects() method is then called to do the drawing:

```
left = width + 15;
drawFilledRects(g, left, top, width, height);
```

The drawRects() method uses a simple while loop to decrease the size of the drawn rectangle by 10 pixels until the current height of the rectangle is no longer a positive value. The drawFilledRects() method first sets the current colour to black before uses a similar while loop to draw each filled rectangle. After the rectangle is drawn a test is carried out to change the colour.

Rounded Rectangles

Rounded rectangles are the same as ordinary ones except that they have rounded corners, and are drawn using the methods drawRoundRect() and fillRoundRect(). Here is the syntax for these methods:

```
g.drawRoundRect(xStart, yStart, width, height, arcWidth, arcHeight);
g.fillRoundRect(xStart, yStart, width, height, arcWidth, arcHeight);
```

The first four arguments are the same as for the previous rectangle-drawing methods, the x and y coordinates of the upper left-hand corner and the width and height, and there are two extra arguments – the width and height of the arcs which form the rounded corners of the rectangle. The arc width is the horizontal distance from the corner to the point at which you want the arc to begin. The arc height is the vertical distance. Therefore, the greater the values of the arc width and height arguments, the more rounded the rectangle.

Figure 12.4: *The RoundRectangles applet (see Listing 12.4)*

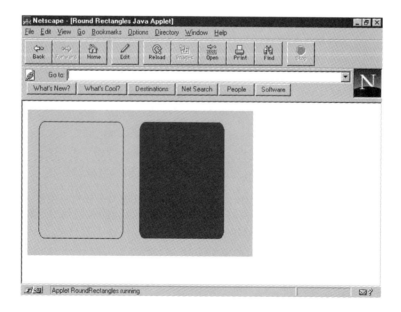

The following code draws two rounded rectangles (see Figure 12.4). The same overall width and height are used with rounded corners. The corners begin 20 pixels along the horizontal and 30 pixels along the vertical.

Listing 12.4:
Rounded rectangles example (see Figure 12.4)

```
import java.awt.*;
import java.applet.Applet;
public class RoundRectangles extends Applet
    {
    public void paint(Graphics g)
        {
        g.drawRoundRect(20, 20, 150, 200, 20, 30);
        g.setColor(Color.blue);
        g.fillRoundRect(200, 20, 150, 200, 20, 30);
        }
    }
```

3D Rectangles

Three-dimensional rectangles are drawn with a shadow which gives the effect of the rectangle appearing raised or indented. The draw3DRect() method requires five arguments:

```
g.draw3DRect(xStart, yStart, width, height, raised);
```

The first four are the usual ones – the x and y coordinates of the upper left corner and the width and height of the rectangle – the fifth argument, raised, is a boolean value which determines whether the rectangle is to be raised (true) or indented (false). Here are some three-dimensional rectangles, the top two are drawn using the draw3DRect() method – one is raised and one indented – and the bottom rectangle uses the fill3DRect() method and is indented:

Listing 12.5:
Example displaying 3D rectangles (see Figure 12.5)

```
import java.awt.*;
import java.applet.Applet;
public class ThreeDRectangles extends Applet
    {
    public void paint(Graphics g)
        {
        g.setColor(Color.lightGray);
        g.draw3DRect(20, 20, 125, 75, true);
        g.draw3DRect(200, 20, 125, 75, false);
```

```
        g.fill3DRect(20, 120, 305, 75, false);
        }
    }
```

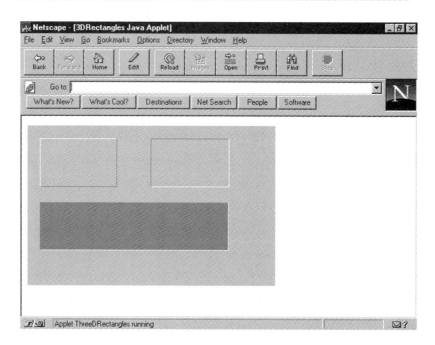

You will find that 3D rectangles don't look very 3D if you draw them in
any other colour apart from light grey on the usual light grey background. Also, they look pretty uninspiring if you just use the
draw3DRect() method as supplied in the Java Graphics class library. By
experimenting a little you can produce output that looks a little more
interesting than the standard 3D rectangles. For instance, by combining two calls to draw3DRect(), one raised and one indented, a reasonable looking frame can be created. The following example draws two
frames that illustrate this, one with a raised appearance, one that is
indented:

Listing 12.6:
*Raised and
indented frames
(see Figure 12.6)*

```
import java.awt.*;
import java.applet.Applet;
public class DrawFrames extends Applet
    {
    public void paint(Graphics g)
        {
```

```
    drawFrame(g, 20, 20, 150, 200, 6, true);
    drawFrame(g, 200, 20, 150, 200, 6, false);
    }
public void drawFrame(Graphics g, int left, int top,
int width, int height, int frameWidth, boolean raised)
    {
    g.setColor(Color.lightGray);
    if (raised)
        {
        g.draw3DRect(left, top, width, height, true);
        g.draw3DRect(left+frameWidth, top+frameWidth,
            width-(2*frameWidth), height-(2*frameWidth), false);
        }
    else
        {
        g.draw3DRect(left, top, width, height, false);
        g.draw3DRect(left+frameWidth, top+frameWidth,
            width-(2*frameWidth), height-(2*frameWidth), true);
        }
    }
}
```

Figure 12.6: *The DrawFrames applet (see Listing 12.6)*

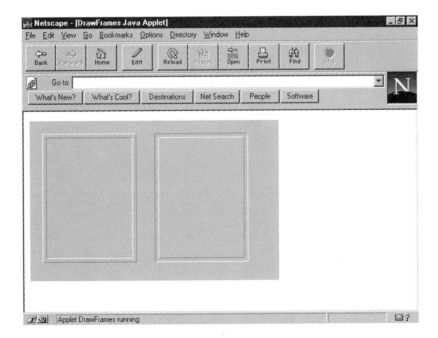

The drawFrame() method expects the usual four rectangle arguments plus a frameWidth and a raised argument. If the last argument, raised, is set to true the method will draw a frame, with a thickness equal to frameWidth, that is raised. If false is passed as the last argument the frame will appear indented.

Drawing Ovals and Circles

The methods used for drawing ovals, drawOval() and fillOval(), expect the same four arguments as the plain rectangle methods:

```
g.drawOval(xStart, yStart, width, height);
g.fillOval(xStart, yStart, width, height);
```

The x and y coordinates of the upper left corner and the width and height are of an imaginary "bounding box" rectangle which encloses the oval you wish to draw. To position the oval you must therefore calculate where the upper left corner of this enclosing rectangle would be. If the width and height arguments are equal, a circle will be drawn. Here is an example program which draws a set of ever-decreasing ovals on the left and a series of circles, alternately filled in black and white, on the right:

Listing 12.7:
Example showing how ovals and circles are drawn (see Figure 12.7)

```java
import java.awt.*;
import java.applet.Applet;
public class Ovals extends Applet
{
    public void paint(Graphics g)
    {
        int left = 5;
        int top = 5;
        int width = (this.size().width) / 2 - 10;
        int height = this.size().height - 10;
        drawOvals(g, left, top, width, height);
        left = width + 15;
        height = width;
        top = (this.size().height - height) / 2;
        drawFilledOvals(g, left, top, width, height);
    }
    public void drawOvals(Graphics g, int l, int t, int w, int h)
    {
        while (h > 0)
            {
```

```
            g.drawOval(l, t, w, h);
            l += 10;
            t += 10;
            w -= 20;
            h -= 20;
            }
        }
    public void drawFilledOvals(Graphics g, int l, int t, int w, int h)
        {
        g.setColor(Color.black);
        while (h > 0)
            {
            g.fillOval(l, t, w, h);
            l += 10;
            t += 10;
            w -= 20;
            h -= 20;
            if (g.getColor() == Color.white)
                g.setColor(Color.black);
            else
                g.setColor(Color.white);
            }
        }
    }
```

Figure 12.7: *The Ovals applet (see Listing 12.7)*

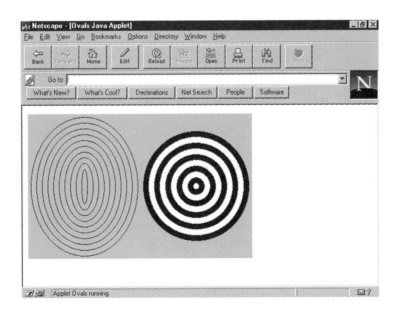

Drawing Arcs

Arcs are sections of an oval. As usual, there are two drawing methods, drawArc() and fillArc(). Here is the syntax:

```
g.drawArc(xStart, yStart, width, height, startAngle, arcAngle);
g.fillArc(xStart, yStart, width, height, startAngle, arcAngle);
```

To draw an arc you must first visualise the oval (or circle) on which it will be based. The first four arguments of the methods are the upper left corner coordinates and width and height of the "bounding box" rectangle of the oval. The *startAngle* argument is the angle at which to start drawing the arc, where 0 degrees is at the 3 o'clock position, 90 degrees is at 12 o'clock, 180 degrees is at 9 o'clock and 270 degrees is 6 o'clock. The *arcAngle* argument is the number of degrees round the oval or circle that you want the arc to be drawn. Positive values of *arcAngle* indicate counter-clockwise rotations, negative values of *arcAngle* are drawn clockwise. To draw an arc based on a circle with a bounding square with upper left corner of (50, 50) and width and height of 100 with the arc beginning at the 90 degrees (or 12 o'clock) point and continuing around the circle for 270 degrees, ending at the 0 degrees position (or 3 o'clock), you would use the following code:

```
g.drawArc(50, 50, 100, 100, 90, 270);
```

The same arc can be drawn by starting at the other endpoint and using a negative value for the arc angle. This line of code draws the same arc:

```
g.drawArc(50, 50, 100, 100, 0, -270);
```

The fillArc() method fills the arcs in a pie section format, a radius line is drawn from each endpoint to form the area to be filled. The following applet shows the above arc in its outline form and filled in. The fillArc() method draws the arc using a negative arcAngle argument.

Listing 12.8:
Drawing arcs (see Figure 12.8)

```
import java.awt.*;
import java.applet.Applet;
public class Arcs extends Applet
    {
    public void paint(Graphics g)
        {
        g.drawArc(50, 50, 100, 100, 90, 270);
        g.setColor(Color.blue);
        g.fillArc(200, 50, 100, 100, 0, -270);
        }
    }
```

Figure 12.8:
*The Arcs applet
(see Listing 12.8)*

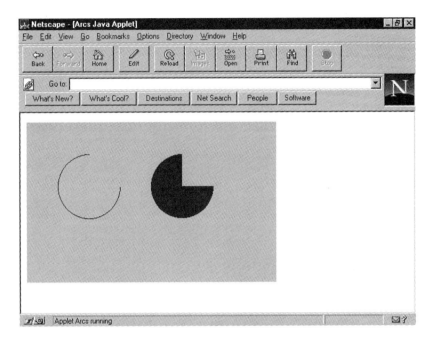

Here is an applet which uses the fillArc() method to draw a pie chart:

Listing 12.9:
*Example using
fillArc() (see
Figure 12.9)*

```
import java.awt.*;
import java.applet.Applet;

public class PieChart extends Applet
    {
    int sectionSizes[] = {60, 150, 30, 45, 75};
    Color sectionColours[] = {Color.blue, Color.red, Color.cyan,
        Color.green, Color.yellow};
    public void paint(Graphics g)
        {
        drawPieChart(g, 50, 20, 200, 200, 90, sectionSizes,
            sectionColours);
        }
    public void drawPieChart(Graphics g, int l, int t, int w, int h,
        int start, int sizes[], Color colours[])
        {
        for (int i = 0; i < sizes.length; i++)
            {
            g.setColor(colours[i]);
```

```
                    g.fillArc(l, t, w, h, start, sizes[i]);
                    start += sizes[i];
                    }
                }
            }
```

Figure 12.9: *The*
PieChart applet
(see Listing 12.9)

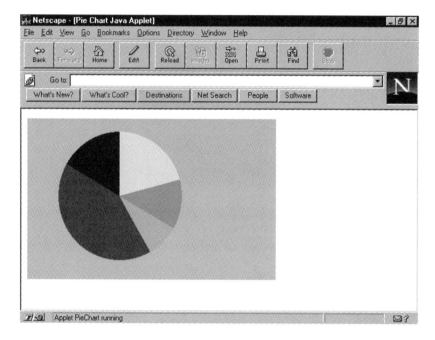

Two array variables are created – sectionsSizes[], to hold the values of each section's arc size in degrees and sectionColours[], which holds the colour of each section in the pie chart.

The drawPieChart() method does the work of drawing the pie chart and is passed eight arguments: the Graphics object, the four standard values for defining the bounding box rectangle, the starting point in the circle at which to start drawing each section and the two array objects holding the sizes and colours of the pie chart sections.

A for loop is used to draw the sections of the pie, using the values held in the array objects passed to it, the length method being used to find out the number of values held in the sizes array. In the body of the loop the fill colour for the section is made the current colour, the fillArc() method is called to draw the section and the start angle is then updated to point to the start of the next section.

Drawing Polygons

A polygon is a shape with any number of sides. As with previous graphical shapes, there are two methods provided in Java for drawing polygons, drawPolygon() and fillPolygon(). The figure is drawn by passing to the methods the x and y coordinates of each point in the polygon. Lines are drawn to connect each point. The coordinates can be passed to the drawing methods in two different forms.

The first form expects two integer arrays – one for the x coordinates and one for the y coordinates – and an integer holding the total number of points. The two arrays must obviously have the same number of elements. The second form expects an object of type Polygon as the argument. Here is the syntax for the first form:

```
g.drawPolygon(x-coordinates, y-coordinates, totalPoints);
g.fillPolygon(x-coordinates, y-coordinates, totalPoints);
```

As usual, the fill() method fills the shape with the current Graphics object colour.

The following program illustrates the use of the coordinate arrays as arguments. Two star shapes are drawn, one in outline form and one filled:

Listing 12.10:
Drawing polygons in Java (see Figure 12.10)

```
import java.awt.*;
import java.applet.Applet;
public class Polygons1 extends Applet
    {
    public void paint(Graphics g)
        {
        int totalPoints = 6;
        int xPoints1[] = {110, 50, 200, 20, 170, 110};
        int yPoints1[] = {20, 190, 80, 80, 190, 20};
        g.drawPolygon(xPoints1, yPoints1, totalPoints);
        int xPoints2[] = {310, 250, 400, 220, 370, 310};
        int yPoints2[] = {20, 190, 80, 80, 190, 20};
        g.setColor(Color.blue);
        g.fillPolygon(xPoints2, yPoints2, totalPoints);
        }
    }
```

Figure 12.10: *The* Polygons1 *applet (see Listing 1210)*

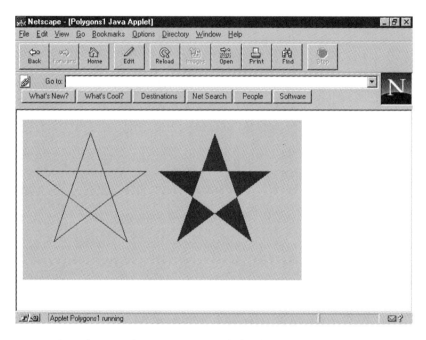

Notice that the coordinate arrays include the starting point again at the end. Java does not automatically close a polygon shape so you must always return to the starting point.

The above example also shows that Java uses what is called the *alternate filling method* when filling polygons. This means that it only fills in those interior parts of the polygon that are accessible from the outside of the polygon by crossing an odd number of lines. Any other interiors are not filled. In the example above the centre of the star is not filled because, to reach it from outside, the polygon would require crossing two lines, an even number.

To use the second method of drawing polygons, you must first create an instance of the Polygon class. There are two ways of doing this. You can either create a finished Polygon shape object from integer arrays like the ones used above or you can create an empty Polygon object and add points to it afterwards.

The following applet, which draws two diamond shapes in outline and filled form, shows both ways of creating Polygon objects:

```java
import java.awt.*;
import java.applet.Applet;
public class Polygons2 extends Applet
  {
  public void paint(Graphics g)
    {
    // first way of creating a Polygon object
    int xPoints[] = {100, 150, 100, 50, 100};
    int yPoints[] = {20, 120, 220, 120, 20};
    int totalPoints = 5;
    Polygon polygon1 = new Polygon(xPoints, yPoints, totalPoints);
        g.drawPolygon(polygon1);
    // second way of creating a Polygon object
    Polygon polygon2 = new Polygon();
    polygon2.addPoint(300, 20);
    polygon2.addPoint(350, 120);
    polygon2.addPoint(300, 220);
    polygon2.addPoint(250, 120);
    polygon2.addPoint(300, 20);
    g.setColor(Color.blue);
    g.fillPolygon(polygon2);
    }
  }
```

To create the first polygon object we define two integer arrays for the x and y coordinates of each point in the diamond and define an integer to hold the number of points:

```java
int xPoints[] = {100, 150, 100, 50, 100};
int yPoints[] = {20, 120, 220, 120, 20};
int totalPoints = 5;
```

The polygon object is then created using the new operator, passing the above arrays and integer as arguments:

```java
Polygon polygon1 = new Polygon(xPoints, yPoints, totalPoints);
```

The diamond-shaped polygon is then drawn:

```java
g.drawPolygon(polygon1);
```

For the filled diamond shape we have first created an empty polygon object:

```java
Polygon polygon2 = new Polygon();
```

We have then added each of the points in the diamond shape using the addPoint() method of the Polygon class. This way of creating polygons is useful if you need to create a shape on the fly:

```
polygon2.addPoint(300, 20);
polygon2.addPoint(350, 120);
polygon2.addPoint(300, 220);
polygon2.addPoint(250, 120);
polygon2.addPoint(300, 20);
```

Finally, the colour is set and the fillPolygon() method is called to draw the filled diamond:

```
g.setColor(Color.blue);
g.fillPolygon(polygon2);
```

Figure 12.11: *The*
Polygons2 applet
(see Listing 12.11)

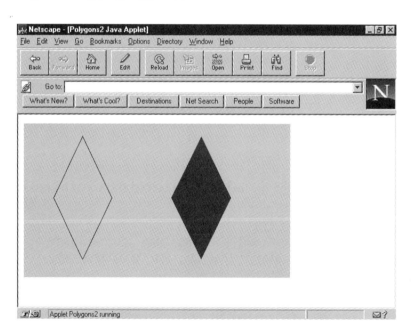

Clearing, copying and moving rectangles

Java provides two methods which enable you to clear all or part of your applet or to move or copy rectangular areas from one location to another.

To clear an area of your applet you can use the clearRect() method. This will clear a rectangular area, setting it to the background colour of the applet. It requires the same arguments as the drawRect() method – the x and y coordinates of the upper left-hand corner and the width and height of the rectangle you want cleared.

The copyArea() method allows you to copy a rectangular area of the applet to another location. It can be combined with the clearRect() method to move areas of the screen. It requires six arguments – the first four are the same four arguments that are always used for defining a rectangle, the upper left corner coordinates, width and height. The other two arguments are the horizontal and vertical distances that you want the rectangular area moved.

The following code extract will draw a 50x50 rectangle and then move it 100 pixels to the right and 200 pixels down:

```
g.drawRect(20, 20, 50, 50);
g.copyArea(20, 20, 50, 50, 100, 200);
g.clearRect(20, 20, 50, 50);
```

Improving the Graphics Class Methods

The applet presented in this section illustrates how you can improve the functionality of the graphics drawing methods as they are supplied in Java.

The following methods (drawRect(), drawRoundRect(), draw3DRect(), drawOval() and drawArc())have been overloaded to accept three extra arguments: a graphics object, an integer line width argument and a Color object. Using these methods gives you the ability to draw shapes with a line thickness greater than one and specify which colour you want the shape to be. Each method saves the current graphics colour before carrying out the drawing and then resets the colour back to it's original setting afterwards.

All of the corresponding fill methods have also been included. In most cases the colour is passed as an argument. In the case of fill3DRect(), a line thickness is also passed, the 3D part of the rectangle being drawn in white and dark grey with the colour argument referring to the inside of the rectangle.

Two other methods have also been included: drawFrame() and drawText(). The drawFrame() method has already been covered earlier in the chapter. The `drawText()` method allows you to specify a font and a colour when drawing a text string. The current font and colour settings are saved and reset after the string has been drawn.

Here is a screenshot of the applet:

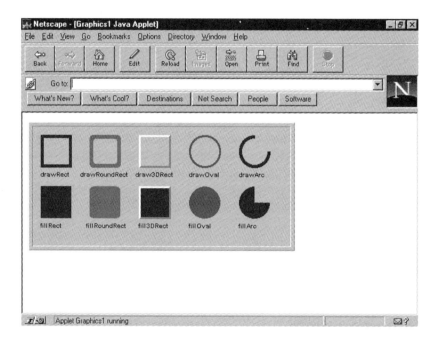

This is the complete source code:

```java
import java.awt.*;
import java.applet.Applet;

public class Graphics1 extends Applet
   {
   private Font f;
   public void init()
      {
      f = new Font("Helvetica", Font.BOLD, 10);
      }
   public void paint(Graphics g)
      {
      drawFrame(g, 0, 0, this.size().width-1, this.size().height-1,
         6, true);
```

```
      drawRect(g, 20, 20, 50, 50, 5, Color.blue);
      drawText(g, "drawRect", 20, 85, f, Color.black);
      drawRoundRect(g, 100, 20, 50, 50, 10, 15, 6, Color.magenta);
      drawText(g, "drawRoundRect", 85, 85, f, Color.black);
      draw3DRect(g, 180, 20, 50, 50, 3, Color.lightGray, true);
      drawText(g, "draw3DRect", 175, 85, f, Color.black);
      drawOval(g, 260, 20, 50, 50, 3, Color.red);
      drawText(g, "drawOval", 260, 85, f, Color.black);
      drawArc(g, 340, 20, 50, 50, 90, 270, 5, Color.blue);
      drawText(g, "drawArc", 340, 85, f, Color.black);

      fillRect(g, 20, 100, 50, 50, Color.blue);
      drawText(g, "fillRect", 20, 165, f, Color.black);

      fillRoundRect(g, 100, 100, 50, 50, 20, 10, Color.magenta);
      drawText(g, "fillRoundRect", 95, 165, f, Color.black);

      fill3DRect(g, 180, 100, 50, 50, 4, Color.blue, true);
      drawText(g, "fill3DRect", 180, 165, f, Color.black);

      fillOval(g, 260, 100, 50, 50, Color.red);
      drawText(g, "fillOval", 260, 165, f, Color.black);

      fillArc(g, 340, 100, 50, 50, 90, 270, Color.blue);
      drawText(g, "fillArc", 340, 165, f, Color.black);
      }
   public void drawRect(Graphics g, int left, int top,
      int width, int height, int lineWidth, Color colour)
      {
      Color savedColour = g.getColor();
      g.setColor(colour);
      if (lineWidth < 1)
         lineWidth = 1;
      for(int i=0; i < lineWidth; i++)
         {
         g.drawRect(left, top, width, height);
         left++;
         top++;
         width -= 2;
         height -= 2;
         }
      g.setColor(savedColour);
```

```
        }
public void fillRect(Graphics g, int left, int top,
    int width, int height, Color colour)
    {
    Color savedColour = g.getColor();
    g.setColor(colour);
    g.fillRect(left, top, width, height);
    g.setColor(savedColour);
    }
public void drawRoundRect(Graphics g, int left, int top,
    int width, int height,
    int arcWidth, int arcHeight,
    int lineWidth, Color colour)
    {
    Color savedColour = g.getColor();
    g.setColor(colour);
    if (lineWidth < 1)
       lineWidth = 1;
    for(int i=0; i < lineWidth; i++)
       {
       g.drawRoundRect(left, top, width, height,
              arcWidth, arcHeight);
       if (i < lineWidth - 1)
          {
          g.drawRoundRect(left, top, width-1, height-1,
             arcWidth, arcHeight);
          g.drawRoundRect(left+1, top, width-1, height-1,
             arcWidth, arcHeight);
          g.drawRoundRect(left, top+1, width-1, height-1,
             arcWidth, arcHeight);
          g.drawRoundRect(left+1, top+1, width-1, height-1,
             arcWidth, arcHeight);
          left++;
          top++;
          width -= 2;
          height -= 2;
          }
       }
    g.setColor(savedColour);
    }
public void fillRoundRect(Graphics g, int left, int top,
        int width, int height, int arcWidth, int arcHeight,
```

```
      Color colour)
   {
   Color savedColour = g.getColor();
   g.setColor(colour);
   g.fillRoundRect(left, top, width, height, arcWidth,
      arcHeight);
   g.setColor(savedColour);
   }
public void draw3DRect(Graphics g, int left, int top,
      int width, int height, int lineWidth, Color colour,
      boolean raised)
   {
   Color savedColour = g.getColor();
   g.setColor(colour);
   if (lineWidth < 1)
      lineWidth = 1;
   for(int i=0; i < lineWidth; i++)
      {
      g.draw3DRect(left, top, width, height, raised);
      left++;
      top++;
      width -= 2;
      height -= 2;
      }
   g.setColor(savedColour);
   }
public void fill3DRect(Graphics g, int left, int top,
      int width, int height, int lineWidth, Color colour,
      boolean raised)
   {
   Color savedColour = g.getColor();
   g.setColor(Color.lightGray);
   if (lineWidth < 1)
      lineWidth = 1;
   for(int i=0; i < lineWidth-1; i++)
      {
      g.draw3DRect(left, top, width, height, raised);
      left++;
      top++;
      width -= 2;
      height -= 2;
      }
```

```java
            g.setColor(colour);
            g.fillRect(left, top, width+1, height+1);
            g.setColor(savedColour);
            }
        public void drawOval(Graphics g, int left, int top,
            int width, int height,
            int lineWidth, Color colour)
            {
            Color savedColour = g.getColor();
            g.setColor(colour);
            if (lineWidth < 1)
                lineWidth = 1;
            for(int i=0; i < lineWidth; i++)
                {
                g.drawOval(left, top, width, height);
                if (i < lineWidth - 1)
                    {
                    g.drawOval(left, top, width-1, height-1);
                    g.drawOval(left+1, top, width-1, height-1);
                    g.drawOval(left, top+1, width-1, height-1);
                    g.drawOval(left+1, top+1, width-1, height-1);
                    left++;
                    top++;
                    width -= 2;
                    height -= 2;
                    }
                }
            g.setColor(savedColour);
            }
        public void fillOval(Graphics g, int left, int top,
            int width, int height, Color colour)
            {
            Color savedColour = g.getColor();
            g.setColor(colour);
            g.fillOval(left, top, width, height);
            g.setColor(savedColour);
            }
        public void drawArc(Graphics g, int left, int top,
            int width, int height, int startAngle, int arcAngle,
            int lineWidth, Color colour)
            {
            Color savedColour = g.getColor();
```

```java
        g.setColor(colour);
        if (lineWidth < 1)
           lineWidth = 1;
        for(int i=0; i < lineWidth; i++)
           {
           g.drawArc(left, top, width, height, startAngle, arcAngle);
           if (i < lineWidth - 1)
              {
              g.drawArc(left, top, width-1, height-1,
                 startAngle, arcAngle);
              g.drawArc(left+1, top, width-1, height-1,
                 startAngle, arcAngle);
              g.drawArc(left, top+1, width-1, height-1,
                 startAngle, arcAngle);
              g.drawArc(left+1, top+1, width-1, height-1,
                 startAngle, arcAngle);
              left++;
              top++;
              width -= 2;
              height -= 2;
              }
           }
        g.setColor(savedColour);
        }
    public void fillArc(Graphics g, int left, int top, int width,
        int height, int startAngle, int arcAngle,
        Color colour)
        {
        Color savedColour = g.getColor();
        g.setColor(colour);
        g.fillArc(left, top, width, height, startAngle, arcAngle);
        g.setColor(savedColour);
        }
    public void drawFrame(Graphics g, int left, int top, int width,
        int height, int frameWidth, boolean raised)
        {
        g.setColor(Color.lightGray);
        if (raised)
           {
           g.draw3DRect(left, top, width, height, true);
           g.draw3DRect(left+frameWidth, top+frameWidth,
              width-(2*frameWidth), height-(2*frameWidth), false);
```

```
        }
      else
        {
        g.draw3DRect(left, top, width, height, false);
        g.draw3DRect(left+frameWidth, top+frameWidth,
            width-(2*frameWidth), height-(2*frameWidth), true);
        }
      }
    public void drawText(Graphics g, String s, int x, int y,
                          Font f, Color colour)
      {
      if (s != null)
        {
        Font savedFont = g.getFont();
        Color savedColour = g.getColor();
        g.setFont(f);
        g.setColor(colour);
        g.drawString(s, x, y);
        g.setColor(savedColour);
        g.setFont(savedFont);
        }
      }
    }
```

Summary

The Java Graphics class provides methods for drawing a number of different graphical shapes: lines, rectangles, ovals, circles, arcs and polygons. The methods are, however, quite limited in what they can produce. All drawing is carried out using a line thickness of one pixel and the 3D rectangles are not very inspiring.

To improve the functionality of the drawing methods we have included a section containing some methods that improve a little upon the existing ones.

13

Mouse and Keyboard Events

Introduction

Like all other programming languages that have a graphical user interface, Java makes use of events to respond to the actions of the user. Whenever a particular event, like a mouse click or keypress, occurs we can include in our program the instructions that we want carried out in response to that event.

When an event occurs Java automatically saves the information about that event in an instance of the Event class. This Event object is passed as an argument to an event message that we can override to respond to individual events. Each Event object contains information about that event. All events use the same Event class so the fields within an event object are always the same.

However, not all fields are used for each event – it depends on the event type. For instance, if the event is a mouse click then the click-Count field will contain the number of consecutive clicks. If the event is a keyboard event the key field will contain the key that was pressed.

Events are continuously being generated within an application or applet. For instance, each time a window is opened, moved or re-sized a paint() method will be generated. (Actually, Java calls the update() method in this situation. The update() method erases the background and then calls the paint() method. Most of the time we can ignore the update() method and just override the paint() procedure.) Whatever instructions you have included in your overriding paint() method will be carried out whenever something happens which requires the screen to be redrawn.

The most common events that you will probably be interested in are those involving the mouse and the keyboard. Whenever you want to control what happens when a user clicks the mouse button, or moves the mouse or presses a certain key, you can tell Java what you want to happen by overriding the event method involved.

Most of the classes that we have used so far, like the Graphics, Color and Font classes, are part of Java's Abstract Windowing Toolkit package, or AWT. AWT manages and generates all the events that occur in a Java application or applet.

Mouse Events

There are a number of events associated with the mouse that you can make use of. Most user interactions involve the mouse and by defining your own mouse event methods you can provide the user with the ability to, say, select different actions by clicking the mouse button or even allow them to draw things on the screen.

Note   In Java, if a user has more than one button on their mouse, you cannot distinguish between them. For instance, under Windows a mouseDown event will be generated whether the left or right mouse button is pressed. This is necessary because the Macintosh platform uses a one-button mouse and Java has to cater for every platform.

When the mouse button is clicked, two events are generated: a mouse-Down event and a mouseUp event. The mouseDown event occurs when the button is first pressed and the mouseUp event when it is released. The two events allow you to differentiate between the mouse first being pressed and being released, either immediately, if the user is just clicking the button, or after a period of time if the user was holding the button down while, for instance, drawing something.

While the mouse button is held down another event is generated – the mouseDrag event. One mouseDrag event is generated for every pixel that the mouse is moved with the button held down. These different events allow you to initiate different actions for each stage of the process, when the mouse is first pressed down, while it is being moved and when the button is released.

Another mouse event is the mouseMove event. This is similar to the mouseDrag event but occurs when the mouse is simply being moved around the application or applet display without the button being pressed. A mouseMove event happens when the mouse is moved a pixel.

The other two events involving the mouse are the mouseEnter and mouseExit events. These are called when the mouse pointer enters or exits the applet display area.

Here is the signature of a mouse event method, in this case the mouse-Down method (all the mouse event methods have the same signature):

```
public boolean mouseDown(Event event, int x, int y)
    {
    ...
    }
```

The first argument is an instance of the Event class. An Event object contains various information about the event, like when it happened, what type of event it is, if it was a keyboard event the key that was pressed and so on. The other two arguments are the x and y co-ordinates of where the event occurred. This means that you will know precisely where within the applet display area a mouse click, for instance, has taken place.

Mouse events return a boolean true or false value. The significance of this will become more apparent when we start talking about the AWT user interface components in a future chapter. Returning true or false in an event handler determines whether the event is passed any further up the hierarchy of interface components. If you return true from your event method no further forwarding of the event will take place.

Mouse clicks

We will now look at an example which illustrates how an applet can respond to mouse clicks by intercepting the mouseDown event. This applet waits for the user to click anywhere in the display window. When the user presses the mouse button, causing a mouseDown event to be triggered, it responds by drawing a very small rectangle at the location where the mouse was clicked and displays the x and y co-ordinates of that location. Here is the source code:

Listing 13.1:
Responding to mouse clicks (see Figure 13.1)

```
import java.awt.*;
import java.applet.Applet;
public class MouseClicks extends Applet
    {
```

```
private Point thePoint;
public boolean mouseDown(Event event, int x, int y)
   {
   if (thePoint == null)
      {
      thePoint = new Point(x, y);
      }
   else
      {
      thePoint.x = x;
      thePoint.y = y;
      }
   repaint();
   return true;
   }
public void paint(Graphics g)
   {
   g.drawString("Click anywhere in this applet", 100, 20);
   g.fillRect(thePoint.x, thePoint.y, 2, 2);
   g.drawString("[" + thePoint.x + "," + thePoint.y + "]",
         thePoint.x+2, thePoint.y+15);
   }
}
```

This is what the applet looks like after a mouse click:

Figure 13.1: *The MouseClicks applet (see Listing 13.1)*

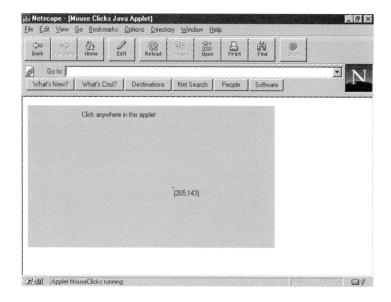

Let's go through the code to see what is happening. We begin with our usual import statements:

```
import java.awt.*;
import java.applet.Applet;
```

Because we will be using events in our applet we need to import the class Event. However, this is part of the java.awt package along with other classes like the Graphics class. As we are using the statement import java.awt.*; all of the classes that are included in the java.awt package will be imported so we don't have to specifically import the Event class.

We need something in our MouseClicks class to hold the x and y co-ordinates of the point where the mouse click has occurred. We will use an object of type Point (the Point class is also part of the awt package) to hold the data:

```
private Point thePoint;
```

A point represents an (x, y) co-ordinate and the Point class contains two integer instance variables, x and y.

Next we add our method to override the mouseDown() method so that the actions we define in the method will be carried out every time there is a mouseDown event:

```
public boolean mouseDown(Event event, int x, int y)
    {
    if (thePoint == null)
        {
        thePoint = new Point(x, y);
        }
    else
        {
        thePoint.x = x;
        thePoint.y = y;
        }
    repaint();
    return true;
    }
```

The first thing the method does is check to see if a click has occurred previously. It does this by testing whether the variable thePoint has been created yet. If the variable is still set to null then we have to create the point object using the new operator. We pass the x and y coordinates to the constructor that were received by the `mouseDown` event. If the object has already been created we just reset it's x and y variables to the new co-ordinates.

Once we have stored the point co-ordinates we call the `repaint()` method. Whenever you have changed what needs to be drawn in your applet you can trigger a `paint()` method by calling the `repaint()` method.

The final statement in the `mouseDown()` method returns the boolean value `true`. All the methods we have written so far have all been declared as `void` methods, which means that they don't return a value. However, all the event methods must return a boolean value. As we want to handle the `mouseDown` event ourselves we return the value `true` so that the event is not passed on to any other event-handling procedures.

Finally, we redefine the `paint()` method to do our drawing:

```
public void paint(Graphics g)
    {
    g.drawString("Click anywhere in this applet", 100, 20);
    g.fillRect(thePoint.x, thePoint.y, 2, 2);
    g.drawString("[" + thePoint.x + "," + thePoint.y + "]",
        thePoint.x+2, thePoint.y+15);
    }
```

The first line is a `drawString()` instruction to display a message telling the user to click anywhere in the applet. This is followed by a call to `fillRect()` to draw a 2 pixel square at the co-ordinates held in the point object. Finally, we draw the x and y co-ordinates next to the point.

Each time the `paint()` method is called the background is cleared. This means that the current point only will appear on the display. If you want every point at which the user clicks to be displayed and left on the screen the applet will have to record each click in a `Point` array and then every point will have to be redrawn each time the `paint()` method is called.

The other point to notice is that because we are only handling the `mouseDown` event the user can press the mouse button, (at which time the co-ordinates will be displayed) and then drag the mouse around with the button held down and nothing else will happen. This is because we are not overriding the `mouseDrag` or `mouseUp` events.

If you want to only initiate an action when the user double-clicks the mouse button, you must check the value of the `clickCount` variable of the `Event` object. This is only used for the `mouseDown` event and will contain the number of consecutive clicks. It will be set to 1 for single-clicks, 2 for double-clicks, and so on. For example, if you wanted to amend the MouseClicks applet so that it only displayed the point co-ordinates when the user double-clicked the mouse, you would use the following piece of code:

```
public boolean mouseDown(Event event, int x, int y)
  {
  if (event.clickCount >= 2)// test for double-click
    {
    if (thePoint == null)
      {
      thePoint = new Point(x, y);
      }
    else
      {
      thePoint.x = x;
      thePoint.y = y;
      }
    repaint();
    }
  return true;
  }
```

Dragging the mouse

This next example illustrates how the combination of the `mouseDown`, `mouseDrag` and `mouseUp` methods can be used. When the user drags the mouse, the applet will continuously displays an oval which changes in size and shape as the mouse is moved around the applet's drawing area. The bounding rectangle of the oval will have it's starting co-ordinates at the point where the mouse button is first held down and will be re-sized and re-drawn according to the movement of the mouse.

Here is the complete code for the applet:

Listing 13.2:
Example showing the use of the MouseDrag *event (see Figure 13.2)*

```
import java.awt.*;
import java.applet.Applet;
public class MouseDrag extends Applet
  {
```

```
private Rectangle rect;
public boolean mouseDown(Event event, int x, int y)
    {
    rect = new Rectangle(x, y, 0, 0);
    repaint();
    return true;
    }
public boolean mouseDrag(Event event, int x, int y)
    {
    rect.resize(x - rect.x, y - rect.y);
    repaint();
    return true;
    }
public boolean mouseUp(Event event, int x, int y)
    {
    rect.resize(x - rect.x, y - rect.y);
    repaint();
    return true;
    }
public void paint(Graphics g)
    {
    Dimension app = this.size();
    int x = rect.x;
    int y = rect.y;
    int width = rect.width;
    int height = rect.height;
    if (rect != null)
        {
        if (width < 0)
            {
            width = 0 - width;
            x = x - width + 1;
            if (x < 0)
                {
                width += x;
                x = 0;
                }
            }
        if (height < 0)
            {
            height = 0 - height;
            y = rect.y - height + 1;
```

```
            if (y < 0)
               {
                 height += y;
                 y = 0;
               }
            }
        if ((x + width) > app.width)
            width = app.width - x;

        if ((y + height) > app.height)
            {
            height = app.height - y;
            }
        g.drawOval(x, y, width - 1, height - 1);
        }
    }
}
```

Figure 13.2: *The MouseDrag applet (see Listing 13.2)*

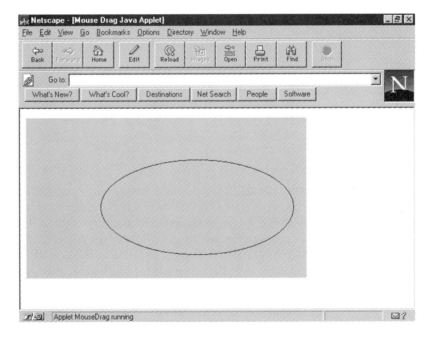

In the MouseClicks applet we stored the click location in an instance of the class Point. In the MouseDrag applet we use an instance of the class Rectangle to store the dimensions of the "bounding" rectangle of the oval. The Rectangle class includes the instance variables for the x and y co-ordinates of the upper left corner and the width and height of the rectangle. The Rectangle class is part of the `java.awt` package so will be imported along with all the other classes in that package.

Lets take a look at the three mouse event methods. The first is the `mouseDown` method:

```
public boolean mouseDown(Event event, int x, int y)
    {
    rect = new Rectangle(x, y, 0, 0);
    repaint();
    return true;
    }
```

When the mouse button is pressed down this routine will create a new instance of the Rectangle class with the co-ordinates of the upper left corner set to the x and y co-ordinates of the current mouse pointer location and a width and height set to zero. The `repaint()` method is then called to re-draw the applet which will have the effect of clearing the current display.

While the mouse button is held down `mouseDrag` events will continuously be triggered:

```
public boolean mouseDrag(Event event, int x, int y)
    {
    rect.resize(x - rect.x, y - rect.y);
    repaint();
    return true;
    }
```

The `mouseDrag()` method contains a call to the `resize()` method of the Rectangle class. This method sets the width and height of the rectangle to the values of the two arguments passed to it. In this case we subtract the current width and height of the rectangle from the new co-ordinates of the mouse pointer to arrive at the new width and height of the rectangle. Again, the `repaint()` method is called so the oval is continuously re-drawn.

The `mouseUp()` method contains the same instructions as the `mouseDrag()` procedure. When the mouse button is released the bounding rectangle of the oval will therefore be set to the final size according to the mouse pointer co-ordinates.

The only other method defined in the applet is the `paint()` method which, as usual, is where all the drawing actually takes place. First we will need to set some variables:

```
public void paint(Graphics g)
    {
    Dimension app = this.size();
    int x = rect.x;
    int y = rect.y;
    int width = rect.width;
    int height = rect.height;
    }
```

The `Dimension` object is used to hold the width and height of the applet itself. A call to the `size()` method obtains these values. We then record the current values of the bounding rectangle in four integer variables. The next piece of code handles the situation caused by the mouse pointer being dragged to the left and/or above the origin of the rectangle:

```
if (rect != null)
    {
    if (width < 0)
        {
        width = 0 - width;
        x = x - width + 1;
        if (x < 0)
            {
            width += x;
            x = 0;
            }
        }
    if (height < 0)
        {
        height = 0 - height;
        y = rect.y - height + 1;
        if (y < 0)
            {
            height += y;
            y = 0;
            }
        }
    }
```

The draw and fill methods in Java will not draw anything if either the width or the height are negative. The above piece of code therefore checks to see whether the width and the height are negative. If they are it means that the mouse has been dragged left or upwards to "flip over" the oval. If they are negative, the x and y values must be reset to what has now become the upper left corner of the bounding rectangle. The width and height are made positive so that the drawOval() method will work. The final bit of code makes sure that the bounding rectangle of the oval doesn't extend beyond the drawing area of the applet:

```
if ((x + width) > app.width)
    width = app.width - x;

if ((y + height) > app.height)
    {
height = app.height - y;
    }
```

If we didn't include this last piece of code it wouldn't stop the oval from being drawn. It would just mean that only the part within the drawing area of the applet would actually be seen. The last line of code in the paint method draws the oval:

```
g.drawOval(x, y, width - 1, height - 1);
```

Moving the mouse

The next example illustrates the use of the mouseMove event. While the mouse pointer is being moved around the drawing area of the applet a mouseMove event is generated for every pixel the mouse is moved. The mouse button does not have to be pressed to trigger a mouseMove.

The applet consists of four rectangles drawn in outline form in a row. As the mouse pointer is moved over a rectangle, it will be filled in black. Once the mouse pointer leaves a rectangle it will revert back to the outline form. We have also included code which implements the mouseEnter and mouseExit events. A message is displayed whenever the mouse pointer enters or exits the applet drawing area. Here is the full source code:

Listing 13.3:
Responding to the
MouseMove *event*
(see Figure 13.3)

```
import java.awt.*;
import java.applet.Applet;
public class MouseMove extends Applet
    {
```

```
private static final int NUMRECTS = 4;
private Rectangle rectangles[] = new Rectangle[NUMRECTS];
private boolean inRect[] = new boolean[NUMRECTS];
private String message;
public void init()
   {
   int x = 20;
   int y = 20;
   int width = 50;
   int height = 100;
   for (int i = 0; i < NUMRECTS; i++)
      {
      inRect[i] = false;
      rectangles[i] = new Rectangle(x, y, width, height);
      x += (width+20);
      }
   }
public boolean mouseEnter(Event event, int x, int y)
   {
   message = "The mouse has entered the applet";
   repaint();
   return true;
   }
public boolean mouseExit(Event event, int x, int y)
   {
   message = "The mouse has left the applet";
   repaint();
   return true;
   }
public boolean mouseMove(Event event, int x, int y)
   {
   boolean change = false;
   for (int i = 0; i < NUMRECTS; i++)
      {
      if (!inRect[i] && rectangles[i].inside(x, y))
         {
         inRect[i] = true;
         change = true;
         }
      if (inRect[i] && !rectangles[i].inside(x, y))
         {
         inRect[i] = false;
```

```
          change = true;
          }
      }
   if (change)
      repaint();
   return true;
   }
public void paint(Graphics g)
   {
   for (int i = 0; i < NUMRECTS; i++)
      {
      if (inRect[i] == true)
         g.fillRect(rectangles[i].x, rectangles[i].y,
               rectangles[i].width, rectangles[i].height);
      else
         g.drawRect(rectangles[i].x, rectangles[i].y,
               rectangles[i].width, rectangles[i].height);
      }
   g.drawString(message, 50, 140);
   }
}
```

Figure 13.3:
The MouseMove
applet (see Listing
13.3)

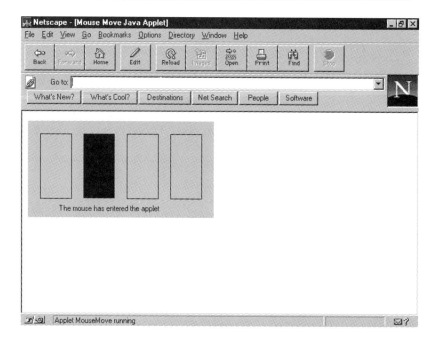

We will now look at each section of the applet code. First of all, we have some instance variable definitions:

```
public class MouseMove extends Applet
    {
    private static final int NUMRECTS = 4;
    private Rectangle rectangles[] = new Rectangle[NUMRECTS];
    private boolean inRect[] = new boolean[NUMRECTS];
    private String message;
    }
```

The `rectangles[]` array will hold the starting corner co-ordinates, width and height of each of the four rectangles we will be displaying.

The `inRect[]` array of boolean values will contain a `true` value if the mouse pointer is inside the boundaries of the rectangle, `false` if not. The `message` string will inform the user whether the mouse has entered or exited the applet.

The first two methods override the `mouseEnter()` and `mouseExit()` methods:

```
public boolean mouseEnter(Event event, int x, int y)
    {
    message = "The mouse has entered the applet";
    repaint();
    return true;
    }
public boolean mouseExit(Event event, int x, int y)
    {
    message = "The mouse has left the applet";
    repaint();
    return true;
    }
```

Whenever the mouse pointer enters the drawing area of the applet, a `mouseEnter` event is triggered and we display the relevant message. The same thing happens when the mouse leaves the applet area.

Next we have the `mouseMove()` method:

```
public boolean mouseMove(Event event, int x, int y)
    {
    boolean change = false;
    for (int i = 0; i < NUMRECTS; i++)
        {
```

```
        if (!inRect[i] && rectangles[i].inside(x, y))
          {
          inRect[i] = true;
          change = true;
          }
        if (inRect[i] && !rectangles[i].inside(x, y))
          {
          inRect[i] = false;
          change = true;
          }
        }
    if (change)
      repaint();
      return true;
    }
```

This method contains a for loop which tests each rectangle in turn to
see whether the mouse pointer lies within the rectangle. For this we use
the inside() method of the Rectangle class. This method is passed the
x and y co-ordinates of the current mouse position and returns a true
value if that point lies within the rectangle. If the mouse pointer has
just entered the confines of one of the rectangles or has just left a rectangle we update the value held in the corresponding inRect element
and set the boolean variable change to true. After the loop has been
exited, we test for a true value in the change variable and, if true, call
the repaint() method.

Lastly, we come to the ubiquitous paint() method:

```
    public void paint(Graphics g)
      {
      for (int i = 0; i < NUMRECTS; i++)
        {
        if (inRect[i] == true)
          g.fillRect(rectangles[i].x, rectangles[i].y,
            rectangles[i].width, rectangles[i].height);
        else
          g.drawRect(rectangles[i].x, rectangles[i].y,
            rectangles[i].width, rectangles[i].height);
        }
      g.drawString(message, 50, 140);
      }
```

The paint() method also contains a for loop. This checks the value of each inRect element. If it is set to true, then the corresponding rectangle is drawn with the fillRect() method. If it is false, the drawRect() method is used. Finally, the message string containing the mouse enter or exit message is displayed.

Keyboard Events

When the user presses a key on the keyboard a keyboard event is generated. When the key is pressed down, a keyDown event is generated and when the key is released, a keyUp event is generated. It is highly unlikely that you would ever want to distinguish between a keyDown event and a keyUp event so we shall just focus on the keyDown method. The signature of the keyDown method is slightly different from the mouseDown method:

```
public boolean keyDown(Event event, int key)
    {
    ...
    }
```

As you would expect, an instance of the Event class is passed as one of the arguments. The other argument, key, is an integer value representing the ASCII character value of the key that has been pressed if it is in the standard character set. The cursor movement keys and the function keys have special codes which are passed as the key argument. These special codes are defined as class variables in the Event class and their names can be used in your programs to make the code more meaningful. Table 13.1 lists the defined control keys and their code values.

The Event class contains a modifiers instance variable which you can test to see whether the Shift, Control, Alt or Meta keys have been pressed. Class variables have also been defined in the Event class to represent the mask values for these keys. To get the state of any of them you can use the AND operator with the modifiers value and one of the following flags:

- Event.SHIFT_MASK
- Event.CTRL_MASK
- Event.ALT_MASK
- Event.META_MASK

Table 13.1: *Control keys and their code values*

Key	Class Variable	Value
The Home key	Event.HOME	1000
The End key	Event.END	1001
The Page Up key	Event.PGUP	1002
The Page Down key	Event.PGDN	1003
The Up arrow key	Event.UP	1004
The Down arrow key	Event.DOWN	1005
The Left arrow key	Event.LEFT	1006
The Right arrow key	Event.RIGHT	1007
The F1 function key	Event.F1	1008
The F2 function key	Event.F2	1009
The F3 function key	Event.F3	1010
The F4 function key	Event.F4	1011
The F5 function key	Event.F5	1012
The F6 function key	Event.F6	1013
The F7 function key	Event.F7	1014
The F8 function key	Event.F8	1015
The F9 function key	Event.F9	1016
The F10 function key	Event.F10	10017
The F11 function key	Event.F11	1018
The F12 function key	Event.F12	1019

For instance, to check whether the Shift key has been held down you can carry out the following bit masking:

```
if (event.modifiers & Event.SHIFT_MASK) != 0)
    {
    // true if Shift key held down
    }
```

As an easier alternative, you can make use of some predefined methods in the Event class which will return true if the Shift, Control or Meta keys are held down. Here is the same test as above:

```
if (event.shiftDown())
    {
    // true if Shift key held down
    }
```

Note   At the time of writing the Shift key seemed to be the only one that could be properly tested for. By the time you read this the problem might be fixed.

The following program example illustrates all of the above points. It is an applet which display a square in the centre of the drawing area that can be moved around by pressing one of the cursor keys: up, down, left or right. If the key combination, Shift + r, is pressed, the square will return to it's original, central position. If Shift + f is pressed, the square will become filled, and if Shift + e is pressed it will become empty again. The ASCII or special code for each key and its character representation are displayed at the top of the display area. Here is the full source code:

Listing 13.4:
Responding to keyboard events (see Figure 13.4)

```
import java.awt.*;
import java.applet.Applet;
public class KeyEvents extends Applet
    {
    private Rectangle rect;
    private boolean filled = false;
    private String message;
    public void init()
        {
        int x = (this.size().width/2) - 50;
        int y = (this.size().height/2) - 50;
        int width = 100;
        int height = 100;
        rect = new Rectangle(x, y, width, height);
        }

public boolean keyDown(Event event, int key)
        {
        char ch;
        switch (key)
```

```java
            {
        case Event.UP:
            if (rect.y > 4)
                rect.y -= 5;
            break;
        case Event.DOWN:
            if ((rect.y + rect.height) < (this.size().height - 5))
                rect.y += 5;
            break;
        case Event.LEFT:
            if (rect.x > 4)
                rect.x -= 5;
            break;
        case Event.RIGHT:
            if ((rect.x + rect.width) < (this.size().width - 5))
                rect.x += 5;
            break;
        default:
            ch = (char)key;
            if (event.shiftDown())
                {
                if (ch == 'r' || ch == 'R')
                    {
                    rect.x = (this.size().width/2) - 50;
                    rect.y = (this.size().height/2) - 50;
                    rect.width = 100;
                    rect.height = 100;
                    }
                if (ch == 'f' || ch == 'F')
                    filled = true;
                if (ch == 'e' || ch == 'E')
                    filled = false;
                }
            }
    message = "ASCII value = " + key +", Key pressed = " +
        getKeyName(key);
    repaint();
    return true;
    }
public void paint(Graphics g)
    {
    if (filled == true)
```

```
            g.fillRect(rect.x, rect.y,rect.width, rect.height);
        else
            g.drawRect(rect.x, rect.y,rect.width, rect.height);
            g.drawString(message, 20, 20);
        }
    public String getKeyName(int key)
        {
        switch(key)
            {
            case Event.HOME: return "Home";
            case Event.END: return "End";
            case Event.PGUP: return "Page Up";
            case Event.PGDN: return "Page Down";
            case Event.UP: return "Up arrow";
            case Event.DOWN: return "Down arrow";
            case Event.LEFT: return "Left arrow";
            case Event.RIGHT: return "Right arrow";
            case Event.F1: return "F1";
            case Event.F2: return "F2";
            case Event.F3: return "F3";
            case Event.F4: return "F4";
            case Event.F5: return "F5";
            case Event.F6: return "F6";
            case Event.F7: return "F7";
            case Event.F8: return "F8";
            case Event.F9: return "F9";
            case Event.F10: return "F10";
            case Event.F11: return "F11";
            case Event.F12: return "F12";
            default:
                char c = (char)key;
                return String.valueOf(c);
            }
        }
    }
```

Here is an example of the output:

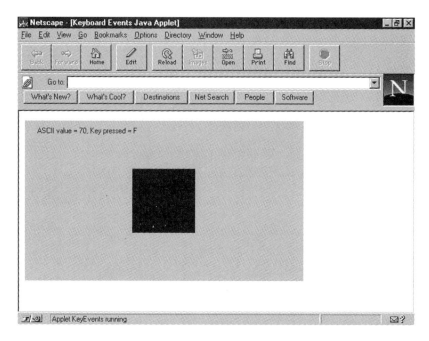

The code for this applet is pretty simple. First we define three instance variables to hold the co-ordinates and dimensions of the square, the current state of the square, ie. empty or filled, and a message string to hold the string we will display to show the current code and character of the key that has been pressed.

The init() method contains instructions to set the starting co-ordinates and dimensions of the square and assigns them to a new Rectangle object.

The next method is the keyDown event method. A switch statement is used to test which key has been pressed. The first four case statements handle the movement of the square if one of the arrow keys has been pressed:

```
switch (key)
    {
    case Event.UP:
        if (rect.y > 4)
            rect.y -= 5;
        break;
    case Event.DOWN:
        if ((rect.y + rect.height) < (this.size().height - 5))
```

```
        rect.y += 5;
      break;
   case Event.LEFT:
      if (rect.x > 4)
         rect.x -= 5;
      break;
   case Event.RIGHT:
      if ((rect.x + rect.width) < (this.size().width - 5))
         rect.x += 5;
      break;
   }
```

The switch statement default then converts the ASCII code to a character and then performs a test to see whether the Shift key is being held down. If it is then the program performs the required actions for the keys that we want to trap:

```
default:
ch = (char)key;
if (event.shiftDown())
   {
   if (ch == 'r' || ch == 'R')
      {
      rect.x = (this.size().width/2) - 50;
      rect.y = (this.size().height/2) - 50;
      rect.width = 100;
      rect.height = 100;
      }
   if (ch == 'f' || ch == 'F')
      filled = true;
   if (ch == 'e' || ch == 'E')
      filled = false;
   }
```

The message string is then constructed using the code value and a call to the getKeyName() method:

```
message = "ASCII value = " + key + ",
Key pressed = " + getKeyName(key);
```

The paint() method is very straightforward. If the filled flag is set to true it draws a filled rectangle, otherwise it uses drawRect(). Finally, the getKeyName() method has the current key code passed to it and uses a switch statement to test for the keys defined as constants in the Event class. If there is a match, a descriptive string is returned. If the key is not one of these control keys, it simply converts it to a character using the (cast) operator and returns it as a string.

Summary

Within this chapter we have looked at how you manage mouse movement and keyboard entry, the two fundamental input methods for any Java program. In the case of a mouse movement there are a number of events associated with it. These actions are up to you to define for your specific requirements. This could range from simply allowing a user to move around a certain area and click objects – such as a button – or actually drag a graphical object around the screen.

One thing to remember about Java is that it cannot distinguish between the buttons pressed on a mouse. Remember that Java is a cross-platform language, and whilst PC users may be used to a two buttoned mouse, Apple Macintosh users are not. They have a single button and Java respects this.

In Java when a mouse button is pressed two events are generated: a mouseDown event when it is first pressed followed by a mouseUp when it is released. Now whilst a mouse button is held down a third event is generated – mouseDrag. One mouseDrag event is generated for every pixel that a mouse is moved over whilst the button is held down. Another event generated by a mouse is called mouseMove. This is similar to mouseDrag but is simply a locator command. It tracks the movement of a mouse without a button being depressed.

With the keyboard whenever a key is depressed a keyDown event is generated and when it is released a keyUp event is generated. Why you would want to worry about a keyUp event is a mystery, but it is there if you find a reason why!

Handling these events is not difficult. But in order for you to make a Java application or applet functional mastering their programming syntax must become second nature.

14

Handling Images and Sound in Java

Images

Java supports two types of images that can be displayed in your applets: GIF and JPEG format files. Images, which must reside on the web site server, must first be loaded before they can be displayed. This involves getting the image from where it is stored on your web site and loading it into the java applet running in a user's browser. Once the image has been loaded, it can then be displayed.

Loading Images

Image files are normally stored in a separate directory in a web site as `*.gif` or `*.jpg` files.

Images are loaded into an applet using the `getImage()` method, part of the Applet class. The `getImage()` method has two forms. Here is the syntax of the first form:

```
Image image = getImage(url)
```

The argument to the `getImage()` method is an instance of the class URL, or Uniform Resource Locator. As the use of the World Wide Web relies on URLs to provide a means of identifying locations it is not a surprise to find that Java contains a URL class. A URL object can be created in different ways but the most common is to provide a string specifying the URL location. For instance:

```
URL url = new URL("http://www.website.co.uk/");
```

You can also take an existing URL object and create a new one from it. This second form of the URL constructor takes two arguments, an existing base URL and a string specifying a relative path from that base. This example creates a URL pointing to a documents sub-directory:

```
URL urlDocs = new URL(url, "documents/picture.gif");
```

A third constructor takes as arguments the protocol (ie. http), the name of the host computer (eg. www.website.co.uk) and a path specifying the resource location (eg. documents/picture.gif). The fourth uses these same arguments but includes a port number as well.

For our discussion of the getImage() method we will only make use of the first form of the URL constructor.

The URL object passed as the argument to getImage() must specify an absolute URL. The image pointed to by the URL is loaded into an instance of the Image class (which is created for you). Here is an example:

```
Image image = getImage(new URL("http://www.website.co.uk/documents/picture.gif"));
```

The drawback with this form of the getImage() method comes when the image is moved to another location. Because the URL is hard-coded into the applet you will have to re-compile the source code with the amended URL.

The second form of the getImage() method provides a way of getting round this problem. Here is the syntax:

```
Image image = getImage(url, relativePath)
```

This time there are two arguments. The first is a URL object again, but this time it acts as a base location for the image. The second argument is a string which contains the location of the image, relative to the url argument. For example, you might decide to store all of your image files in a directory called images below the documents directory specified in the previous example. You could then call getImage() with the arguments:

```
Image image = getImage(new URL("http://www.website.co.uk/documents/"),"images/picture.gif");
```

This is fine if you continue to keep your images directory under the documents directory. However, if you decide to change the name of the documents directory you will have to change the coding in your applet and re-compile it. Fortunately, there are two other methods in the Applet class which provide a better way of specifying the base URL argument. They are getDocumentBase() and getCodeBase(). They both return URL objects.

The first one, getDocumentBase(), returns the URL of the directory that holds the HTML page containing the applet. So, if the HTML page is in the directory

```
http://www.website.co.uk/documents,
```

the getDocumentBase() method would return a URL pointing at that directory. Therefore, if your images directory was under the documents directory you could use the following getImage() call:

```
Image image = getImage(getDocumentBase(), "images/picture.gif");
```

Now, as long as you didn't move the image file from the images directory and always kept the images directory as a sub-directory of the HTML page directory, you would not need to re-compile the applet if you moved the HTML file to a different location.

The other method, getCodeBase(), returns the URL of the path where the applet class file is situated. If you haven't used the CODEBASE attribute of the <APPLET> tag in your HTML file this will be the same directory as the HTML document. If, however, you have specified the CODEBASE attribute as say, "classes", then the getCodeBase() method will return the URL pointing at

```
http://www.website.co.uk/documents/classes
```

If you located your image file in the same directory as the applet class file, you could make the following call to getImage():

```
Image image = getImage(getCodeBase(), "picture.gif");
```

An error won't occur if the image file isn't where you've specified it and stop the applet from running. It just won't display the image when you come to draw it. An important point to make is that the getImage() method will return immediately but the image won't be loaded straight away. It will not be retrieved until you actually come to display it. The purpose of this is to keep to a minimum the time taken to download images and the amount of memory that is used.

Drawing Images

Once you have used getImage() to create an instance of the Image class, you must use the drawImage() method of the Graphics class to actually display the image. The drawImage() method has several forms. This is the syntax of the simplest:

```
g.drawImage(image, x, y, ImageObserver)
```

The first argument is the image you obtained with the getImage() call. The image is positioned according to the x and y co-ordinates which specify where you want the upper left corner of the image. The last argument is an object which implements the ImageObserver interface, part of the Image class. The ImageObserver class can be used to track the progress of the image loading process and enables you to draw partial images or wait until a complete image is loaded. It is mainly used for handling a series of images that you are loading to produce an animation.

For most cases of loading a simple image you can just use the this keyword as the last argument. The Applet class will provide the necessary methods to enable the image to be drawn. The drawImage() method returns true once the image has been completely loaded and drawn; otherwise it returns false.

Let's look at a very simple applet which just loads an image using getImage() and then displays it using drawImage:

Listing 14.1: *An example to display an image (see Figure 14.1)*

```
import java.awt.*;
import java.applet.Applet;
public class SimpleImage extends Applet
    {
    Image image;
    public void init()
        {
        image  = getImage(getCodeBase(), "images/duke.gif");
        }
    public void paint(Graphics g)
        {                                    ImageObserver
        g.drawImage(image, 100, 100, this);
        }
    }
```

Here is a screen shot of the displayed image:

Figure 14.1: *The
SimpleImage
applet (see Listing
14.1)*

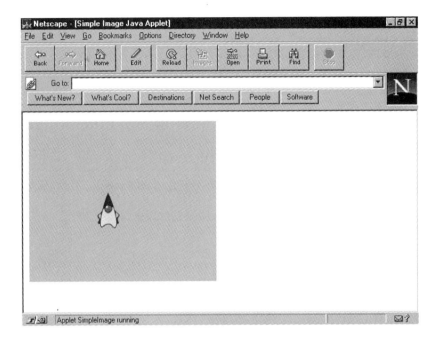

Figure 14.1: *The SimpleImage applet (see Listing 14.1)*

Another form of the `drawImage()` method contains a couple of extra arguments: the width and height of the image to be displayed. Here is the syntax:

```
g.drawImage(image, x, y, width, height, ImageObserver)
```

The `width` and `height` arguments are both integers. These parameters can be used to scale the image if they are specified different to the actual width and height of the image. Images can therefore be made larger or smaller than they actually are, or can be squeezed or flattened to fit into a particular space. It must be pointed out however, that if you expand or contract images the quality of the image might be impaired.

Here is an applet which illustrates the use of this form of the drawImage() method to scale the image. It uses the keyboard event handling that we introduced in the last chapter to allow you to make the image larger or smaller or to stretch or contract the image in the horizontal or vertical planes. Pressing L will make the image larger by scaling the width and height by similar amounts, S will make it smaller and R will reset it to it's original size. The up and down arrow keys will stretch the image in the vertical plane and the left and right keys will stretch it horizontally. If you hold down the shift key while pressing the arrow keys the image will be contracted. Here is the full source code:

| **Listing 14.2:** <br> *Scaling an image* <br> *(see Figure 14.2)* | ```java
import java.awt.*;
import java.applet.Applet;
public class ScaleImage extends Applet
   {
   Image image;
   int width, height;
   int wScale = 0;
   int hScale = 0;
   public void init()
      {
      image = getImage(getCodeBase(), "images/mail.gif");
      }
   public boolean keyDown(Event event, int key)
      {
      char ch;
      switch (key)
         {
         case Event.UP:
         case Event.DOWN:
            if (event.shiftDown())
               hScale -= 10;
            else
               hScale += 10;
            break;
         case Event.LEFT:
         case Event.RIGHT:
            if (event.shiftDown())
               wScale -= 10;
            else
               wScale += 10;
            break;
         default:
            ch = (char)key;
            if (ch > 'a' && ch < 'z')
               ch = (char)(ch - ' ');
            if (ch == 'R')
               {
               wScale = 0;
               hScale = 0;
               }
            if (ch == 'l' || ch == 'L')
               {
``` |
```

```
                wScale += 10;
                hScale += 10;
                }
            if (ch == 's' || ch == 'S')
                {
                wScale -= 10;
                hScale -= 10;
                }
        }
    repaint();
    return true;
    }
public void paint(Graphics g)
    {
    width = image.getWidth(this) + wScale;
    height = image.getHeight(this) + hScale;
    int x = (this.size().width - width) / 2;
    int y = (this.size().height - height) / 2;
    g.drawImage(image, x, y, width, height, this);
    }
}
```

Here is a screen shot of the applet showing the image in an enlarged form:

Figure 14.2: *The ScaleImage applet (see Listing 14.2)*

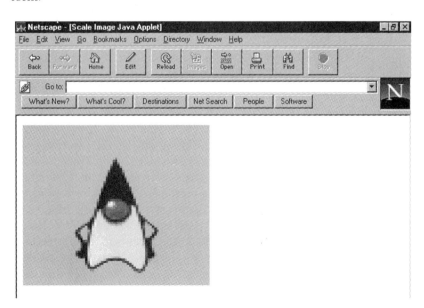

The only new code in this program is in the `paint()` method. The first two lines set the width and height parameters that we pass to the draw-Image() method:

```
width = image.getWidth(this) + wScale;
height = image.getHeight(this) + hScale;
```

We make use of a couple of methods defined in the Image class, `getWidth()` and `getHeight()`. These methods return the width and height of the actual image. They take an argument of type `ImageObserver` but again we can just use `this`. Using these methods you can keep the same ratio between the width and height when you scale an image so that it does not become distorted.

There are two other forms of the `drawImage()` method. They differ from the two we have mentioned in that they include an extra argument for the colour to be drawn underneath the image. Here is the syntax for both:

```
g.drawImage(image, x, y, bgColour, ImageObserver)
g.drawImage(image, x, y, width, height, bgColour, ImageObserver)
```

If you use one of these forms, any transparent pixels in the image that you are drawing will be drawn in the colour you specify as *bgColour*. You can therefore match the transparent parts of your image to the background you are using in your applet.

Manipulating Images

We have already seen how you can change images by scaling them. Java provides other interfaces and classes within the `java.awt.image` package that enable you to manipulate images. We will end this discussion of images with a look at how image filters can be used to change the appearance of an image.

We have already mentioned one of the interfaces within the Image class, `ImageObserver`. There are two other interfaces within the Image class that are necessary for image production. The `ImageProducer` interface specifies the methods that all image producers must implement. An image producer is an object which adheres to the `ImageProducer` interface and creates the data used by an `Image` object. Every image contains an image producer which can reconstruct the image whenever it is needed by an image consumer. The data created by an image producer is sent to an object implementing the `ImageConsumer` interface.

An image filter is an object that is based on the `ImageConsumer` interface and sits between an image producer and an image consumer, changing the image data before it reaches the consumer. Don't worry if this seems a little confusing. You can still make use of an image filter without being aware of what is happening behind the scenes. If you want to write your own image filters you will have to take a closer look at the `Image` class and these interfaces. That is beyond the scope of this book. However, using an existing image filter is quite easy so we will take a look at one of the filters that is defined in the `java.awt.image` package – the `CropImageFilter`.

The `CropImageFilter` is based on the `ImageFilter` class and will allow you to extract a rectangular region of an existing image and create a brand new image containing only the cropped extract. The following applet first loads an image and displays it. Each time the mouse button is clicked the image will be cropped so that a different quarter of the image is displayed. Here is the full source code:

Listing 14.3:
Example illustrating the use of an image filter (see Figure 14.3)

```
import java.awt.*;
import java.awt.image.*;
import java.applet.Applet;
public class CropImage extends Applet
{
Image sourceImage;
Image croppedImage;
int cx, cy;
int sx, sy;
int sWidth, sHeight;
boolean fullImage = true;
int qtr = 1;
public void init()
    {
    sourceImage  = getImage(getCodeBase(), "images/rbplogo.gif");
    }
public void CropTheImage()
    {
    switch (qtr)
        {
        case 1:
            cx = 0;
            cy = 0;
            break;
        case 2:
            cx = sWidth / 2;
```

```
            cy = 0;
            break;
        case 3:
            cx = sWidth / 2;
            cy = sHeight / 2;
            break;
        case 4:
            cx = 0;
            cy = sHeight / 2;
            break;
        }
    if (qtr == 4)
        qtr = 1;
    else
        qtr++;
    ImageFilter cropFilter = new CropImageFilter(cx, cy,
                sWidth / 2, sHeight / 2);
    ImageProducer producer = new FilteredImageSource(
                sourceImage.getSource(),cropFilter);
    croppedImage = createImage(producer);
    repaint();
    }
public boolean mouseDown(Event event, int x, int y)
    {
    CropTheImage();
    fullImage = false;
    repaint();
    return true;
    }
public void paint(Graphics g)
    {
    if (fullImage)
        {
        sWidth = sourceImage.getWidth(this);
        sHeight = sourceImage.getHeight(this);
        sx = (this.size().width - sWidth) / 2;
        sy = (this.size().height - sHeight) / 2;
        g.drawImage(sourceImage, sx, sy, this);
        }
    else
        {
        g.drawImage(croppedImage, sx+cx, sy+cy, this);
        }
    }
}
```

Figure 14.3: *The*
CropImage applet
(see Listing 14.3)

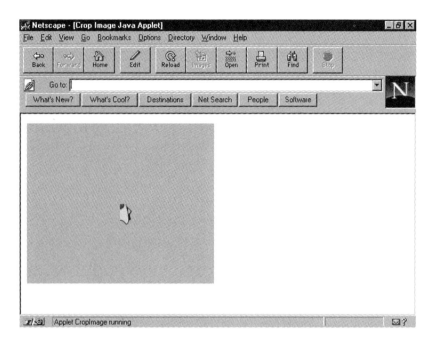

There are a few things that need to be explained about this applet. First of all, we have added the `import` statement:

```
import java.awt.image.*
```

This will import the classes that we require that are included in the `java.awt.image` package.

The first step to be carried out when implementing an image filter is to obtain the source image, using the `getImage()` method. We have done this in the `init()` method. The other important section of code is situated in the `CropTheImage()` method. The following three lines carry out the image filtering:

```
ImageFilter cropFilter = new CropImageFilter(cx, cy,
                    sWidth / 2, sHeight / 2);
ImageProducer producer = new FilteredImageSource(
                    sourceImage.getSource(),cropFilter);
croppedImage = createImage(producer);
```

First, we create an instance of the image filter which we call `cropFil-ter`. The `CropImageFilter` constructor takes four arguments: the x and y locations of the upper left corner of the rectangle to be extracted (in relation to the source image) and the width and height of the rectangle to be extracted:

```
ImageFilter cropFilter = new CropImageFilter(cx, cy,
                         sWidth / 2, sHeight / 2);
```

Next, we create a `FilteredImageSource` object. The first argument the constructor requires is the image source, or image producer, that produces the pixels for this image, which we can obtain by using the `Image` class `getSource()` method. The other argument is the filter object that we created in the previous line.

The final line of code uses the `createImage()` method of the `Component` class to create the new, cropped, image. The only argument is the `FilteredImageSource` object created above.

```
croppedImage = createImage(producer);
```

The same code, with minor changes, is all that is required to use any image filter. The steps can be summarised as:

```
Image sourceImage = getImage(arguments);
ImageFilter filter = new AnyImageFilter(constructor arguments);
ImageProducer producer = new FilteredImageSource(
        sourceImage.getSource(), filter);
Image newImage = createImage(producer);
```

Sound

Java currently supports only one format for playing sounds, the .au format from Sun. This is an 8-bit, single-channel format and doesn't produce sounds of particularly high quality. It's main advantage is that the sound files are quite small which helps keep loading times down to a minimum. The playing of sound files is supported in the `Applet` class and it's `AudioClip` interface. There are two ways of retrieving and playing sound files. The first method, `play()`, is part of the `Applet` class and has the same arguments as the `getImage()` method used for retrieving images. It is different from `getImage()`, however, in that it will both load the audio clip and play it as soon as it has obtained it from the server. The syntax is as follows:

```
play(url)
```

or

```
play(url, relativePath)
```

The first form takes a URL object as the argument, loading and playing the sound clip at that location. In the second case, the first argument is a base URL location and the second argument is a string which contains the location of the audio clip, relative to the url argument. As with the getImage() method, the getDocumentBase() and getCodeBase() methods can be used to obtain the base URL. An example might be:

```
play(getDocumentBase(), "audio/sound.au");
```

where the sound files are stored in a directory called audio under the directory where the HTML documents are held.

Here is a very simple applet which will display a string and play an audio clip:

Listing 14.4:
Playing an
audio clip

```
import java.awt.*;
import java.applet.Applet;
import java.applet.AudioClip;

public class SimpleAudio extends Applet
    {
    AudioClip clip;
    public void init()
        {
        play(getCodeBase(), "audio/train.au");
        }
    public void paint(Graphics g)
        {
        g.drawString("This is a simple audio applet", 20, 20);
        }
    }
```

An important point to bear in mind is that the applet will "pause" while the sound is loaded – it will appear to be doing nothing. Therefore, if you put a play() method in the init() method as we have done here, the user won't be able to interact with the applet until the sound has been loaded and played. If play() can't find the sound clip file than nothing will be heard and no error will be returned.

Another restriction on the play() method is that it will only play the audio clip once. If you know that you will want to play the clip more than once or repeatedly, it is better to use the getAudioClip() method and make use of the methods found in the AudioClip interface in the Applet class. The getAudioClip() method is used to load the sound only and returns an instance of the AudioClip class. There are two forms of the method and the arguments are the same as for the play method above.

This is the syntax:

```
AudioClip clip = getAudioClip(url)
```

or

```
AudioClip clip = getAudioClip(url, relativePath)
```

Once you have created an AudioClip object you can make use of the following methods, defined in the AudioClip interface:

- play() – which plays the clip once,
- loop() – which plays the clip repeatedly, and
- stop() – which stops the playing.

The getAudioClip() method differs with respect to the Applet play() method in that it will return null if it can't find the specified sound file. You should test for this as the AudioClip methods, play(), loop() and stop(), will produce an error if you try using them on a null object.

The following applet illustrates the use of the AudioClip methods. The init() method loads the audio clip, creating an instance of the class AudioClip called clip. When the mouse button is clicked the sound will be played repeatedly, using the loop() method, until the mouse is clicked again. Here is the source code:

Listing 14.5:
Playing an audio clip repeatedly

```
import java.awt.*;
import java.applet.*;
public class LoopAudio extends Applet
   {
   AudioClip clip;
   boolean looping = false;
   public void init()
      {
      clip = getAudioClip(getCodeBase(), "audio/train.au");
      }
   public boolean mouseDown(Event event, int x, int y)
      {
      if (looping)
         {
         looping = false;
         clip.stop();
```

```
                showStatus("Stopped playing sound");
                }
            else
                {
                looping = true;
                clip.loop();
                showStatus("Playing sound");
                }
            return true;
            }
    public void stop()
            {
            if (looping)
                clip.stop();
            }
    public void start()
            {
            if (looping)
                clip.loop();
            }
    public void paint(Graphics g)
            {
            g.drawString("Click mouse button to start or stop sound
            loop", 20, 20);
            }
        }
```

One thing to note is that if the loop() method is used to play a sound repeatedly the sound will not stop playing if the user moves to another page. We have therefore included a test in the stop() method to stop the sound loop if it is looping until the page is reloaded when it will be started again in the start() method.

One other new thing in this program is the use of the ShowStatus() method. This is an Applet method which will display a message in the status bar of the browser.

Summary

Two image file formats are supported by Java – GIF and JPEG. Images must be loaded from the web site server, using the getImage() method, before they can be displayed. A URL object is used as an argument to specify the location of the image. Once the image is loaded the `drawImage()` method can be used to actually display it.

Images can be manipulated in various ways: they can be made larger or smaller and stretched in either direction. The quality of the image is likely to be affected if it's form is altered too much.

The only sound file format that is supported at the moment is the .au format from Sun. Although these files are quite small, allowing fast download times, the quality of the sound they produce is not of a high quality.

15

Animation

Introduction

In this chapter we are going to be covering the use of animation in Java. We will begin by discussing threads – an important ingredient in Java animation – before moving on to explain how to create animations through the use of a number of examples. The first examples cover animation using text, based around the infamous Ticker Tape applet that anyone that who has surfed the World Wide Web will have come across numerous times.

We then include an example involving the use of text shadows and mouse movements, which is not strictly an animation, but contains a number of techniques that overlap with animations.

Finally, we include an example of animation involving images. This is the Duke character that anyone familiar with the JavaSoft Web site will have already come across.

Threads – an Introduction

Multitasking vs Multithreading

Multitasking, which has been around for some time now, is the ability to run more than one program at the same time. For instance, an operating environment like Windows 3.x allows the user to print a word processing document while updating a spreadsheet at the same time. Two programs, the word processor and the spreadsheet application, are running at the same time. Both are sharing the processing cycles of a computer.

Most computers are single processor machines and can only do one thing at a time. The illusion is given that two or more things are being carried out simultaneously because the operating system allocates time and resources to every program that is running one after the other. Because people cannot type or issue commands as fast as the processor can work the CPU is actually idle a lot of the time. The processor is therefore actually allocating the resources sequentially, but because it operates so fast it appears that things are happening simultaneously.

Multitasking comes in two forms – pre-emptive and non-preemptive. Pre-emptive multitasking means that the operating system decides when one program has had enough of the resources and allocates a time slice to the next program. One program cannot "hog" the resources and lock out all the others. Unix, Windows NT and Windows 95 (32-bit programs) are pre-emptive operating systems.

Programs running under a non-preemptive operating system (like Windows 3.x) must co-operate with any other programs by letting go of the system resources periodically so that other programs can run. If a program does not co-operate by relinquishing control of the processor no other applications can run properly. The control of resources is in the hands of the application, not the operating system.

A classic example of how a non-preemptive operating systems works is to imagine the software running a nuclear power station. The computer system is running two programs. One monitors the temperature of the core and the second is a chess program which an operator is using to play the computer.

The chess program is engaged in a rather tricky situation (checkmate in two moves) and is puzzling away to figure out how to avoid this. Meanwhile the core goes critical. Sadly the rather dumb operating system (sorry Windows 3.x) would just let the core go critical while the chess program (which at that time was hogging the system) worried more about its King than a big bang.

Multithreading, which is a fairly recent innovation provided by 32-bit operating systems, is the ability for a process to contain more than one path or stream of execution at any one time. So, instead of waiting for a long calculation to be completed before continuing processing, a multi-threaded program can be performing the calculation in one thread while other threads carry out other tasks, such as obtaining further user input. Within an application you can have one thread displaying an image while another thread is downloading the next image ready to be displayed when required.

As this chapter progresses you will see just how important a thread is when it comes to manipulating images using Java, especially over low-bandwidth communication links like the Internet and Web browsers.

Multithreading is different from multitasking in that threads share resources. They can all access the same objects, methods and variables within an application. This has its advantages and its disadvantages. On the positive side it provides much greater connectivity between the threads. Threads can communicate with each other to perform interrelated tasks.

This is not possible with multitasking processes. On the negative side, this ability to share resources can have undesirable results. If a thread is in the middle of a set of instructions which involves accessing a variable which another thread is in the process of updating, the outcome could be that the first thread uses an incorrect value for that variable depending on when the second variable updates it. Java fortunately provides ways of preventing this sort of thing from happening. We will cover this in a later chapter. *concurrency control*

The example applets that we have looked at so far have all been single thread programs – only one execution path was present. In fact, the Java run-time system maintains other threads – the automatic garbage collection which tidies up the memory is a thread.

Using Threads in Applets

There are two ways of creating a thread in Java. One way is to derive a class from the `Thread` class and place the code that implements the thread task in the `run()` method of that class. You define the main task of the thread by overriding the `run()` method derived from the `Thread` class and that is what is executed when you start the thread running. We will be covering this and other aspects of the `Thread` class in far more detail in a later chapter. For the moment, we are more interested in performing some animation in a Java applet.

Why use threads for animation? Well, to create animation in an applet we obviously have to include the main body of the animation code – the code that actually moves the text or images to give the illusion of animation – in a loop. Unfortunately, this means that the applet will continue to loop indefinitely, stopping any other applets on the page from obtaining system resources. The solution to this problem is to create the animation as a thread. That way it can continue running, obtaining a regular time slice of the system resource, without preventing other threads, ie. applets, from carrying out their tasks.

As we just mentioned, to create a thread you would normally derive a class from the `Thread` class. However, we are creating an applet by extending the `Applet` class. There is no multiple inheritance in Java so we cannot derive from more than one parent class. Because we cannot derive from both the `Applet` class and the `Thread` class we have to use an interface.

Java provides the `runnable` interface precisely for this purpose. Methods are defined in an interface which may be common to a number of classes. The methods are *abstract*, with no method body, and act as templates that are only defined in the classes that require that behaviour and actually *implement* the interface.

To create an applet that uses threads you must change the class definition to implement the `runnable` interface. The first line of the class definition must therefore appear like this:

```
public class ThreadsApplet extends Applet implements Runnable
    {
    ...
    }
```

The applet class is derived from `Applet` as usual but now implements the `runnable` interface.

The only method in the `runnable` interface is the abstract `run()` method. The applet must therefore include a definition for the `run()` method. The code defined in the `run()` method is the code that you want to run as a separate thread:

```
public void run()
    {
    ...   // thread code goes here
    }
```

You must also include a thread object as an instance variable:

```
Thread myThread;
```

When the thread object is created it takes a reference to a `Runnable` object as an argument to its constructor. The `run()` method defined for that object will be run when the thread is started. This is normally done in the `start()` method of the applet. The code will usually look like this:

```
public void start()// start method of the applet
   {
   if (myThread == null)
      {
      myThread = new Thread(this);
      myThread.start();
      }
   }
```

The `start()` method first checks to see if the thread has already been created by testing to see if its value is `null`. If it is `null`, it creates a new thread object, passing as an argument to the constructor, the reference to the applet class, using the `this` keyword. The `start()` method of the thread is then called to execute the thread (not to be confused with the applet `start()` method). When the thread `start()` method is called the code defined in the applet `run()` method is executed. When the user leaves the page containing the thread we need to stop it executing. This is usually carried out in the applet `stop()` method:

```
public void stop()
   {
   if (myThread != null)
      {
      myThread.stop();
      myThread = null;
      }
   }
```

The best way to make the use of threads easier to understand is to look at some programming examples.

Example One: TickerTape Applet

Our first example of text animation is a Java standard – the TickerTape applet. A text string is moved slowly across the screen in an imitation of a ticker tape display used in stock exchanges to display the latest prices. The text message, the font to be used and the size of the font are all passed as <APPLET> tag parameters. Here is the HTML code for the example:

```
<HTML>
<HEAD>
<TITLE> Ticker Tape Java Applet </TITLE>
</HEAD>
<BODY>
<APPLET CODE="TickerTape" WIDTH=400 HEIGHT=40>
<PARAM NAME=text VALUE="Some text to display in the Ticker Tape">
<PARAM NAME=font VALUE="Times Roman">
<PARAM NAME=size VALUE="20">
</APPLET>
</BODY>
</HTML>
```

The following screen shot shows the output from Listing 15.1:

Figure 15.1: *The* TickerTape *applet (see Listing 15.1)*

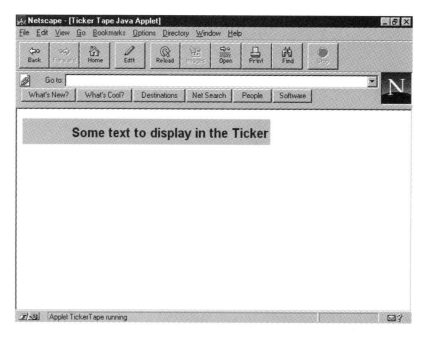

Here is the full source code of the applet:

Listing 15.1: *The* TickerTape *example applet (see Figure 15.1)*

```
import java.awt.*;
import java.applet.Applet;
public class TickerTape extends Applet implements Runnable
{
```

```
Thread tickerThread;
int currXPos = 0;
int currYPos = 0;
int textWidth = 0;
int startXPos = 0;
int moveDistance = 10;
int delay = 150;
String textMsg;
Font textFont;
String fontName;
int textSize;
Image OffScrImage;
Graphics OffScrGC;
int appWidth;
int appHeight;
public void init()
   {
   GetParams();
   SetDimensions();
   }
public void GetParams()
   {
   textMsg = getParameter("text");
   if (textMsg == null)
      textMsg = "No text parameter provided!";
   fontName = getParameter("font");
   if (fontName == null)
      fontName = "Helvetica";
   String strSize = getParameter("size");
   if (strSize == null)
      textSize = 18;
   else
      textSize = Integer.parseInt(strSize);
   }
public void SetDimensions()
   {
   textFont = new Font(fontName, Font.BOLD, textSize);
   FontMetrics fm = getFontMetrics(textFont);
   textWidth = fm.stringWidth(textMsg);
   appHeight = this.size().height;
   appWidth = this.size().width;
   currYPos = ((appHeight - textSize)/2) + fm.getAscent();
   startXPos = appWidth;
   currXPos = startXPos;
```

```java
      }
public void run()
    {
    tickerThread.setPriority(Thread.MIN_PRIORITY);
    OffScrImage = createImage(appWidth, appHeight);
    OffScrGC = OffScrImage.getGraphics();
    repaint();
    while(tickerThread != null)
        {
        MoveText();
        try
            {
            Thread.sleep(delay);
            }
        catch(InterruptedException e) {}
        }
    }
public void MoveText()
    {
    currXPos -= moveDistance;
    if ((currXPos + textWidth) < 0)
        currXPos = startXPos;
    repaint();
    }
public void update(Graphics g)
    {
    paint(g);
    }
public void paint(Graphics g)
    {
    OffScrGC.setColor(Color.lightGray);
    OffScrGC.fillRect(0, 0, appWidth, appHeight);
    OffScrGC.setColor(Color.black);
    OffScrGC.setFont(textFont);
    OffScrGC.drawString(textMsg, currXPos, currYPos);
    g.drawImage(OffScrImage, 0, 0, this);
    }
public void start()
    {
    if(tickerThread == null)
        {
        tickerThread = new Thread(this);
        tickerThread.start();
        }
```

```
      }
  public void stop()
      {
      if((tickerThread != null) && tickerThread.isAlive())
          {
          tickerThread.stop();
          }
      currXPos = appWidth;
      tickerThread = null;
      }
  }
```

We will now look at the program code step by step. The imports statements are standard. The Thread class is included in the java.lang
package which is automatically imported so we don't have to worry
about that. Here is the first line of the class definition:

```
  public class TickerTape extends Applet implements Runnable
      {
      ...
      }
```

The applet class is derived as usual from the Applet class. The extra bit,
implements Runnable, gives us access to the Runnable interface. The
first instance variable is the Thread that we will use to perform the animation:

```
  Thread tickerThread;
```

We then have a number of other instance variables. Their use will be
explained as we go through the code within the method definitions.
The init() method calls two functions which perform all the required
initialisation for the applet:

```
  public void init()
      {
      GetParams();
      SetDimensions();
      }
```

The GetParams() method obtains the parameters passed from the
<APPLET> tag in the HTML document, textMsg, which will hold the text
to be displayed in the tickertape, fontName, which holds the name of
the font to be used and textSize, which will define the size of the font.
As usual, we make sure that all of the parameters have been included in

the HTML. If any have been omitted `getParameter()` will return `null` so we need to set default values:

```
public void GetParams()
   {
   textMsg = getParameter("text");
   if (textMsg == null)
      textMsg = "No text parameter provided!";
   fontName = getParameter("font");
   if (fontName == null)
      fontName = "Helvetica";
   String strSize = getParameter("size");
   if (strSize == null)
      textSize = 30;
   else
      textSize = Integer.parseInt(strSize);
   }
```

The next method, `SetDimensions()`, initialises the variables used to keep track of the text position:

```
public void SetDimensions()
   {
   textFont = new Font(fontName, Font.BOLD, textSize);
   FontMetrics fm = getFontMetrics(textFont);
   textWidth = fm.stringWidth(textMsg);
   appHeight = this.size().height;
   appWidth = this.size().width;
   currYPos = ((appHeight - textSize)/2) + fm.getAscent();
   startXPos = appWidth;
   currXPos = startXPos;
   }
```

We first create the `textFont` object according to the parameters obtained from the <APPLET> tag. Using the font and the text string we want to display, we can work out the width of the string. This is held in the `textWidth` variable. The width and height dimensions of the applet are assigned to the `appWidth` and `appHeight` variables.

The variable to hold the y coordinate of the text is calculated so that the text is displayed centrally within the height of the applet. The `startXPos` variable is set to the width of the applet because we want the text string to first appear on the right hand edge of the applet. The current x coordinate variable, `currXPos`, is initialised to the same position.

The next method, run(), holds the main code for the thread. This is the method called when the thread is started and contains the main animation loop. The first line sets the priority of the thread using the Thread method, setPriority(). Thread priorities are defined in the Thread class and range from MIN_PRIORITY (value=1) to MAX_PRIORITY (value=10). The standard is NORM_PRIORITY which has a value of 5. Threads with the highest priority will be scheduled more often than those with a low priority. Our animation does not warrant a high priority so we make it MIN_PRIORITY:

```
tickerThread.setPriority(Thread.MIN_PRIORITY);
```

The next two lines require a bit of explanation. Because we want to move the text across the applet display area we will have to repaint the screen each time the text is moved. If we just make a call to repaint() each time, the text will certainly move across the screen as we intended. However, there will be a great deal of flickering on the screen.

The reason for this is that, when repaint() is called, it in turn makes a call to the update() method. The update() method proceeds to clear the screen completely, filling the applet's bounding rectangle with the background colour. It then makes a call to paint(), which performs the drawing on the screen. This two stage process of clearing the display before painting it is the cause of the flickering.

Double Buffering

The most straightforward solution to this problem is called *double buffering*. Double buffering involves the creation of an offscreen graphics image. All of the painting is carried out to the offscreen image and, when complete, the whole image is then transferred to the actual applet display. That way, no partial updating of the screen image is accidentally carried out and a smooth transition takes place during the animation.

The other thing that we have to do to prevent flickering is to override the update() method so that it doesn't clear the screen before calling the paint() method. The overridden version should just call paint():

```
public void update(Graphics g)
    {
    paint(g);
    }
```

Returning to the run() method, these two lines create an offscreen image and a graphics context for that image. The variables created will be used in the paint() method as you will see shortly:

```
OffScrImage = createImage(appWidth, appHeight);
OffScrGC = OffScrImage.getGraphics();
```

After a call to an initial repaint() function we move into the main loop of the animation:

```
while(tickerThread != null)
   {
   MoveText();
   try
      {
      Thread.sleep(delay);
      }
   catch(InterruptedException e) {}
   }
```

The loop cycles while tickerThread is running. Each iteration of the loop calls the method, MoveText(), which updates the position of the text string and calls repaint(). There are then some lines of code which introduce a delay into the loop. The sleep() method of the Thread class causes the thread, and therefore the annimation, to pause. Without it, the text would fly past too fast to follow. The argument passed to the sleep() method is the length of the pause in milliseconds. We have used a value of 150 milliseconds in this example. Try experimenting by changing the value of the delay variable to see how it affects the speed of the animation.

The try and catch statements either side of the sleep command are Java exception handling statements. If another thread interrupts the current thread while it is sleeping an exception will be thrown and Java requires that any method that has been declared to throw an exception must be enclosed by the try/catch combination. We will be covering exception handling in a later chapter. For the moment it is only necessary to know that these statements must always enclose a sleep() statement.

The MoveText() method is quite straightforward. Each time it is called it moves the current x coordinate of the start of the text string move-Distance pixels to the left until the whole text string has disappeared off the left hand side of the screen, in which case it resets the current x coordinate back to the start position on the right hand edge of the screen. The `repaint()` method is then called to paint the screen.

We have already mentioned the `update()` method so lets move on to the `paint()` method:

```
public void paint(Graphics g)
    {
    OffScrGC.setColor(Color.lightGray);
    OffScrGC.fillRect(0, 0, appWidth, appHeight);
    OffScrGC.setColor(Color.black);
    OffScrGC.setFont(textFont);
    OffScrGC.drawString(textMsg, currXPos, currYPos);
    g.drawImage(OffScrImage, 0, 0, this);
    }
```

As you can see, all of the drawing is being carried out in the offscreen graphics context. First the background is set to light grey. Then the text is drawn at the current x and y coordinates (`currYPos` doesn't actually change during the lifetime of the applet once it has been initialised).

Finally, the `drawImage()` method paints the offscreen image on the visible graphics context. The second and third arguments are the coordinates of the upper left corner of the image. As both the onscreen and offscreen images have the same dimensions one will replace the other.

The applet `start()` method is implemented as it was discussed earlier in the chapter. The applet `stop()` method first determines whether the thread is active and, if it is, stops it, sets the thread to `null` and resets the x coordinate back to the initial position.

Example Two: Nervous TickerTape Applet

This applet is a variation on the TickerTape applet we have just presented. It uses the idea of "nervous text" that is included as a demo program in the JDK. Instead of moving across the screen in an orderly fashion, the letters jump up and down randomly, making the animation a little more interesting and eye-catching. Here is a screenshot showing what it looks like:

Figure 15.2: *The*
"nervous text"
TickerTape *applet*
(see Listing 15.2)

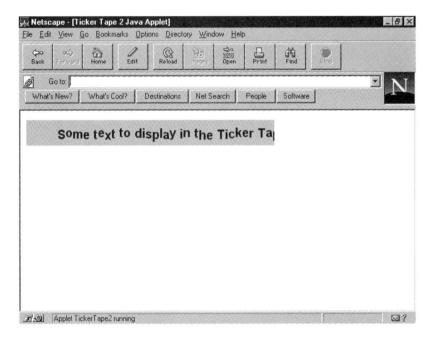

The main difference between this applet and the previous one is that the letters have to move independently of each other. This means that we have to be able to control the position of each character separately. Obviously, we can't do this by using the drawString() method that we have used before. This time we will use the drawChars() method of the Graphics class. This lets us individually draw each character of an array of characters.

We will look at the sections of code that are different from the first TickerTape applet to see what changes we need to make. First, there are some extra instance variables:

```
int xOffset[];
int yOffset;
int yAdj;
char textChars[];
```

The char array, textChars, will be used to store the individual characters of the text string being displayed. The xOffset integer array will contain the horizontal offset from the start of the text string to the position where each character will be displayed. Each element of the xOffset array relates to the corresponding character in the textChars array.

The yOffset integer variable will contain the amount the text should be offset from the top of the display area based on the height of the applet and the size of the font. The yAdj integer variable will be multiplied with a randomly generated number between 0 and 1 to arrive at the distance each letter should be shifted vertically.

Only two methods have been changed – SetDimensions() and paint(). Lets take a look at the changes to SetDimensions(). Firstly, the initialisation of yAdj and yOffset has been added:

```
yAdj = textSize / 4;
yOffset = ((appHeight - textSize)/2) + fm.getAscent() - (yAdj/2);
```

Next, the char array, textChars, is created with a size equal to the length of the text string:

```
textChars = new char [textMsg.length()];
```

The String method, getChars(), is then used to populate the character array with all the characters from the textMsg string:

```
textMsg.getChars(0, textMsg.length(), textChars, 0);
```

Next, the xOffset integer array is created with the same number of elements as the textChars array:

```
xOffset =  new int[textMsg.length()];
```

Each element of the xOffset array will contain the horizontal offset from the start position of the text string for the corresponding character in the textChars array. The first element is set to zero and then a for loop is used to populate the rest of the array:

```
xOffset[0] = 0;
int totalWidth = 0;
for(int i = 0; i < textMsg.length(); i++)
   {
   totalWidth += fm.charWidth(textChars[i]);
   if(i+1 < textMsg.length())
       xOffset[i+1] = totalWidth;
   }
```

The FontMetrics charWidth() method is used to obtain the width of each character and this is added to a running total which is then allocated to the xOffset element.

In the paint() method the call to drawString(), that was used in the previous TickerTape example, has been replaced by a loop:

```
for(int i = 0; i < textMsg.length(); i++)
  {
  currYPos = (int) (Math.random() * yAdj + yOffset);
  OffScrGC.drawChars(textChars, i, 1,
     currXPos + xOffset[i], currYPos);
  }
```

This sets the current y coordinate, currYPos, for each character using the random() method from the Math class. This returns a pseudo random number between 0 and 1. We multiply this number by yAdj to give a value which corresponds to the size of the font. The drawChars() method is then used to actually draw the character.

The drawChars() method has the following syntax:

```
g.drawChars(charArray, offset, numberOfChars, xPos, yPos)
```

The first argument, *charArray*, is the array of characters to be displayed. *offset* is the position in the array from which you want to start displaying characters. *numberOfChars* is the number of characters you actually want to display. The *xPos* and *yPos* arguments are the x and y coordinates of the screen position where you want to start displaying the characters.

Within our loop we set the numberOfChars argument to 1 for each iteration so that we only display one character at a time. We do this because the x and y coordinates of each character have to be calculated separately.

Having created our off screen image we again use drawImage() to actually display the text on the screen.

Here is the full source code:

Listing 15.2:
*The code for the
"nervous text"
TickerTape applet
(see Figure 15.2)*

```
import java.awt.*;
import java.applet.Applet;
public class TickerTape2 extends Applet implements Runnable
  {
  Thread tickerThread = null;
  int currXPos = 0;
  int currYPos = 0;
  int textWidth = 0;
  int startXPos = 0;
  int moveDistance = 10;
  int delay = 150;
  String textMsg;
```

```
Font textFont;
String fontName;
int textSize;
Image OffScrImage;
Graphics OffScrGC;
int appWidth;
int appHeight;
int xOffset[];
int yOffset;
int yAdj;
char textChars[];
public void init()
    {
    GetParams();
    SetDimensions();
    }
public void GetParams()
    {
    textMsg = getParameter("text");
    if (textMsg == null)
       textMsg = "No text parameter provided!";
    fontName = getParameter("font");
    if (fontName == null)
       fontName = "Helvetica";
    String strSize = getParameter("size");
    if (strSize == null)
       textSize = 30;
    else
       textSize = Integer.parseInt(strSize);
    }
public void SetDimensions()
    {
    textFont = new Font(fontName, Font.BOLD, textSize);
    FontMetrics fm = getFontMetrics(textFont);
    textWidth = fm.stringWidth(textMsg);
    appHeight = this.size().height;
    appWidth = this.size().width;
    startXPos = appWidth;
    currXPos = startXPos;
    yAdj = textSize / 4;
    yOffset = ((appHeight - textSize)/2) +
                   fm.getAscent() - (yAdj/2);
```

```java
            textChars =  new char [textMsg.length()];
            textMsg.getChars(0, textMsg.length(), textChars, 0);
            xOffset =  new int[textMsg.length()];
            xOffset[0] = 0;
            int totalWidth = 0;
            for(int i = 0; i < textMsg.length(); i++)
               {
               totalWidth += fm.charWidth(textChars[i]);
               if(i+1 < textMsg.length())
                  xOffset[i+1] = totalWidth;
               }
            }
      public void run()
         {
         tickerThread.setPriority(Thread.MIN_PRIORITY);
         OffScrImage = createImage(appWidth, appHeight);
         OffScrGC = OffScrImage.getGraphics();
         repaint();
         while(tickerThread != null)
            {
            MoveText();
            try
               {
               Thread.sleep(delay);
               }
            catch(InterruptedException e) {}
            }
         }
      public void MoveText()
         {
         currXPos -= moveDistance;
         if ((currXPos + textWidth) < 0)
            currXPos = startXPos;
         repaint();
         }
      public void update(Graphics g)
         {
         paint(g);
         }
      public void paint(Graphics g)
         {
         OffScrGC.setColor(Color.lightGray);
```

```
    OffScrGC.fillRect(0, 0, appWidth, appHeight);
    OffScrGC.setColor(Color.black);
    OffScrGC.setFont(textFont);
    for(int i = 0; i < textMsg.length(); i++)
        {
        currYPos = (int) (Math.random() * yAdj + yOffset);
        OffScrGC.drawChars(textChars, i, 1,
            currXPos + xOffset[i], currYPos);
        }
    g.drawImage(OffScrImage, 0, 0, this);
    }
public void start()
    {
    if(tickerThread == null)
        {
        tickerThread = new Thread(this);
        tickerThread.start();
        }
    }
public void stop()
    {
    if((tickerThread != null) && tickerThread.isAlive())
        {
        tickerThread.stop();
        }
    currXPos = appWidth;
    tickerThread = null;
    }
}
```

Example Three: Moving Shadow Applet

Our third example isn't strictly text animation as such and doesn't make use of threads. It does, however, involve movement on the screen and makes use of double buffering so we have included it in this chapter.

When the page containing this applet is first displayed the applet will display a text string which casts a shadow. To enhance the effect the shadow is drawn slightly larger than the actual text to give it a more natural appearance.

The more interesting aspect of the applet is manifested when the user moves the mouse cursor over the applet. The shadow will start changing position according to where the cursor arrow is moved. The effect achieved is that the cursor arrow controls the position of the light source which determines where the shadow will be cast.

Figure 15.3: *The* MovingShadow *applet (see Listing 15.3)*

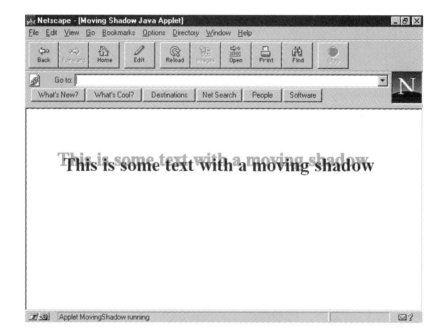

Here is the full source code of the applet:

Listing 15.3: *Applet which displays text with a shadow that moves in relation to the mouse position (see Figure 15.3)*

```
import java.awt.*;
import java.applet.*;

public class MovingShadow extends Applet
    {
    int shadowXOffset = 3;
    int shadowYOffset = 3;
    Color shadowColour;
    Color fg = Color.black;
    Color bg = Color.white;
    String textMsg = "This is some text with a moving shadow";
    Font textFont;
    int textWidth, textHeight;
```

```
int appWidth, appHeight;
Image offScrImage;
Graphics offScrGC;

public void init()
   {
   appWidth = this.size().width;
   appHeight = this.size().height;
   offScrImage = createImage(appWidth, appHeight);
   offScrGC = offScrImage.getGraphics();
   textFont = new Font("TimesRoman", Font.BOLD, 30);
   FontMetrics fm = getFontMetrics(textFont);
   textWidth = fm.stringWidth(textMsg);
   textHeight = fm.getHeight();
   shadowColour = new Color(170, 170, 170);
   }

public void update(Graphics g)
   {
   paint(g);
   }

public void paint(Graphics g)
   {
   int x, y;

   offScrGC.setFont(textFont);
   offScrGC.setColor(bg);
   offScrGC.fillRect(0, 0, appWidth, appHeight);

   x = ((appWidth - textWidth) / 2) + shadowXOffset;
   y = ((appHeight - textHeight) / 2) + shadowYOffset;

   offScrGC.setColor(shadowColour);
   for(int i = 0; i < 2; i++)
      for(int j = 0; j < 2; j++)
         offScrGC.drawString(textMsg, x + i, y + j);

   x = (appWidth - textWidth) / 2;
   y = (appHeight - textHeight) / 2;

   offScrGC.setColor(fg);
```

```
            offScrGC.drawString(textMsg, x, y);
            g.drawImage(offScrImage, 0, 0, this);
            }

        public boolean mouseMove(Event evt, int x, int y)
            {
            shadowXOffset = (appWidth/2 - x)/10;
            shadowYOffset = (appHeight/2 - y)/10;
            repaint();
            return true;
            }
        }
```

There is nothing really new in the list of instance variables. We will explain what each one does when it first appears in the code.

The init() method kicks off by setting the appWidth and appHeight variables to the dimensions of the applet. The off screen graphics image and graphics context is then created. Next, the font object is created and the width and height of the text string obtained using the FontMetrics methods., stringWidth() and getHeight(). Lastly, we create a Color object, shadowColour, and assign it a combination of RGB values to arrive at a suitable shade of grey.

As usual we override the update method to stop the screen being cleared. All it does is call the paint() method, which does just about all the work in this applet. We are using double buffering to eliminate any flickering so all the drawing is being carried out on the off screen graphics context, offScrGC. The font is set to the one we have chosen – TimesRoman in this instance, and the background colour is set to white:

```
        offScrGC.setFont(textFont);
        offScrGC.setColor(bg);
        offScrGC.fillRect(0, 0, appWidth, appHeight);
```

As we obviously want the shadow to appear behind the actual text, we must draw it first. The next six lines accomplish this. First we have to work out the x and y screen coordinates where we want the shadow drawn. This is done by calculating the starting coordinates for the text so that it will be drawn centrally within the applet display and then adding an offset to each:

```
        x = ((appWidth - textWidth) / 2) + shadowXOffset;
        y = ((appHeight - textHeight) / 2) + shadowYOffset;
```

Initially, the shadow offset is set to 3. This will ensure that the shadow is drawn slightly to the right and below the actual text.

The current colour is then set to the grey we are using for the shadow and a nested loop is used to draw it:

```
offScrGC.setColor(shadowColour);
for(int i = 0; i < 2; i++)
    for(int j = 0; j < 2; j++)
        offScrGC.drawString(textMsg, x + i, y + j);
```

There are two iterations of each loop so the shadow is drawn four times. In the first iteration of the outer loop the text is first drawn at the coordinates specified by the x and y variables and then again one pixel lower. In the second iteration, the x coordinate has been incremented so the text is drawn one pixel to the right and then again one pixel down. The result is a shadow that is one pixel larger than the actual text in each of the positive x and y directions.

Having drawn the shadow we must now draw the text itself. First the x and y coordinates of the starting position for the text must be recalculated:

```
x = (appWidth - textWidth) / 2;
y = (appHeight - textHeight) / 2;
```

As you can see, all we are doing is centering the string within the applet display space. Next, we set the current colour to black and then use drawString() to draw the text:

```
offScrGC.setColor(fg);
offScrGC.drawString(textMsg, x, y);
```

Finally, we use drawImage() to paint the offscreen image on to the visible graphics context:

```
g.drawImage(offScrImage, 0, 0, this);
```

If we just wanted to display some text with a shadow that is all we would have to do. The point of this applet, however, is to move the position of the shadow according to the current position of the mouse cursor. This is, in fact, quite simple. All we have to do is override the mouseMove() event method:

```
public boolean mouseMove(Event evt, int x, int y)
    {
    shadowXOffset = (appWidth/2 - x)/10;
    shadowYOffset = (appHeight/2 - y)/10;
```

```
repaint();
return true;
}
```

The shadow coordinate offsets, `shadowXOffset` and `shadowYOffset`, are recalculated each time a `mouseMove` event is generated and a call is made to repaint the screen. This results in the shadow being drawn at coordinates that move in relation to the position of the mouse cursor. As you move the cursor down the screen the shadow will move up, move the cursor to the left and the shadow will shift to the right – giving the impression that the mouse cursor is being used to control the position of a light source.

Animation Using Images

For our final example involving animation we present an applet that displays the Java mascot, Duke, waving his arm. The animation consists of ten images, which are displayed one at a time, with a suitable delay between each change. All the images are loaded first, into an array of images, and once we know that the loading process has completed, we start to display each of the images in turn. We use the same approach that was used for the Ticker Tape applets, running the animation in a thread that is created when the applet begins execution.

Figure 15.4: *The* ImageAnimation *applet (see Listing 15.4)*

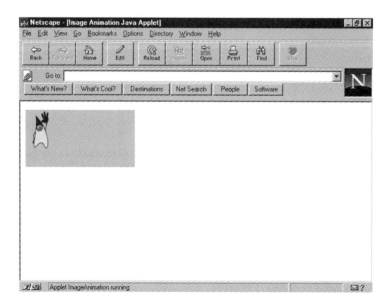

It would be possible to load all the images into the array using the getI-mage() method. This, however, can have the unwanted side effect of the images being displayed before they have been completely loaded. This happens because getImage() returns immediately and does not actually fetch the pixels of the image – that happens when drawImage() is used to display the image. You can therefore reach the situation where the image display loop is trying to display the images before they have all been loaded.

Fortunately there is a solution for this in the form of the MediaTracker class. The MediaTracker class provides methods that allow you to download a series of images and keep track of the progress. They give you the flexibility to begin displaying images before the complete set has been downloaded, or waiting until the complete set of images have obtained before beginning the display process.

MediaTracker will also report on any errors that have been encountered whilst downloading the image data. Another benefit is that the images will be loaded much faster using MediaTracker. The methods that obtain each image use background threads to speed up the data transmission.

The basic structure of this applet is the same as the preceding text animation applets. We create an applet from the Applet class and implement the Runnable interface. As before, the thread containing the animation loop is situated in the run() method, the image displaying is carried out in the paint() method and the start() and stop() methods control the thread execution when the user leaves or enters the page.

Here is the source code for the applet. After the listing we will discuss the differences from the earlier examples.

Listing 15.4: *An example showing how images can be animated (see Figure 15.4)*

```
import java.awt.*;
import java.applet.Applet;

public class ImageAnimation extends Applet implements Runnable
    {
    Thread animationThread = null;
    int appWidth;
    int appHeight;
    int delay = 150;

    Image OffScrImage;
```

```
Graphics OffScrGC;

Image[] images;
int frameNo;
MediaTracker mTracker;

public void init()
    {
    images = new Image[10];
    mTracker = new MediaTracker(this);
    frameNo = 0;
    for (int i = 1; i <= 10; i++)
        {
        images[i-1] = getImage(getCodeBase(),
                        "images/T"+i+".gif");
        mTracker.addImage(images[i-1], 0);
        }
    appHeight = this.size().height;
    appWidth = this.size().width;
    }

public void run()
    {
    animationThread.setPriority(Thread.MIN_PRIORITY);
    OffScrImage = createImage(appWidth, appHeight);
    OffScrGC = OffScrImage.getGraphics();

    repaint();

    try
        {
        mTracker.waitForAll();
        } catch (InterruptedException e) {}

    while(animationThread != null)
        {
        frameNo++;
        repaint();
        try
            {
            Thread.sleep(delay);
            }
```

```
                catch(InterruptedException e) {}
            }
        }

    public void update(Graphics g)
        {
        paint(g);
        }

    public void paint(Graphics g)
        {
        if (mTracker.checkAll())
            {
            OffScrGC.setColor(getBackground());
            OffScrGC.fillRect(0, 0, appWidth, appHeight);
            OffScrGC.setColor(Color.black);

            OffScrGC.drawImage(images[frameNo % 10], 0, 0, this);

            g.drawImage(OffScrImage, 0, 0, this);
            }
        else
            {
            g.clearRect(0, 0, appWidth, appHeight);
            g.drawString("Loading images...Please wait",
                        10, appHeight/2);
            }
        }

    public void start()
        {
        if(animationThread == null)
            {
            animationThread = new Thread(this);
            animationThread.start();
            }
        }

    public void stop()
        {
        if((animationThread != null) && animationThread.isAlive())
            {
```

```
            animationThread.stop();
            }
        animationThread = null;
        }
    }
```

We still have to make use of double buffering to prevent any flickering in our animation so the offscreen graphics image instance variables are still required. We also still need the delay variable to slow the animation down to a reasonable speed. The extra instance variables are an array of images to hold the frames that make up the animation, an integer variable to keep track of the frame currently being displayed and an instance of the MediaTracker class.

The init() method contains the code for creating the image array object and the MediaTracker object. The argument for the latter's constructor is a component object – in this case the applet. The media tracker registers the applet with the image producers of the images it maintains (*see the chapter on Images and Sound*). The images are loaded into the image array in a loop.

The addImage() method of the media tracker adds each image to the list of images that it is to maintain. The second argument is an id – in this case set to zero. Media tracker associates all of the images in the set with this id. The images can then be regarded as one image, giving us the ability to wait for all the images in our animation to be loaded, without error, before we start using any of them.

In the run() method, the thread is given a low priority and the off screen graphics image is created. A call is then made to the wait-ForAll() method of media tracker:

```
try
    {
    mTracker.waitForAll();
    }
catch (InterruptedException e) {}
```

waitForAll() only returns when all the images have been loaded. The method is declared to throw an InterruptedException exception so we have to enclose it within the try/catch combination. The main animation loop follows. The only difference from our text animation examples is that the image frame number is incremented for each iteration.

The paint() method contains the code for displaying each image. The checkAll() method is used to make sure that all the images have been loaded before we begin the animation. A "please wait" message is displayed while the loading process takes place.

We have kept this example applet fairly simple to illustrate the important aspects of image animation, using the media tracker. There are a number of other methods available within the MediaTracker class that will enable you to manage the image loading process in whatever way you want. It is worth looking at the demo applet, Animator, included with the JDK. This applet provides an excellent framework for creating your own animations.

Summary

We began this chapter on animation by introducing the concept of threads. The differences between multitasking and multithreading were discussed in order to explain why multithreading can provide a number of advantages. Multithreading is the ability for a process to contain more than one path of execution at any one time. Therefore, a number of different threads can be running at the same time, each one performing a different task.

Threads are particularly useful when including animation in a program. By placing the code that carries out the animation inside a thread, the animation can run without preventing any other threads from running, as it will be given a regular time slice of the system resources.

To include threads inside applets, the applet class must implement the Runnable interface.

We saw how double buffering can help with animations by preventing the flickering effect that occurs when a screen display is repeatedly cleared and redrawn. Double buffering involves the creation of an off-screen graphics image. Any painting is carried out to the offscreen image and, when complete, the whole image is transferred to the actual screen display.

In the example illustrating image animation, we saw how the MediaTracker class can be used to control the loading of images, thus preventing the image animation loop from trying to display a series of images before they have all been downloaded.

Designing a User Interface

Introduction

Components and Containers

The Java AWT class provides a number of different *components* that can be used for creating a user interface in Java. The components include common GUI elements such as buttons, checkboxes, text fields and lists. These components must always be placed inside other Java objects called *containers*.

In Windows, the container would be a parent window and the components would be the controls placed in that window. In X-Windows, the components are called widgets and are placed within container widgets.

Containers are themselves components – components, inside which, other components can be placed. The most commonly used container is the panel. A panel is a rectangular area, invisible to the user, which can be used to divide up the display area so that components can be positioned, according to your design wishes, within a window.

The Applet class is in fact derived from the panel class. Therefore, an applet is itself a container and components can be placed in an applet without any other panels being created. As you will see later on, however, to create a user interface that requires more than one or two components, you must make extensive use of panels.

A major difference from constructing graphical user interfaces under other operating systems is that Java components are not placed or sized according to any kind of coordinate system. In Windows, for instance, when a dialog box is to be included in an application, the resource description for that dialog will include the x and y coordinates of all the controls within it. Java applets and applications, on the other hand, must run on a number of different platforms.

The user interface for your Java application must look correct no matter what machine and operating system it is being run on. For instance, fonts and therefore font metrics can be different and buttons can be different sizes and shapes. Java overcomes these problems by providing *layout managers* to handle all the painting and positioning of components in your interface.

There are five layout managers – flow layout, border layout, grid layout, grid bag layout and card layout. Before you start placing any components you must specify which layout you want to use. Once you have done that you can start adding the components and the layout manager will take care of the positioning of the components within the interface. The only thing you have to consider is the order that you use for adding the components. You will see why shortly.

Here is a list of the available components and their uses:

- **Button** – used to invoke a command when clicked on by the user.
- **Canvas** – used for drawing graphics or text in a user interface.
- **Checkboxes** – allows one or more options to be selected by the user.
- **Checkbox Group** – allows only one checkbox option in a group to be selected at one time.
- **Choice list** – provides a drop-down list from which the user can select their choice.
- **Label** – used to display a non-editable text string on the user interface.
- **List** – provides a scrollable list of items from which multiple choices may be made.
- **Scrollbar** – provides a sliding scale to allow values to be chosen from a specific range.
- **TextField** – allows the user to enter and edit a line of text.
- **TextArea** – allows the user to enter and edit text in a multiple line area.

Buttons

The first component that we will look at is the button component. Whenever you need a command to be invoked in your applet the usual answer is to use a button. A button object is created in the usual manner, using the new operator. For instance to create a button with the label "OK" you would use the following command:

```
btnOk = new Button("OK");
```

Having created the button, it can be added to the applet display by using the add command:

```
add(btnOk);
```

The button class contains two constructors:

- Button(String) creates a button with a label set to String.
- Button() creates a button with no label.

Our button example applet will contain three buttons – OK, Cancel and Help. This is what the applet will look like:

Figure 16.1: *The* Button2 *applet (see Listing 16.1)*

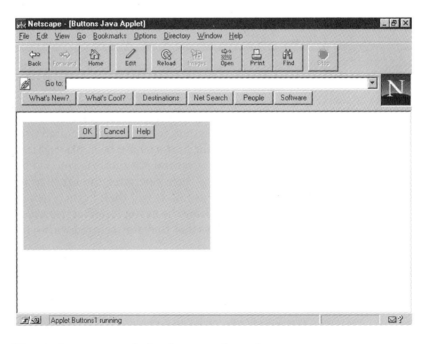

Here is the source code for the example applet:

| **Listing 16.1:** *Displaying buttons in an applet (see Figure 16.1)* | ```
import java.awt.*;
import java.applet.*;
public class Buttons1 extends Applet
    {
    public void init()
        {
        Button btnOk = new Button("OK");
        Button btnCancel = new Button("Cancel");
        Button btnHelp = new Button("Help");
        add(btnOk);
        add(btnCancel);
        add(btnHelp);
        }
    }
``` |

Button methods

- `public String getLabel()` returns a string containing the button's label.
- `public void setLabel(String label)` sets the label of the button to the string.

Flow Layout

In the preceding example the flow layout manager has been used. This is the default layout system for applets so we didn't need to specify it first. As you can see, the buttons have been placed across the top of the applet display area in a central position. As you add buttons, the flow layout manager places them one after the other in a row across the screen until that row is full. It will then begin a new row underneath the first. If you try resizing the example applet you will see that the buttons will be redrawn so that they stay centred within the applet display area.

In our example, we haven't used a command to set the layout. We do this by using the `setLayout()` method of the panel class. This tells the panel what layout manager it should use. Here is the method:

```
setLayout(new FlowLayout);
```
```

You can control whether the buttons are centred, as they are by default, left-aligned or right-aligned. If we wanted to display the buttons left-aligned, we would need to include an alignment constant in the FlowLayout constructor. Here is the source for displaying the buttons left-aligned:

Listing 16.2:
*Using the Flow
Layout to display
left-aligned
buttons (see
Figure 16.2)*

```
import java.awt.*;
import java.applet.*;
public class Buttons2 extends Applet
    {
    public void init()
      {
      Button btnOk = new Button("OK");
      Button btnCancel = new Button("Cancel");
      Button btnHelp = new Button("Help");
      setLayout(new FlowLayout(FlowLayout.LEFT));
      add(btnOk);
      add(btnCancel);
      add(btnHelp);
      }
    }
```

Our example will now look like this:

Figure 16.2: *The
Buttons2 applet
(see Listing 16.2)*

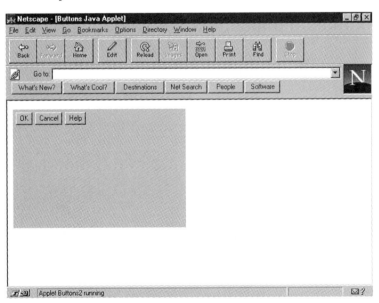

The other two alignment constants are FlowLayout.CENTER and Flow-Layout.RIGHT. If we add a lot more buttons to our example applet you can see how the FlowLayout object starts another row of buttons under the first. We will align them centrally:

Listing 16.3:
Example showing how Flow Layout displays a number of buttons (see Figure 16.3)

```java
import java.awt.*;
import java.applet.*;
public class Buttons3 extends Applet
    {
    public void init()
        {
        Button btnOk = new Button("OK");
        Button btnCancel = new Button("Cancel");
        Button btnHelp = new Button("Help");
        Button btnYes = new Button("Yes");
        Button btnNo = new Button("No");
        Button btnAbort = new Button("Abort");
        Button btnRetry = new Button("Retry");
        Button btnTom = new Button("Tom");
        Button btnDick = new Button("Dick");
        Button btnHarry = new Button("Harry");
        setLayout(new FlowLayout(FlowLayout.CENTER));
        add(btnOk);
        add(btnCancel);
        add(btnHelp);
        add(btnYes);
        add(btnNo);
        add(btnAbort);
        add(btnRetry);
        add(btnTom);
        add(btnDick);
        add(btnHarry);
        }
    }
```

Figure 16.3 shows the output.

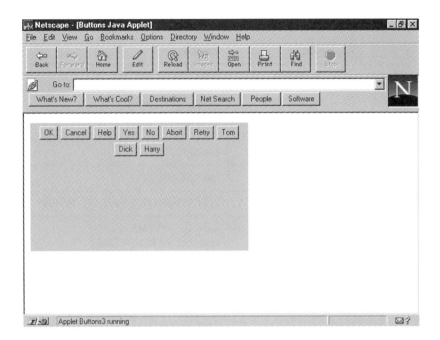

Figure 16.3: *The*
Buttons3 *applet*
(see Listing 16.3)

Handling events in a user interface

When you click one of the buttons in our example program the button changes it's appearance as though it has been pushed, but nothing else happens. How do we get a button to respond to a mouse click and invoke a command? The answer is events.

Every time an event is generated, it is passed to a handleEvent() method. The handleEvent() method is passed an event object. Every event object has an id field which identifies what kind of event it is. The handleEvent() method uses this event id to call a specific method for that event type. Table 16.1 lists of all the event handling methods followed by the id of the event type each one handles:

Table 16.1: *Events and methods*

Method	Event id
action()	Event.ACTION_EVENT
mouseEnter()	Event.MOUSE_ENTER

Table 16.1: *Events and methods (continued)*

Method	Event id
mouseExit()	Event.MOUSE_EXIT
mouseMove()	Event.MOUSE_MOVE
mouseDown()	Event.MOUSE_DOWN
mouseDrag()	Event.MOUSE_DRAG
mouseUp()	Event.MOUSE_UP
keyDown()	Event.KEY_PRESS or Event.KEY_ACTION
keyUp()	Event.KEY_RELEASE or Event.KEY_ACTION_RELEASE
gotFocus()	Event.GOT_FOCUS
lostFocus()	Event.LOST_FOCUS

We have already looked at the events relating to the mouse and keyboard. To respond to mouse clicks or movement we had to define methods to override the mouseDown and mouseMove events. If we had wanted to, we could have dealt with any keyboard and mouse events by overriding the handleEvent() method and testing for the appropriate event id.

This could, however, lead to confusion if we are attempting to deal with a large number of events. It is much safer and clearer dealing with events in the event handler relating to that type of event.

Every time a button or any other component is pressed an action event is generated. Therefore, to respond to a button click we must define an action() method which will contain the code we want to be run whenever the button is pressed.

Here is the signature of an action event method:

```
public boolean action(Event event, Object arg)
    {
    ...
    }
```

As you can see it is pretty much the same as one of the mouse or keyboard events. An event object is passed as the first argument. The second argument, however, can be any type of object. This is because an action event can be generated by any UI component. A different second argument will be passed depending upon the component that originated the event.

For instance, in the case of a button press, the label of the button is passed as the second argument. As we introduce the other UI components, like Check boxes and Lists, we will specify what is passed as the arg argument in each case.

The fact that an action event can be generated by any one of a number of different components means that you must include some code in the action method to determine which type of object actually generated the event. To allow you to do this, the object that generates the action is passed as the target instance variable of the event object.

Our next example applet illustrates how to intercept the action event when a button is pressed and so invoke a command. The addition of the action() method is the only difference from the previous example. Here is the full source code:

Listing 16.4:
Making buttons respond when clicked (see Figure 16.4)

```java
import java.awt.*;
public class ButtonEvents extends java.applet.Applet
   {
   Button btnOk, btnCancel, btnHelp;
   public void init()
      {
      btnOk = new Button("OK");
      btnCancel = new Button("Cancel");
      btnHelp = new Button("Help");
      add(btnOk);
      add(btnCancel);
      add(btnHelp);
      }
   public boolean action(Event evt, Object arg)
      {
      if (evt.target == btnOk)
         {
         showStatus("OK pressed");
         return (true);
         }
      else if (evt.target == btnCancel)
         {
         showStatus("Cancel pressed");
```

```
            return (true);
            }
        else if (evt.target == btnHelp)
            {
            showStatus("Help pressed");
            return (true);
            }
        return (false);
        }
    }
```

Figure 16.4: *The ButtonsEvent applet (see Listing 16.4)*

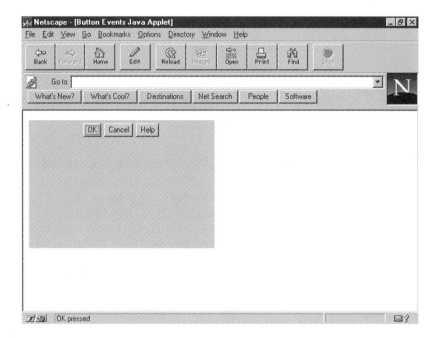

Notice in the action() method that the event target instance variable is being tested to find out which button has been pressed. The showStatus() method is then used to display a relevant message in the status bar. Note also that we return a true value if we are handling the event, false otherwise. By returning true we stop the event being handled by any component further up the component hierarchy.

As we have already mentioned, when a button is pressed the label of the button is passed as the second argument, arg, to the action()

method. We could therefore write the method in the following form and get the same results:

```
public boolean action(Event evt, Object arg)
  {
  if (arg == "OK")
     {
     showStatus("OK pressed");
     return (true);
     }
  else if (arg == "Cancel")
     {
     showStatus("Cancel pressed");
     return (true);
     }
  else if (arg == "Help")
     {
     showStatus("Help pressed");
     return (true);
     }
  return (false);
  }
```

Border Layout

The border layout manager positions components according to five locations within a container. The locations are called North, South, East, West and Center. The container is divided into five areas and the components placed accordingly. The components are drawn in the following sequence: North, South, West and East. Enough space is allocated to draw each of the components and the Center component gets all the remaining space.

When you add a component to a container you must specify one of these locations, in a string argument, by its name, which is case-sensitive. For instance, to add a button on the north side of a container, you would use the following command:

```
add("North", new Button("OK"));
```

Here is an example where buttons are placed in each of the five locations:

Figure 16.5: *The*
BorderLayout
*example (see
Listing 16.5)*

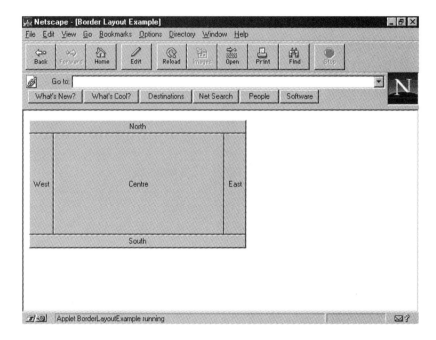

This is the source code:

Listing 16.5:
*Using the Border
Layout manager
(see Figure 16.5)*

```java
import java.awt.*;
import java.applet.*;
public class BorderLayoutExample extends Applet
   {
   public void init()
      {
      Button btnNorth = new Button("North");
      Button btnSouth = new Button("South");
      Button btnEast = new Button("East");
      Button btnWest = new Button("West");
      Button btnCentre = new Button("Centre");

      setLayout(new BorderLayout());
      add("North", btnNorth);
      add("South", btnSouth);
      add("East", btnEast);
      add("West", btnWest);
      add("Center", btnCentre);
      }
   }
```

You can specify a gap between each of the components by amending the constructor arguments for the layout to include the required horizontal and vertical gaps in pixels. By changing the setLayout() command in the example above to this:

```
setLayout(new BorderLayout(5, 10));
```

the components will be drawn with a horizontal gap between the components of 5 pixels, and a vertical gap between each of 10 pixels.

Although you cannot use a location more than once in a container, you can omit some if you choose. In the following example, we have only drawn three buttons – in the South, East and Center locations:

Listing 16.6:
Example omitting some border widths (see Figure 16.6)

```
import java.awt.*;
import java.applet.*;

public class PartialBorder extends Applet
    {
    public void init()
        {
        Button btnSouth = new Button("South");
        Button btnEast = new Button("East");
        Button btnCentre = new Button("Centre");

        setLayout(new BorderLayout());

        add("South", btnSouth);
        add("East", btnEast);
        add("Center", btnCentre);
        }
    }
```

As you can see from Figure 16.6, the Center button has expanded to fill up all the remaining space, after the first two buttons have been drawn.

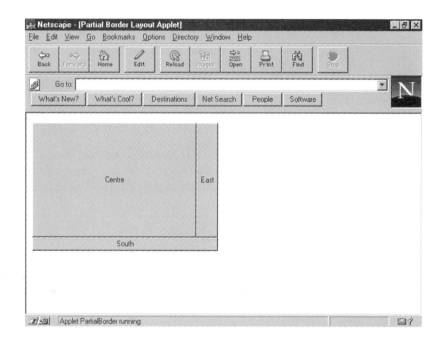

Figure 16.6: *The* `PartialBorder` *applet (see Listing 16.6)*

Panels

Up until now, we have just been using one container in each of our examples, the applet class itself. Obviously, the interfaces we can build in one container, using one layout manager, are very restricted. To get round this limitation we can make use of *panels*. As we mentioned earlier, a container is itself a component. Therefore, as panels are components they can thus be nested within other panels.

We can use panels to divide up the main container, say, the applet, into a number of smaller containers, each using different layout managers if necessary. This way, components can be placed in an accurate fashion, wherever you want them to be, by adding your components to panels, and then adding the panels to the main window.

For instance, our first buttons example, using the flow layout only, displayed the buttons in a row across the top. If we wanted the buttons to appear along the bottom of the applet display we could use the following code:

Listing 16.7:
Using Border Layout to place buttons (see Figure 16.7)

```java
import java.awt.*;
import java.applet.*;
public class BorderButtons extends Applet
    {
    public void init()
        {
        Button btnOk = new Button("OK");
        Button btnCancel = new Button("Cancel");
        Button btnHelp = new Button("Help");
        Panel p = new Panel();
        p.setLayout(new FlowLayout());
        p.add(btnOk);
        p.add(btnCancel);
        p.add(btnHelp);

        setLayout(new BorderLayout());
        add("South", p);
        }
    }
```

After the button objects are created, a panel, p, is created and the layout for the panel is set to flow layout. The buttons are added and will be drawn in a row. The layout for the applet is then set to BorderLayout and the panel containing the buttons is added in the South location. Here is the result:

Figure 16.7: *The BorderButtons applet (see Listing 16.7)*

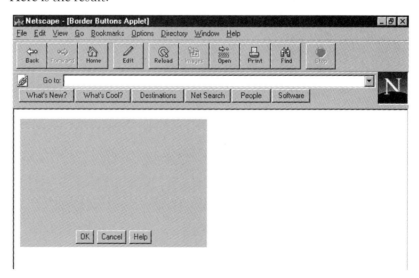

Grid Layout

The grid layout, as you would expect, allows you to draw the components in rows and columns, forming a grid. When you set the layout for a container you must specify how many rows and columns you require. For instance, to draw a grid of three rows and four columns you would use the command:

```
setLayout(new GridLayout(3, 4));
```

Figure 16.8 shows the GridLayoutExample applet created using the code shown in Listing 16.8.

Figure 16.8: *The* GridLayoutExample *applet (see Listing 16.8)*

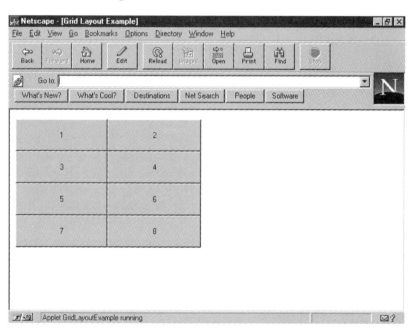

The following simple example draws a grid of buttons with 4 rows and 2 columns:

Listing 16.8: *Using the Grid Layout manager (see Figure 16.8)*

```
import java.awt.*;
import java.applet.*;
public class GridLayoutExample extends Applet
  {
  public void init()
    {
```

```
        setLayout(new GridLayout(4, 2));
        add(new Button("1"));
        add(new Button("2"));
        add(new Button("3"));
        add(new Button("4"));
        add(new Button("5"));
        add(new Button("6"));
        add(new Button("7"));
        add(new Button("8"));
        }
    }
```

If the applet is resized the grid will redrawn with the same number of rows and columns. The buttons will be resized to fit the new overall size.

You can also specify a gap between each of the components in the grid layout by amending the constructor arguments to include the required horizontal and vertical gaps. By changing the setLayout() command in the example above to this:

```
    setLayout(new GridLayout(4, 2, 10, 20));
```

the grid will be drawn with a horizontal gap between the columns of 10 pixels, and a vertical gap between each row of 20 pixels.

Canvases

Canvases are similar to panels in that they are both rectangular areas that you can place in your user interface and which are invisible to the user. However, panels are containers which are used to place components according to a particular layout whereas canvases are used for drawing text or graphics within your GUI. If you are using a number of panels to control the design of your user interface, it doesn't make sense to draw directly on a panel where the drawn items could be obscured by other components or conflict with their operation.

To draw something on a canvas you must derive a new class from the Canvas class and provide the methods required to carry out the drawing. This will usually include overriding the paint() method of your new canvas class.

This next example illustrates the use of a canvas. The applet contains a panel, which in turn contains three buttons, and a canvas, which is used for displaying a text string. By pressing a button you can select the font that will be used for drawing the text – Helvetica, Times Roman or Courier. Figure 16.9 shows what the applet looks like after the Times Roman button has been pressed.

This is the full source code:

Listing 16.9:
Using a Canvas for drawing text (see Figure 16.9)

```
import java.awt.*;
import java.applet.*;
public class CanvasExample extends Applet
    {
    Button btnHelv, btnTimes, btnCourier;
    DisplayCanvas txtDisplay;

    public void init()
        {
        btnHelv = new Button("Helvetica");
        btnTimes = new Button("TimesRoman");
        btnCourier = new Button("Courier");

        Panel pnlButtons = new Panel();
        pnlButtons.setLayout(new GridLayout(3, 1));

        pnlButtons.add(btnHelv);
        pnlButtons.add(btnTimes);
        pnlButtons.add(btnCourier);

        setLayout(new BorderLayout());

        add("West", pnlButtons);

        txtDisplay = new DisplayCanvas();
        add("Center", txtDisplay);
        }

    public boolean action(Event evt, Object arg)
        {
        if (evt.target instanceof Button)
            {
            txtDisplay.setFont((String)arg);
            return (true);
            }
        return (false);
        }
```

```
public Insets insets()
    {
    return new Insets(10, 10, 10, 10);
    }
}

class DisplayCanvas extends Canvas
    {
    public DisplayCanvas()
        {
        setFont("Helvetica");
        }
    public void setFont(String fontName)
        {
        setFont(new Font(fontName, Font.PLAIN, 20));
        repaint();
        }
    public void paint(Graphics g)
        {
        g.drawString("Canvas Example", 10, 50);
        }
    }
```

Figure 16.9: *The CanvasExample applet (see Listing 16.9)*

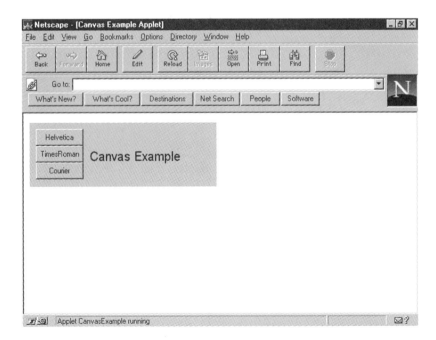

As you can see, we have defined two classes – CanvasExample, derived from the Applet class, and DisplayCanvas, derived from Canvas.

The CanvasExample class includes three Button instance variables and an instance of the DisplayCanvas class, txtDisplay. In the init() method the three buttons are created and then added to a panel, pnl-Buttons. A grid layout is set for this panel using three rows and one column. We then set the layout for the applet to BorderLayout and add the pnlButtons panel using the "West" string argument. This ensures that the buttons will be placed down the left side of the applet. The DisplayCanvas object, txtDisplay, is then added to the applet using the "Center" string argument so that it will occupy the rest of the available display area. To handle the button clicks we include the following code in the action method:

```
if (evt.target instanceof Button)
    {
    txtDisplay.setFont((String)arg);
    return (true);
    }
```

The instanceof operator is used to confirm that a button has originated the action event. If true the setFont() method of the Display-Canvas object is called and the button label is passed as a parameter. In the definition of the DisplayCanvas class we have defined a constructor method which simply calls the setFont() method to display the text "Canvas Example" in the Helvetica font. The setFont() method itself merely sets the current font to that passed as an argument to the method, and then calls the repaint() method. The paint() method has been overridden to draw the string "Canvas Example".

Insets

The CanvasExample applet includes an extra method definition, Insets:

```
public Insets insets()
    {
    return new Insets(10, 10, 10, 10);
    }
```

The Insets class is used to provide a gap around the outside of any panel. All you have to do is override the insets() method within the panel class. The four arguments to the constructor are the gap you require, in pixels, from the top, bottom, left and right edges of the panel. By overriding the insets() method within the applet class in the above example, a gap of 10 pixels will be included from each edge of the applet.

Text Fields

To make our example applet a bit more flexible we will now add a Text Field component. This will allow the user to input the text string that will then be displayed in the canvas. Text fields are usually only used for one line fields as they cannot scroll. If you want to allow larger amounts of text to be input and edited you should use a Text Area. We will be covering Text Areas later on in the chapter.

A text field is added to a container in the usual manner for components – first the object is created and then the add() method of the container is used to actually place it within the container. This section of code creates a text field component and adds it to the container:

```
TextField txtEntry = new TextField("Enter text here", 30);
add(txtEntry);
```

The string passed as the first argument of the constructor will be placed in the text field when it is first displayed. If an empty string is passed, the text field will appear empty. The second argument of the constructor is the required width of the text field in characters. Java uses the average width of a character in the font you are currently using. This doesn't always result in a field width that is of sufficient size so it is usually worth including a safety factor when you create the text field.

Whatever width you set the field to, it doesn't prevent the user from entering more characters than can be displayed within the field. As the user continues to type in the field, the characters will scroll across to the left.

To obtain the text that has been entered by the user you must call the getText() method. For instance, the following command will extract the text from the txtEntry text field and place it in the string str:

```
String str = txtEntry.getText();
```

You can also use the setText() method to set the contents of the text field to a string that you pass as a parameter. This command will place the string "Please enter some text" in the text field:

```
txtEntry.setText("Please enter some text");
```

TextField methods

- `public int getColumns()` returns the number of columns in the text field.

- `public char getEchoChar()` returns the echo character for the text field.

- `public void setEchoCharacter(char c)` sets the echo character for the text field. Any character that the user types in the text field is echoed in this text field as the echo character.

Labels

When a text field component is placed in a container there is nothing to indicate to the user what belongs in that field. To identify a text field you must use a `Label` component. A `Label` is a string of text which can be displayed in a container but cannot be edited by the user.

To place a label in front of a text field you could use the following command:

```
add(new Label("Enter text to be displayed"));
```

Here is a screen shot of the amended applet:

Figure 16.10: *The* `TextFieldExample` *applet (see Listing 16.10)*

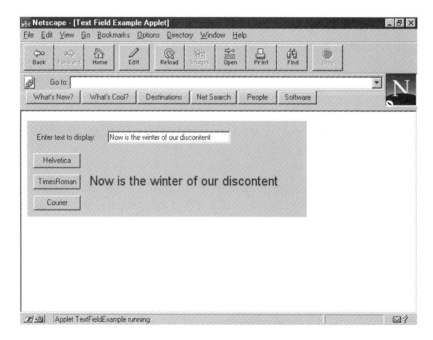

This is the full source code:

```
import java.awt.*;
import java.applet.*;

public class TextFieldExample extends Applet
    {
    Button btnHelv, btnTimes, btnCourier;
    DisplayCanvas txtDisplay;
    TextField txtEntry;

    public void init()
        {
        btnHelv = new Button("Helvetica");
        btnTimes = new Button("TimesRoman");
        btnCourier = new Button("Courier");
        Panel pnlButtons = new Panel();
        pnlButtons.setLayout(new GridLayout(3, 1, 10, 10));
        pnlButtons.add(btnHelv);
        pnlButtons.add(btnTimes);
        pnlButtons.add(btnCourier);
        Panel pnlText = new Panel();
        pnlText.setLayout(new FlowLayout(FlowLayout.LEFT));
        txtEntry = new TextField("", 30);
        pnlText.add(new Label("Enter text to display:"));
        pnlText.add(txtEntry);
        setLayout(new BorderLayout(5,10));
        add("North", pnlText);
        add("West", pnlButtons);
        txtDisplay = new DisplayCanvas();
        add("Center", txtDisplay);
        }
    public boolean action(Event evt, Object arg)
        {
        if (evt.target instanceof Button)
            {
            txtDisplay.setFont((String)arg, txtEntry.getText());
            return (true);
            }
        return (false);
        }
```

```
public Insets insets()
    {
    return new Insets(10, 10, 10, 10);
    }
}
class DisplayCanvas extends Canvas
    {
    String displayText;
    public DisplayCanvas()
        {
        setFont("Helvetica", "Enter text in the field above");
        }
    public void setFont(String fontName, String s)
        {
        setFont(new Font(fontName, Font.PLAIN, 20));
        if (displayText.length() == 0)
            displayText = "No text entered";
        displayText = s;
        repaint();
        }
    public void paint(Graphics g)
        {
        g.drawString(displayText, 10, 50);
        }
    }
```

We have added another panel, pnlText, and included the label and text field within it:

```
Panel pnlText = new Panel();
pnlText.setLayout(new FlowLayout(FlowLayout.LEFT));
txtEntry = new TextField("", 30);
pnlText.add(new Label("Enter text to display:"));
pnlText.add(txtEntry);
```

The panel has then been added at the top of the applet display:

```
add("North", pnlText);
```

An extra parameter has been added to the setFont() method of the DisplayCanvas class to pass the text string obtained from the text field.

Label methods

- `public String getText()` returns the text of the label.
- `public void setText(String label)` sets the text for the label to the specified text.

Checkboxes

Checkboxes are used to offer the user a fixed number of options, from which they can select none or as many choices as they wish. Providing the user with all the available options removes the need for the user to enter their choice in a text field and the subsequent need for the input text to be validated.

To select a checkbox option the user clicks inside it. By clicking in it again the checkbox is unchecked. Within a set of checkboxes there is no limit on how many can be checked. If you want the options to be mutually exclusive, you must create a checkbox group. Checkbox groups are covered in the next section.

When a checkbox is created, using the `new` operator, the text that you want displayed alongside the checkbox to identify it, must be passed as a parameter to the constructor. For instance:

```
chkBold = new Checkbox("Bold");
```

An `action` event is triggered when the user clicks in a checkbox. The name of the checkbox object is passed in the target field of the `event` object. The state of the checkbox, ie. whether it has been selected or not, is obtained by calling the `getState()` method. If the checkbox has been checked, `getState()` returns `true`, otherwise `false` is returned.

The state of any checkbox can be set using the `setState()` method and passing a `true` or `false` value as the argument, depending on whether you want the checkbox to be set or not.

To illustrate the use of checkboxes we are going to add two to the example applet we have been using so far. The checkboxes will allow the user to change the font style by making the font bold, italic or both.

Listing 16.11:	

Listing 16.11:
Adding check-
boxes to the
example (see
Figure 16.11)

```java
import java.awt.*;
import java.applet.*;

public class CheckBoxExample extends Applet
    {
    Button btnHelv, btnTimes, btnCourier;
    DisplayCanvas txtDisplay;
    TextField txtEntry;
    Checkbox chkBold, chkItalic;
    String fontName = "";
    int fontStyle;

    public void init()
        {
        btnHelv = new Button("Helvetica");
        btnTimes = new Button("TimesRoman");
        btnCourier = new Button("Courier");
        Panel pnlButtons = new Panel();
        pnlButtons.setLayout(new GridLayout(3, 1, 10, 10));
        pnlButtons.add(btnHelv);
        pnlButtons.add(btnTimes);
        pnlButtons.add(btnCourier);
        Panel pnlText = new Panel();
        pnlText.setLayout(new FlowLayout(FlowLayout.LEFT));
        txtEntry = new TextField("", 30);
        pnlText.add(new Label("Enter text to display", Label.RIGHT));
        pnlText.add(txtEntry);
        Panel pnlChkBoxes = new Panel();
        pnlChkBoxes.setLayout(new FlowLayout(FlowLayout.LEFT));
        chkBold = new Checkbox("Bold");
        chkItalic = new Checkbox("Italic");
        pnlChkBoxes.add(chkBold);
        pnlChkBoxes.add(chkItalic);
        setLayout(new BorderLayout(5,10));
        add("North", pnlText);
        add("West", pnlButtons);
        add("South", pnlChkBoxes);
        txtDisplay = new DisplayCanvas();
        add("Center", txtDisplay);
        }

    public boolean action(Event evt, Object arg)
```

```
      {
      if (evt.target instanceof Button)
         {
         fontName = (String)arg;
         txtDisplay.setFont(fontName, fontStyle,
         txtEntry.getText());
         return (true);
         }
      if (evt.target instanceof Checkbox)
         {
         fontStyle = 0;
         if (chkBold.getState())
            fontStyle += Font.BOLD;
         if (chkItalic.getState())
            fontStyle += Font.ITALIC;
         txtDisplay.setFont(fontName, fontStyle,
                    txtEntry.getText());
         return (true);
         }
      return (false);
      }

   public Insets insets()
      {
      return new Insets(10, 10, 10, 10);
      }
   }
class DisplayCanvas extends Canvas
   {
   String displayText;

   public DisplayCanvas()
      {
      setFont("Helvetica", Font.PLAIN,
                   "Enter text in the fieldabove");
      }

   public void setFont(String fontName, int style, String s)
      {
      setFont(new Font(fontName, style, 20));
      displayText = s;
      if (displayText.length() == 0)
```

```
            displayText = "No text entered";
        repaint();
        }

    public void paint(Graphics g)
        {
        g.drawString(displayText, 10, 50);
        }
    }
```

Figure 16.11 shows how the applet will now look.

Figure 16.11: *The*
CheckBoxExample
applet (see Listing
16.11)

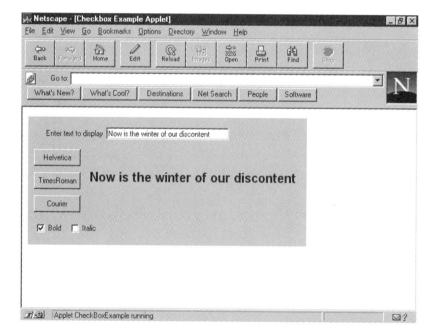

We have added another panel to the applet, pnlChkBoxes, into which we have placed the two checkboxes, chkBold and chkItalic. The panel has then been added using the "South" location of the border layout.

The action() method has been changed so that it now responds when one of the checkboxes is clicked on:

```
public boolean action(Event evt, Object arg)
    {
    if (evt.target instanceof Button)
```

```
            {
            textString = (String)arg;
            txtDisplay.setFont(textString, fontStyle,
                              txtEntry.getText());
            return (true);
            }
        if (evt.target instanceof Checkbox)
            {
            fontStyle = 0;
            if (chkBold.getState())
                fontStyle += Font.BOLD;
            if (chkItalic.getState())
                fontStyle += Font.ITALIC;
            txtDisplay.setFont(textString, fontStyle,
                              txtEntry.getText());
            return (true);
            }
        return (false);
    }
```

The `instanceof` operator has been used to distinguish between a button being pressed and a checkbox being clicked. When a checkbox is checked or unchecked the current state of each is determined and the `fontStyle` variable is set accordingly. We have also had to include the `fontName` variable to hold the current font. In the previous example we just passed the `arg` parameter (which contains the button label) straight to the DisplayCanvas object.

We cannot, however, continue to do this when a checkbox is clicked because the `arg` object is not going to contain the font name. The only other change is the inclusion of the font style as a parameter in the DisplayCanvas `setFont()` method.

Checkbox methods

- `public String getLabel()` returns the label of this check box, or `null` if the check box has no label.

- `public boolean getState()` determines if the check box is checked or unchecked.

- `public void setLabel(String label)` sets the check box's label to be the `String` argument.

- `public void setState(boolean state)` this sets the check box to the the specifed boolean state: `true` indicates checked; `false` indicates unchecked.

Checkbox Groups

When you want the user to only be able to select one choice out of a number of selections you must make use of the checkbox group component. If a series of check boxes are part of a group, when one is checked, the previously selected box in that group is unchecked. In other systems, these "grouped" check boxes are known as *radio buttons*.

Check boxes which form part of a group have a different appearance from stand-alone check boxes – they are round instead of square, with a dot used to indicate selection rather than a cross. To create a check box group you must first create a `CheckboxGroup` object and then create each of the check boxes you want included in the group, passing the CheckboxGroup object as one of the constructor arguments for the boxes.

This code example shows how you would create a check box group to implement the font selection from our applet example:

```
CheckboxGroup chkGroup = new CheckboxGroup();
chkHelv = new Checkbox("Helvetica", chkGroup, true);
chkTimes = new Checkbox("TimesRoman", chkGroup, false);
chkCourier = new Checkbox("Courier", chkGroup, false);
```

The first line creates the group object. The following three lines add the check boxes. The first constructor argument for the check boxes is the label that will appear next to the radio button. The second argument is the `CheckboxGroup` object and the third argument specifies whether the box should be checked or not – true to check it, false otherwise.

An action event is generated each time a box is checked. All you have to do to respond to a user clicking on a grouped check box is to include a test for each box. The box being unchecked does not generate an action event. Here is the action event method code for our next example:

```
public boolean action(Event evt, Object arg)
    {
    if (evt.target instanceof Checkbox)
        {
```

```
            if (evt.target.equals(chkBold) ||
                evt.target.equals(chkItalic))
            {
            fontStyle = 0;
            if (chkBold.getState())
                fontStyle += Font.BOLD;
            if (chkItalic.getState())
                fontStyle += Font.ITALIC;
            txtDisplay.setFont(fontName, fontStyle,
                txtEntry.getText());
            return (true);
            }
        if (evt.target.equals(chkHelv))
                fontName = "Helvetica";
            else if (evt.target.equals(chkTimes))
            fontName = "TimesRoman";
            else if (evt.target.equals(chkCourier))
            fontName = "Courier";
            txtDisplay.setFont(fontName, fontStyle,
                txtEntry.getText());
            return (true);
        }
    return (false);
}
```

As you can see, once we have determined that a check box has been clicked, we just need a series of tests to determine the response for each box. The amended applet now looks like this:

Figure 16.12: *The*
CheckBoxGroup
example (see
Listing 16.12)

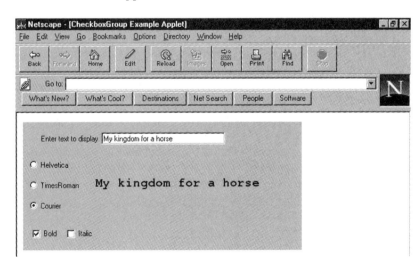

Here is the full source code:

```java
import java.awt.*;
import java.applet.*;

public class CheckBoxGroupExample extends Applet
    {
    Checkbox chkHelv, chkTimes, chkCourier;
    DisplayCanvas txtDisplay;
    TextField txtEntry;
    Checkbox chkBold, chkItalic;
    String fontName = "";
    int fontStyle;

    public void init()
        {
        CheckboxGroup chkGroup = new CheckboxGroup();
        chkHelv = new Checkbox("Helvetica", chkGroup, true);
        chkTimes = new Checkbox("TimesRoman", chkGroup, false);
        chkCourier = new Checkbox("Courier", chkGroup, false);

        Panel pnlChkGroup = new Panel();
        pnlChkGroup.setLayout(new GridLayout(3, 1));

        pnlChkGroup.add(chkHelv);
        pnlChkGroup.add(chkTimes);
        pnlChkGroup.add(chkCourier);

        Panel pnlText = new Panel();
        pnlText.setLayout(new FlowLayout(FlowLayout.LEFT));
        txtEntry = new TextField("", 30);
        pnlText.add(new Label("Enter text to display", Label.RIGHT));
        pnlText.add(txtEntry);

        Panel pnlChkBoxes = new Panel();
        pnlChkBoxes.setLayout(new FlowLayout(FlowLayout.LEFT));
        chkBold = new Checkbox("Bold");
        chkItalic = new Checkbox("Italic");
        pnlChkBoxes.add(chkBold);
        pnlChkBoxes.add(chkItalic);

        setLayout(new BorderLayout(5,10));
```

```
        add("North", pnlText);
        add("West", pnlChkGroup);
        add("South", pnlChkBoxes);
        txtDisplay = new DisplayCanvas();
        add("Center", txtDisplay);
        }

    public boolean action(Event evt, Object arg)
        {
        if (evt.target instanceof Checkbox)
            {
            if (evt.target.equals(chkBold) ||
                        evt.target.equals(chkItalic))
                {
                fontStyle = 0;
                if (chkBold.getState())
                    fontStyle += Font.BOLD;
                if (chkItalic.getState())
                    fontStyle += Font.ITALIC;
                txtDisplay.setFont(fontName, fontStyle,
                        txtEntry.getText());
                return (true);
                }

            if (evt.target.equals(chkHelv))
                fontName = "Helvetica";
            else if (evt.target.equals(chkTimes))
                fontName = "TimesRoman";
            else if (evt.target.equals(chkCourier))
                fontName = "Courier";
            txtDisplay.setFont(fontName, fontStyle,
                    txtEntry.getText());
            return (true);
            }
        return (false);
        }

    public Insets insets()
        {
        return new Insets(10, 10, 10, 10);
        }
    }
```

```
class DisplayCanvas extends Canvas
   {
   String displayText;
   public DisplayCanvas()
      {
      setFont("Helvetica", Font.PLAIN,
            "Enter text in the field above");
      }
   public void setFont(String fontName, int style, String s)
      {
      setFont(new Font(fontName, style, 20));
      displayText = s;
      if (displayText.length() == 0)
         displayText = "No text entered";
      repaint();
      }
   public void paint(Graphics g)
      {
      g.drawString(displayText, 10, 50);
      }
   }
```

Choices

Choice boxes are usually referred to as drop-down lists in other systems. They are especially useful when you are short of space in your user interface as they only take up one line when not being used. When a user clicks clicks on the component a full list of choices will drop down and the user can make a selection.

To include a choice box in your UI you first create an instance of the Choice class and then add each of the items that you want included in the drop-down list. The individual items are added using the addItem() method. For instance, this section of code creates a Choice object and adds three items to generate our font selection example as a choice box:

```
fontChoice = new Choice();
fontChoice.addItem("Helvetica");
fontChoice.addItem("TimesRoman");
fontChoice.addItem("Courier");
```

Items can be added at any time once the `Choice` object has been created. You cannot, however, remove any items once they have been added to the list. The user can also only select one item from the list at a time. (The `List` component, which we will introduce next, is more adaptable and allows multiple selections.)

Responding to a an item being selected from a choice box is fairly straightforward. The event target passed to the `action()` method is the choice component and the `arg` object contains the item string selected.

The text display applet, with a choice box providing the font selection, now looks like this:

Figure 16.13: *The* `ChoiceExample` *applet (see Figure 16.13)*

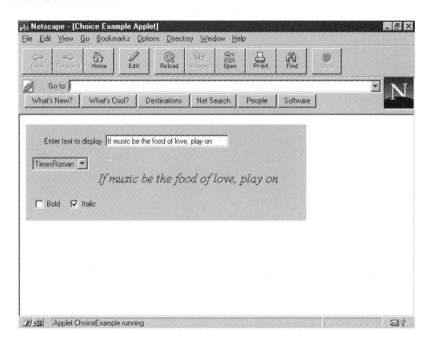

Here is the source code:

Listing 16.13: *The example applet amended to use a choice box (see Figure 16.13)*

```
import java.awt.*;
import java.applet.*;
public class ChoiceExample extends Applet
    {
    Choice fontChoice;
    DisplayCanvas txtDisplay;
    TextField txtEntry;
    Checkbox chkBold, chkItalic;
```

```
String fontName = "";
int fontStyle;

public void init()
    {
    fontChoice = new Choice();
    fontChoice.addItem("Helvetica");
    fontChoice.addItem("TimesRoman");
    fontChoice.addItem("Courier");
    Panel pnlText = new Panel();
    pnlText.setLayout(new FlowLayout(FlowLayout.LEFT));
    txtEntry = new TextField("", 30);
    pnlText.add(new Label("Enter text to display", Label.RIGHT));
    pnlText.add(txtEntry);

    Panel pnlChkBoxes = new Panel();
    pnlChkBoxes.setLayout(new FlowLayout(FlowLayout.LEFT));
    chkBold = new Checkbox("Bold");
    chkItalic = new Checkbox("Italic");
    pnlChkBoxes.add(chkBold);
    pnlChkBoxes.add(chkItalic);

    setLayout(new BorderLayout(5,10));

    add("North", pnlText);
    add("West", fontChoice);
    add("South", pnlChkBoxes);
    txtDisplay = new DisplayCanvas();
    add("Center", txtDisplay);
    }

public boolean action(Event evt, Object arg)
    {
    if (evt.target instanceof Choice)
        {
        fontName = (String)arg;
        txtDisplay.setFont(fontName, fontStyle,
            txtEntry.getText());
        return (true);
        }
    if (evt.target instanceof Checkbox)
        {
        if (evt.target.equals(chkBold) ||
            evt.target.equals(chkItalic))
```

```
                          {
                          fontStyle = 0;
                          if (chkBold.getState())
                             fontStyle += Font.BOLD;
                          if (chkItalic.getState())
                             fontStyle += Font.ITALIC;
                          txtDisplay.setFont(fontName, fontStyle,
                             txtEntry.getText());
                          return (true);
                          }
                    }
            return (false);
            }
        public Insets insets()
            {
            return new Insets(10, 10, 10, 10);
            }
        }
    class DisplayCanvas extends Canvas
        {
        String displayText;
        public DisplayCanvas()
            {
            setFont("Helvetica", Font.PLAIN,
                "Enter text in the field above");
            }
        public void setFont(String fontName, int style, String s)
            {
            setFont(new Font(fontName, style, 20));
            displayText = s;
            if (displayText.length() == 0)
               displayText = "No text entered";
            repaint();
            }
        public void paint(Graphics g)
            {
            g.drawString(displayText, 10, 40);
            }
        }
```

Choice methods

- public void addItem(String item) adds an item to the choice menu.

- `public int countItems()` returns the number of items in the choice menu.
- `public String getItem(int index)` returns the string at the specified index in the choice menu.
- `public int getSelectedIndex()` returns the index of the currently selected item in the choice menu.
- `public String getSelectedItem()` returns a string representation of the currently selected item in the choice menu.
- `public void select(int pos)` sets the selected item in the choice menu to be the item at the specified position.
- `public void select(String str)` sets the selected item in the choice menu to be the choice whose name is equal to the specified string. If more than one choice is equal to the specified string, the one with the smallest index whose name matches is selected.

Lists

The List component gives you the ability to present a list of items to the user, from which they can select one or more items. Where the Choice component only displays one item when first displayed, the List component can be displayed so that all the items, or only some of them, can be displayed from the start. The user can also select more than one item from a List component.

The constructor for the List class has two parameters – the number of items to be displayed at one time and a boolean flag to indicate whether you want to allow multiple selections or not (`true` and `false` respectively). The number of items displayed does not affect the total number of items you can include in the list – if there are more items than the number initially displayed the list will scroll. This command will create a List component that will display six items and won't allow multiple selections:

```
List theList = new List(6, false);
```

After creating the List object, items are added to the list in the same way as the Choice box, by using the `addItem()` method:

```
theList.addItem("First item");
theList.addItem("Second item");
theList.addItem("Third item");
```

```
theList.addItem("Fourth item");
```

The List component provides far more functionality than, say, the Choice component. You have the ability to delete any number of items from an existing list, clear it completely, make initial selections before displaying the list for the first time or deselect items if required.

The example applet we have been using for the last few pages is becoming a bit tedious so we will try and produce an example which is a bit more ambitious to illustrate the use of List boxes. Our lists example presents the user with two List boxes, one containing a list of web site categories and one containing actual web sites. When a category list item is clicked the contents of the web sites list will change to reflect the category chosen. When the *Go to site* button is clicked, the browser will display the web site page in a new window. When this new window is closed the user is returned to the page containing the applet.

This is how the applet appears:

Figure 16.14: *The* `ListExample` *applet (see Listing 16.14)*

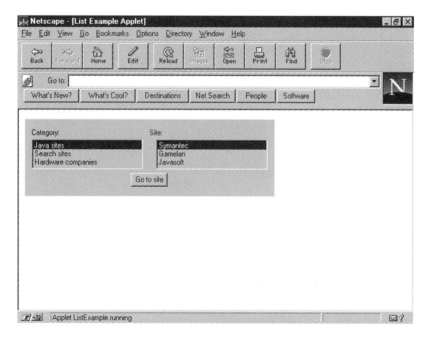

We will list the full source code first and then discuss the methods:

Listing 16.14:
Example using list components (see Figure 16.14)

```java
import java.awt.*;
import java.applet.*;
import java.net.*;

public class ListExample extends Applet
  {
  List listCategories, listSites;
         Button btnGo;
  String categories[] = { "Java sites",
                              "Search sites",
                              "Hardware companies" };
  String sites0[] = { "Symantec",
                         "Gamelan",
                         "Javasoft"};
  String sites1[] = { "Yahoo",
                         "Lycos",
                         "Excite" };
  String sites2[] = { "Compaq",
                         "Dell",
                         "Gateway 2000"};
  String urls0[] = {"http://cafe.symantec.com",
                       "http://www.gamelan.com",
                       "http://java.sun.com" };
  String urls1[] = {"http://www.yahoo.com",
                       "http://www.lycos.com",
                       "http://www.excite.com" };
  String urls2[] = {"http://www.compaq.com",
                       "http://www.dell.com",
                       "http://www.gateway2000.com"};
  public void init()
     {
     DisplayCategoriesList();
     listSites = new List(3, false);
     DisplaySitesList(0);

     Panel pnlLabels = new Panel();
     pnlLabels.setLayout(new GridLayout(1, 2));
     pnlLabels.add(new Label("Category:"));
     pnlLabels.add(new Label("Site:"));

     Panel pnlLists = new Panel();
     pnlLists.setLayout(new GridLayout(1, 2, 20, 0));
```

```
      pnlLists.add(listCategories);
      pnlLists.add(listSites);

      Panel pnlButton = new Panel();
      pnlButton.setLayout(new FlowLayout());
      btnGo = new Button("Go to site");
      pnlButton.add("South", btnGo);

      setLayout(new BorderLayout());
      add("North", pnlLabels);
      add("South", pnlButton);
      add("Center", pnlLists);
      }

  public void DisplayCategoriesList()
      {
      listCategories = new List(3, false);
      for (int i = 0; i < categories.length; i++)
         listCategories.addItem(categories[i]);
      listCategories.select(0);
      }

  public void DisplaySitesList(int selection)
      {
      int listTotal = 0;
      listSites.clear();
      if (selection == 0) listTotal = sites0.length;
      if (selection == 1) listTotal = sites1.length;
      if (selection == 2) listTotal = sites2.length;

      for (int i = 0; i < listTotal; i++)
         {
         if (selection == 0) listSites.addItem(sites0[i]);
         if (selection == 1) listSites.addItem(sites1[i]);
         if (selection == 2) listSites.addItem(sites2[i]);
         }
      listSites.select(0);
      }

  public boolean handleEvent(Event evt)
      {
      if (evt.id == Event.LIST_SELECT &&
```

```
                evt.target.equals(listCategories))
            {
            DisplaySitesList(listCategories.getSelectedIndex());
            return true;
            }
        return super.handleEvent(evt);
        }

    public boolean action(Event evt, Object arg)
        {
        if (evt.target instanceof Button)
            {
            GotoSite(listCategories.getSelectedIndex(),
                        listSites.getSelectedIndex());
            return true;
            }
        return false;
        }

    public void GotoSite(int siteList, int selection)
        {
        String siteURL = "";
        if (siteList == 0) siteURL = urls0[selection];
        if (siteList == 1) siteURL = urls1[selection];
        if (siteList == 2) siteURL = urls2[selection];

        try
            {
            URL u = new URL(siteURL);
            getAppletContext().showDocument(u, "_blank");
            } catch(MalformedURLException e)
                {
                showStatus("URL error " + e);
                }
        }

    public Insets insets()
        {
        return new Insets(10, 10, 10, 10);
        }
    }
```

As well as the the two List instance variables, `listCategories` and `listSites`, and a button variable, `btnGo`, we have defined a number of String arrays that will be used to populate the lists. The first one, `categories[]`, holds the three web site categories. We then have three arrays containing the web site names as they will appear in the lists – one for each of the three categories. There are then three more arrays which contain the web site URLs for each of the web sites. The first method called in the `init()` method is `DisplayCategoriesList()`. This method creates the `listCategories` List component, adds the three categories from the array and then uses the `select()` method to initially select the first item of the list. Continuing with the `init()` method, the method `DisplaySitesList()` is called for the first time, with a 0 passed as the parameter.

The `DisplaySitesList()` method first uses the `clear()` method to remove all the current items from the list. It then obtains the size of the array specified by the selection parameter before populating the `listSites` object with the items held in the relevant `sites[]` array. Having filled the initial lists, three panels are created to locate the titles, lists and the button within the applet display area.

Events are handled slightly differently in this applet. We use both the `action()` and the `handleEvent()` methods. The reason for this is that an `action` event is only triggered for a list box when the user *double-clicks* on an item. This is not the most natural way for users to select an item from a list box – we want the `Sites` list box to be updated whenever the user clicks once on an item in the `Categories` list box.

Fortunately, the `handleEvent()` method provides us with the ability to do this. Each time an item is selected or deselected in a list box an event is generated with an event id of `LIST_SELECT` or `LIST_DESELECT` respectively, which can be intercepted in the `handleEvent()` method.

We are therefore overriding the `handleEvent()` method to handle the list box selections and overriding the `action()` event method to handle the button press. It is of course possible to handle the button press in the `handleEvent()` method as well – an event with the ID `ACTION_EVENT` will be generated – but the code is often easier to follow if the `action` event method is used. The `handleEvent()` method looks like this:

```
public boolean handleEvent(Event evt)
    {
    if (evt.id == Event.LIST_SELECT &&
       evt.target.equals(listCategories))
```

```
        {
        DisplaySitesList(listCategories.getSelectedIndex());
        return true;
        }
    return super.handleEvent(evt);
    }
```

We test for a list item selection in the `Categories` list box and call the `DisplaySitesList()` method, passing it the index of the selected item. The `DisplaySitesList()` method will then clear any existing items from the `Sites` list box and add a new set of items from the required site array.

An important thing to note is that we don't return false in the `handleEvent()` method if we are not handling the event. If `false` is returned, the event is passed to the parent in the *window* hierarchy. In this case the applet window is a top-level window so there is no parent to process the event and call the `action()` method.

With no call made to the `action()` method we have no way of processing the button click. We must return `super.handleEvent(evt)` if we are not handling it. By doing that the event will be passed to the parent in the component hierarchy which will in turn call the `action()` method.

Here is the action method:

```
    public boolean action(Event evt, Object arg)
        {
        if (evt.target instanceof Button)
            {
                GotoSite(listCategories.getSelectedIndex(),
                        listSites.getSelectedIndex());
                return true;
            }
            return false;
        }
```

As there is only one button we just wait for any button press and then call the `GotoSite()` method, passing the index of both lists.

The `GotoSite()` method causes the browser to display the web page of the chosen site:

```
    public void GotoSite(int siteList, int selection)
        {
```

```
String siteURL = "";
if (siteList == 0) siteURL = urls0[selection];
if (siteList == 1) siteURL = urls1[selection];
if (siteList == 2) siteURL = urls2[selection];
try
   {
   URL u = new URL(siteURL);
   getAppletContext().showDocument(u, "_blank");
   } catch(MalformedURLException e)
      {
      showStatus("URL error " + e);
      }
}
```

The siteList parameter tells us which url array to access and the selection parameter provides the index to the string holding the site URL. From this we can create a URL object. The applet context holds information about the applet's environment, in this case, the browser. The showDocument() method of the AppletContext interface causes the browser to display another HTML document.

The second argument of the showDocument() method is the "target" string. Using this argument you can control how the document will be displayed. We have used the "_blank" string, which will cause the new document to be displayed in a new top-level window. See the API documentation for the rest of the target strings.

The URL constructor has been declared to throw an exception – in this case a MalformedURLException – if the URL is not valid, so it must be enclosed by the try/catch combination.

List methods

- public void addItem(String item) adds the specified string to the end of the list.

- public void addItem(String item, int index) adds the specified string to the list at the specified position. The index argument is zero-based. If the index is -1, or greater than or equal to the number of items already in the list, then the item is added at the end of this list.

- public boolean allowsMultipleSelections( ) returns true if the list allows multiple selections; false otherwise.

- public void clear() removes all items from the list.

- `public int countItems()` returns the number of items in the list.
- `public void delItem(int position)` deletes the item at the specified position from the list.
- `public void delItems(int start, int end)` deletes the items in the range start to end from the list.
- `public void deselect(int index)` deselects the item at the specified index of the list.
- `public String getItem(int index)` returns the string of the list at the specified index.
- `public int getRows()` returns the number of visible lines in the list.
- `public int getSelectedIndex()` returns the index of the selected item on the list, or -1 if either no items are selected or more than one item is selected.
- `public int[] getSelectedIndexes()` returns an array of the selected indexes of the list.
- `public String getSelectedItem()` returns the selected item on the list, or `null` if either no items are selected or more than one item is selected.
- `public String[] getSelectedItems()` returns an array of the selected items on the list.
- `public void replaceItem(String newValue, int index)` replaces the item at the given index in the list with the new string.
- `public void select(int index)` selects the item at the specified index in the list.
- `public void setMultipleSelections(boolean flag)` allows the list to accept multiple selections if flag is `true`.

Scrollbars

Scrollbars are used in Java either for creating a "slider" to give a user control over a range of values, or as a scrollbar at the side or bottom of a window to allow scrolling through the window contents.

Scrollbars are created with a default range of 0 to 100. If a user clicks on one of the arrows at either end of the bar, the value will be incremented or decreased by one. If the area between the arrows and the slider is clicked on, the value will be incremented or decreased by 10. (Both these quantities, called the line increment and the page increment respecively, can be changed using the `setLineIncrement()` and `set-PageIncrement()` methods.)

The user can also change the value by "dragging" the slider in either direction. The value will be changed to a new value based on the new position of the slider. At the moment, Java does not support the ability to continuously modify the value as the slider is moved.

There are three forms of the Scrollbar constructor:

1. `Scrollbar()` creates a scrollbar with a vertical orientation.
2. `Scrollbar(int orientation)` creates a scrollbar with the `orientation` specified.

   The class static variables:
   - `Scrollbar.VERTICAL`
   - `Scrollbar.HORIZONTAL`

   are provided.
3. `Scrollbar(int orientation, int initValue, int visible, int minimum, int maximum)`

   This creates a scrollbar with the following configuration:
   - `orientation` is either vertical or horizontal as above;
   - `initValue` is the initial value to be given to the scrollbar;
   - `visible` relates to the visible area of the window and should be set to 0 for sliders;
   - `minimum` is the minimum value of the scrollbar range
   - `maximum` is the maximum value.

If you use one of the first two constructors you must then use the `setValues()` method if you want to change, say, the range of the scrollbar. The `setValues()` method requires the last four values specified for the third form of the constructor.

Scrollbar events must be trapped in the `handleEvent()` method. The current value of a scroll bar can be obtained using the `getValue()` method. We will present an example of the use of scrollbars after the next section on the grid bag layout – a layout manager that will give us more control over the positioning of components than we have had up until now.

Scrollbar methods

- `public int getLineIncrement()` returns the line increment of the scroll bar.

- `public int getMaximum()` returns the maximum value of the scroll bar.

- `public int getMinimum()` returns the maximum value of the scroll bar.

- `public int getOrientation()` determines the orientation of the scroll bar. The value returned is either `HORIZONTAL` or `VERTICAL`.

- `public int getPageIncrement()` returns the page increment for the scroll bar.

- `public int getValue()` returns the current value of the scroll bar.

- `public void setLineIncrement(int l)` sets the line increment of the scroll bar.

- `public void setPageIncrement(int l)` sets the page increment of the scroll bar.

- `public void setValue(int value)` sets the value of the scroll bar to the specified value. If the specified value is below the scroll bar's current minimum or above the current maximum, it becomes the minimum or maximum value, respectively.

- `public void setValues(int value, int visible, int minimum, int maximum)` sets the value of the scroll bar, the amount visible, the maximum value and the minimum value.

Grid Bag Layout

The grid bag layout is the most powerful, flexible and complex of all the layout managers. It gives you the ability to design user interfaces by aligning different sized components according to the number of cells you want each of the components to occupy in a grid.

The components placed using the gridbag layout manager are known collectively as a gridbag. Every component has applied to it a number of gridbag constraints. These constraints control the size of the component within the gridbag and its position in the grid. Each component must have it's gridbag constraints set before being added to the layout.

The full capabilities of the gridbag layout are beyond the scope of this book. What we will now do is to present an example applet, using the scrollbar component that was introduced in the last section, which will hopefully illustrate how the gridbag layout manager is utilised to locate components within a user interface. As we work through the example code, you should get a reasonable idea of how it can help you.

We should stress that the process of creating a user interface using the gridbag layout is very much an iterative process that requires a fair amount of experimentation and testing to arrive at a layout which meets your requirements.

The best thing to do when creating a gridbag layout is to draw your user interface design on a piece of paper and then, over the top of the design, draw a grid pattern so that you can determine how many cells each component will occupy. A component such as a button would normally occupy one cell of the grid.

This is what we want the applet to look like:

Figure 16.15: *The* Colours *applet (see Listing 16.15)*

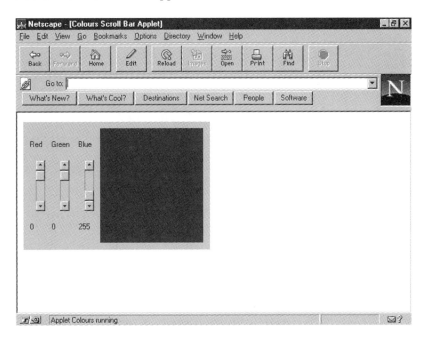

The three scrollbars control the red, green and blue values of a Color object that will be displayed in the canvas on the right side of the applet.

This listing contains the full source code of the applet:

```
import java.awt.*;
import java.applet.*;

public class Colours extends Applet
    {
    Scrollbar red, green, blue;
    Label lblRed, lblGreen, lblBlue;
    Label lblRedVal, lblGreenVal, lblBlueVal;
    Canvas colourCanvas;
    public void init()
        {
        lblRed = new Label("Red");
        lblGreen = new Label("Green");
        lblBlue = new Label("Blue");

        red = new Scrollbar(Scrollbar.VERTICAL, 255, 0, 0, 255);
        green = new Scrollbar(Scrollbar.VERTICAL, 0, 0, 0, 255);
        blue = new Scrollbar(Scrollbar.VERTICAL, 0, 0, 0, 255);

        lblRedVal = new Label(" 255");
        lblGreenVal = new Label("0");
        lblBlueVal = new Label("0");

        colourCanvas = new Canvas();
        colourCanvas.setBackground(new Color(255, 0, 0));

        GridBagLayout gbLayout = new GridBagLayout();
        setLayout(gbLayout);

        GridBagConstraints gbConstraints = new GridBagConstraints();

        gbConstraints.fill = GridBagConstraints.NONE;
        gbConstraints.anchor = GridBagConstraints.WEST;
        gbConstraints.weightx = 10;
        gbConstraints.weighty = 10;

        add(lblRed, gbLayout, gbConstraints, 0, 0, 1, 1);
        add(lblGreen, gbLayout, gbConstraints, 1, 0, 1, 1);
        add(lblBlue, gbLayout, gbConstraints, 2, 0, 1, 1);

        gbConstraints.fill = GridBagConstraints.BOTH;
        gbConstraints.weightx = 100;
```

```
       add(colourCanvas, gbLayout, gbConstraints, 3, 0, 3, 6);

       gbConstraints.fill = GridBagConstraints.VERTICAL;
       gbConstraints.anchor = GridBagConstraints.CENTER;
       gbConstraints.weightx = 10;

       add(red, gbLayout, gbConstraints, 0, 1, 1, 4);
       add(green, gbLayout, gbConstraints, 1, 1, 1, 4);
       add(blue, gbLayout, gbConstraints, 2, 1, 1, 4);

       gbConstraints.anchor = GridBagConstraints.WEST;

       add(lblRedVal, gbLayout, gbConstraints, 0, 5, 1, 1);
       add(lblGreenVal, gbLayout, gbConstraints, 1, 5, 1, 1);
       add(lblBlueVal, gbLayout, gbConstraints, 2, 5, 1, 1);
       }

   private void add(Component component, GridBagLayout layout,
      GridBagConstraints constraints, int x, int y, int w, int h)
      {
      constraints.gridx = x;
      constraints.gridy = y;
      constraints.gridwidth = w;
      constraints.gridheight = h;
      layout.setConstraints(component, constraints);
      add(component);
      }

   public boolean handleEvent(Event evt)
      {
      if (evt.target instanceof Scrollbar)
         {
         lblRedVal.setText("" + red.getValue());
         lblGreenVal.setText("" + green.getValue());
         lblBlueVal.setText("" + blue.getValue());
         colourCanvas.setBackground(new Color(red.getValue(),
                 green.getValue(), blue.getValue()));
         colourCanvas.repaint();
         return true;
         }
      return super.handleEvent(evt);
      }

   public Insets insets()
```

```
        {
        return new Insets(10, 10, 10, 10);
        }
    }
```

We will now work through the example code. You should be able to relate the procedures used back to the design of the grid.

First, we create all of the components that we require: the three scrollbars, the title labels for each scrollbar, the value labels for each and the canvas on which the colour will be displayed. The initial setting of the scrollbars have been set for a range of 0 to 255 and the red value has been given an initial value of 255.

Next, we create an instance of the GridBagLayout class, gbLayout, and make this the layout for the container applet:

```
GridBagLayout gbLayout = new GridBagLayout();
setLayout(gbLayout);
```

Then we must create a GridBagConstraints object:

```
GridBagConstraints gbConstraints = new GridBagConstraints();
```

The GridBagConstraints object contains the information which determines how the components are sized and located within the grid. For each component that we add to the layout, we must first set the constraints for that component. Once the constraints have been specified, the setConstraints() method is used to pass the information to the GridBagLayout object. There are five main constraints:

1. position: the gridx and the gridy constraints determine the column and the row position of the upper left corner of the component. If the component is to be placed in the top left corner of the grid the gridx and gridy constraints should both be 0.

2. size: the gridwidth and gridheight constraints specify the size, in cells, of the component. Therefore, if a component is to be two cells wide and three deep, the gridwidth and gridheight should be set to 2 and 4 respectively.

3. fill: this determines whether the component should be stretched to fill the display area that has been allocated to it. The four fill types are:

   - GridBagConstraints.NONE
   - GridBagConstraints.HORIZONTAL
   - GridBagConstraints.VERTICAL

▪ GridBagConstraints.BOTH.

4. anchor: if the fill constraint has not been set so that the component does not fill the display area, the anchor constraint specifies the components position within it's display area. The anchor values are GridBagConstraints.CENTER (which is the default), and all the points of the compass, ie. NORTH, NORTHEAST, EAST etc.

5. weights: the weightx and weighty constraints determine how Java allocates the space for each area. This constraint, above all others, is worth experimenting with to achieve the desired result. Basically, if you set the weight to 0, that area will never grow beyond its initial size if the container is resized. If the weight of one area is greater than the weight of another, the first will be allocated more of the available space.

Because we always want to specify the position and size constraints we have defined an add method which accepts a component object, the GridBagLayout object, the GridBagConstraints object and the position and size constraints as arguments and sets the constraints for a component before adding it to the layout:

Having created our GridBagConstraints object we now set our initial constraints. We don't want the components to fill their display areas and we want them left-aligned:

```
gbConstraints.fill = GridBagConstraints.NONE;
gbConstraints.anchor = GridBagConstraints.WEST;
gbConstraints.weightx = 10;
gbConstraints.weighty = 10;
```

We can now add the first components, the title labels:

```
add(lblRed, gbLayout, gbConstraints, 0, 0, 1, 1);
add(lblGreen, gbLayout, gbConstraints, 1, 0, 1, 1);
add(lblBlue, gbLayout, gbConstraints, 2, 0, 1, 1);
```

The labels are placed in the first three cells across the top of the grid and each label is given a size of one cell.

Before adding the canvas we change the fill constraint so that the canvas will fill its allocated cells and we increase the weight in the x direction so that the canvas has first claim to the column width:

```
gbConstraints.fill = GridBagConstraints.BOTH;
gbConstraints.weightx = 100;
```

The canvas is allocated a display area three columns wide and six rows deep:

```
add(colourCanvas, gbLayout, gbConstraints, 3, 0, 3, 6);
```

We now want to add the scrollbars. Before doing so we change the `fill` constraint so that the scrollbars will stretch to fill the vertical space available and the `anchor` constraint is changed so that they will be centred horizontally. We also set the `weightx` constraint back to its initial setting:

```
gbConstraints.fill = GridBagConstraints.VERTICAL;
gbConstraints.anchor = GridBagConstraints.CENTER;
gbConstraints.weightx = 10;
```

Each scrollbar is allocated one column width and four rows:

```
add(red, gbLayout, gbConstraints, 0, 1, 1, 4);
add(green, gbLayout, gbConstraints, 1, 1, 1, 4);
add(blue, gbLayout, gbConstraints, 2, 1, 1, 4);
```

Finally, the anchoring is set back to left-alignment before the colour value labels are added:

```
gbConstraints.anchor = GridBagConstraints.WEST;
add(lblRedVal, gbLayout, gbConstraints, 0, 5, 1, 1);
add(lblGreenVal, gbLayout, gbConstraints, 1, 5, 1, 1);
add(lblBlueVal, gbLayout, gbConstraints, 2, 5, 1, 1);
```

The event handling is quite straightforward. We simply create a new `Color` object with the values obtained using the Scrollbar `getValue()` method, set the background of the canvas to that colour and call the `repaint()` method.

Text Areas

Text areas are used when you want to be able to accept text input from a user that is more than one line long. A `TextArea` component can be created with any number of rows and columns and is automatically given scrollbars – the text will scroll if too much is entered. Text fields and text areas are both descended from the `TextComponent` class and so share a number of methods. Getting and setting text is the same for both, as is selecting text. Text areas, however, have more functionality than text fields, notably the ability to insert text at any position, append text and replace selected text.

The user can select text by highlighting it in the usual fashion for a particular platform. Text can also be selected using the methods `select()`, which can select part of the text according to starting and ending positions, and `selectAll()`, which selects all of the text.

It is worth noting that the text will not "word-wrap" when it reaches the end of a line – unless the user inserts a carriage return, the text will just continue to scroll across. If you want to add text to a text area, using the `setText()` method, you must remember to specify carriage returns where you want them by including a `'\n'`.

The usual way to create a text area is to specify the number rows and columns that you require as parameters to the constructor:

```
TextArea txtArea = new TextArea(5, 40);
```

The above code will create a text area consisting 5 lines of 40 columns each. Our example applet contains a text field and a text area. Any text entered in the text field can be transferred to the text area component by pressing one of three buttons – Insert, Append or Replace. If the Insert button is pressed, the text from the text field will be inserted at the current cursor location. If Append is pressed, the text will be appended at the end of the text in the text area and if Replace is pressed, the text field text will replace any text that is selected in the text area.

Figure 16.16: *The* `TextAreaExample` *applet (see Listing 16.16)*

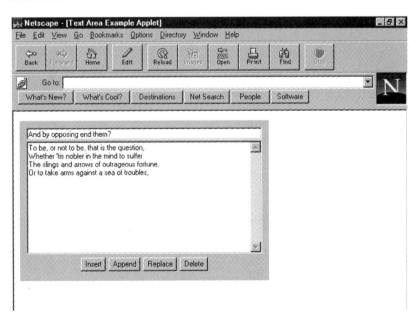

Here is the source code:

```
import java.awt.*;
import java.applet.*;
public class TextAreaExample extends Applet
    {
    TextField txtField;
    TextArea txtArea;
    Button btnInsert, btnAppend, btnReplace, btnDelete;
    public void init()
        {
        txtField = new TextField("Enter text here");
        txtArea = new TextArea();
        btnInsert = new Button("Insert");
        btnAppend = new Button("Append");
        btnReplace = new Button("Replace");
        btnDelete = new Button("Delete");

        Panel pnlButtons = new Panel();
        pnlButtons.setLayout(new FlowLayout());
        pnlButtons.add(btnInsert);
        pnlButtons.add(btnAppend);
        pnlButtons.add(btnReplace);
        pnlButtons.add(btnDelete);

        setLayout(new BorderLayout());
        add("North", txtField);
        add("South", pnlButtons);
        add("Center", txtArea);
        }

    public boolean action(Event evt, Object arg)
        {
        if (evt.target instanceof Button)
            {
            if (arg == "Insert")
                {
                String s = txtField.getText();
                txtArea.insertText(s, txtArea.getSelectionStart());
                }
            else if (arg == "Append")
                {
```

```
                    String s = txtField.getText();
                    txtArea.appendText(s);
                    }
                else if (arg == "Replace")
                    {
                    String s = txtField.getText();
                    txtArea.replaceText(s, txtArea.getSelectionStart(),
                            txtArea.getSelectionEnd());
                    }
                else if (arg == "Delete")
                    {
                    txtArea.setText("");
                    }
                return (true);
                }
            return (false);
            }

        public Insets insets()
            {
            return new Insets(10, 10, 10, 10);
            }
        }
```

The insertText(), appendText() and replaceText() methods do exactly as you would expect. The getSelectionStart() and getSelectionEnd() methods return the starting and ending positions of the current selection. Note that getSelectionStart() can be used to obtain the current cursor position as well. Text can be deleted by simply setting the text to an empty string.

TextArea methods

- public void appendText(String str) appends the given text string to this text area's current text.

- public int getColumns() returns the number of columns in this text area.

- public int getRows() returns the number of rows in this text area.

- public void insertText(String str, int pos) inserts the text, str, at the specified position, pos, in this text area.

- `public void replaceText(String str, int start, int end)` replaces the text in the text area from the position `start` (inclusive) to the position `end` (exclusive) with the new text string `str`.

Card Layout

Card layouts provide an alternative way of displaying components. The other layout managers display all the components at the same time. The card layout manager allows you to lay panels one on top of the other, so that only one is displayed at a time, and provides you with methods which let you display the "cards" in any sequence you like. The procedure for creating a card layout is as follows:

1. Create all the panels that you want to make into cards.
2. Create another panel to contain the cards.
3. Create a `CardLayout` object and use `setLayout()` to apply it to the cards panel.
4. Add each of your panels to the card panel, in the order in which you want to display them if they are to be part of a sequence, and assigning each one a name so that they can be shown individually.

Figure 16.17: *The* `CardLayoutExample` *applet (see Listing 16.17)*

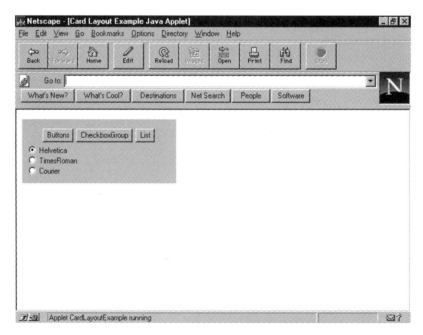

The individual panels can be displayed using the show() method, which allows you to specify a card by name. Alternatively, you can use the first() and last() methods to display the first and last cards in the sequence, or the next() and previous() methods to show the cards according to their order in the sequence. This example applet contains three buttons which, when pressed, will display three different alternatives for selecting a font: buttons, a check box group and a list box. As you click on each of the selector buttons a different method of selecting fonts will appear. Figure 16.17 shows how the applet looks when the check box group card is being displayed. Here is the source code:

Listing 16.17:
Using the Card Layout manager (see Figure 16.17)

```java
import java.awt.*;
import java.applet.*;

public class CardLayoutExample extends Applet
    {
    Button btnButtons, btnCheckboxes, btnList;
    Panel cards;
    CardLayout theLayout;

    public void init()
        {
        btnButtons = new Button("Buttons");
        btnCheckboxes = new Button("CheckboxGroup");
        btnList = new Button("List");
        Panel pnlChoices = new Panel();
        pnlChoices.setLayout(new FlowLayout());
        pnlChoices.add(btnButtons);
        pnlChoices.add(btnCheckboxes);
        pnlChoices.add(btnList);

        Panel pnlButtons = new Panel();
        pnlButtons.setLayout(new GridLayout(3, 1));
        Button btnHelv = new Button("Helvetica");
        Button btnTimes = new Button("TimesRoman");
        Button btnCourier = new Button("Courier");
        pnlButtons.add(btnHelv);
        pnlButtons.add(btnTimes);
        pnlButtons.add(btnCourier);

        CheckboxGroup chkGroup = new CheckboxGroup();
        Checkbox chkHelv = new Checkbox("Helvetica", chkGroup, true);
```

```java
        Checkbox chkTimes =
        new Checkbox("TimesRoman", chkGroup, false);
        Checkbox chkCourier = new Checkbox("Courier", chkGroup, false);
        Panel pnlChkGroup = new Panel();
        pnlChkGroup.setLayout(new GridLayout(3, 1));
        pnlChkGroup.add(chkHelv);
        pnlChkGroup.add(chkTimes);
        pnlChkGroup.add(chkCourier);

        List lstFonts = new List(3, false);
        lstFonts.addItem("Helvetica");
        lstFonts.addItem("TimesRoman");
        lstFonts.addItem("Courier");

        cards = new Panel();
        theLayout = new CardLayout();
        cards.setLayout(theLayout);
        cards.add("Buttons", pnlButtons);
        cards.add("CheckboxGroup", pnlChkGroup);
        cards.add("List", lstFonts);

        setLayout(new BorderLayout());
        add("North", pnlChoices);
        add("Center", cards);
        }

    public boolean action(Event evt, Object arg)
        {
        if (evt.target instanceof Button)
            {
            theLayout.show(cards, (String)arg);
            return (true);
            }

        return (false);
        }

    public Insets insets()
        {
        return new Insets(10, 10, 10, 10);
        }
    }
```

Three individual panels are created: one for the buttons that will allow the user to select a different card for display, pnlChoices, one as a buttons container, pnlButtons, and one as a checkbox group container, pnlChkGroup. The list box, lstFonts, is also created.

We then come to the code that creates the cards panel and the card layout:

```
cards = new Panel();
theLayout = new CardLayout();
cards.setLayout(theLayout);
```

We can then add each of our components to the layout. Notice that they are each given names:

```
cards.add("Buttons", pnlButtons);
cards.add("CheckboxGroup", pnlChkGroup);
cards.add("List", lstFonts);
```

Finally, the selection buttons panel and the cards panel are placed on the applet:

```
setLayout(new BorderLayout());
add("North", pnlChoices);
add("Center", cards);
```

To display each of the card panels we intercept the action event when one of the buttons is pressed and pass the label of each button, which matches the name we gave each card, as a parameter of the layout show() method:

```
theLayout.show(cards, (String)arg);
```

Frames

Frames allow you to create pop-up windows that are not attached to the browser in which your applet is running. The windows that are created from the Frame class have a title bar, a menu bar, and a border and can be moved and resized. The cursor can also be modified when required.

Frames and Dialogs, which we will talk about shortly, are both descended from the Window class. You could derive classes straight from Window but your window would not then have the additional properties mentioned above.

The Frame constructor accepts a string for the title:

```
myFrame = new Frame("This is a frame");
```

The title string can be omitted, in which case the word "Untitled" will appear in the title bar of the frame. Windows, like panels, are derived from the Container class, so can contain other components. One difference from the Panel class is that the default layout for windows is the border layout and not the flow layout.

When a frame is first created, it is not visible. To make the window visible you must use the show() method. Before that, the size of the window has to be set. This is done using the resize() method, which accepts two integer arguments, the width and height of the window.

This code creates a frame window, with a width of 250 pixels and a height of 150 pixels, and then displays it:

```
myFrame = new Frame("This is a frame");
myFrame.resize(250, 150);
myFrame.show();
```

The window can be hidden using the hide() method. If you use the dispose() method, the window will be removed and its resources freed.

Figure 16.18: *The* FrameExample *applet (see Listing 16.18)*

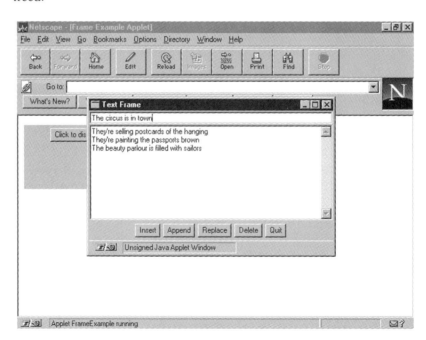

To illustrate the use of frames we have an applet containing a button which, when pressed, will display a window containing the TextArea example that we looked at earlier. The frame will contain the text field, the text area and the buttons that were used before, plus an extra button, Quit, to close the window and return control back to the basic applet.

Here is the source code:

```java
import java.awt.*;
import java.applet.*;

public class FrameExample extends Applet
    {
    public void init()
        {
        add(new Button("Click to display frame"));
        }

    public boolean action(Event evt, Object arg)
        {
        if (evt.target instanceof Button)
            {
            new TextFrame("Text Frame");
            return (true);
            }
        return (false);
        }
    }

class TextFrame extends Frame
    {
    TextField txtField;
    TextArea txtArea;
    Button btnInsert, btnAppend, btnReplace, btnDelete, btnQuit;

    public TextFrame(String title)
        {
        super(title);

        txtField = new TextField("Enter text here");
        txtArea = new TextArea();
        btnInsert = new Button("Insert");
```

```java
        btnAppend = new Button("Append");
        btnReplace = new Button("Replace");
        btnDelete = new Button("Delete");
        btnQuit = new Button("Quit");

        Panel pnlButtons = new Panel();
        pnlButtons.setLayout(new FlowLayout());

        pnlButtons.add(btnInsert);
        pnlButtons.add(btnAppend);
        pnlButtons.add(btnReplace);
        pnlButtons.add(btnDelete);
        pnlButtons.add(btnQuit);

        setLayout(new BorderLayout());

        add("North", txtField);
        add("South", pnlButtons);
        add("Center", txtArea);

        resize(400, 250);
        show();
        }

    public boolean handleEvent(Event evt)
        {
        if (evt.id == evt.WINDOW_DESTROY)
            {
            dispose();
            return true;
            }
        return super.handleEvent(evt);
        }

    public boolean action(Event evt, Object arg)
        {
        if (evt.target instanceof Button)
            {
            if (arg == "Insert")
                {
                String s = txtField.getText();
                txtArea.insertText(s, txtArea.getSelectionStart());
```

```
         }
      else if (arg == "Append")
         {
         String s = txtField.getText();
         txtArea.appendText(s);
         }
      else if (arg == "Replace")
         {
         String s = txtField.getText();
         txtArea.replaceText(s, txtArea.getSelectionStart(),
                 txtArea.getSelectionEnd());
         }
      else if (arg == "Delete")
         {
         txtArea.setText("");
         }
      else if (arg == "Quit")
         {
         dispose();
         }
      return (true);
      }
   return (false);
   }
}
```

The applet class definition is minimal. It just contains an init() method to display the button and an action event method that creates our frame object, TextFrame, when the button is pressed.

The rest of the code is the definition of our TextFrame class, derived from Frame. We have included all of the code for setting up the components in the constructor for the new class. The first command in the frame constructor calls the frame super constructor, passing it the title bar caption. The components included in the earlier example are then created. (We could, of course, omit the setLayout() call for the frame as the border layout is the default for frames.) Lastly, the size of the window is set and the show() method is called to display the window.

We have included a handleEvent() method to test for an event with an ID equal to WINDOW_DESTROY. This event is generated when the user clicks on the close box of the window. If the close box is clicked or the user selects the close option from the system menu, the dispose()

method is called to remove the window. As it happens, we have provided a Quit button to enable the user to close the window but it doesn't hurt to include another escape option.

The action method is just about the same as it was for the TextArea example. The only difference is the test to see if the Quit button has been pressed.

Menus

Any window created from the Frame class can have its own *menu bar*. When one of the names in the menu bar is clicked on, a drop-down *menu* appears containing any number of *menu items*. Each menu item can also have its own submenu. A menu bar is created by creating an instance of the class MenuBar:

```
MenuBar mBar = new MenuBar();
```

The setMenuBar() method is then used to make the newly created menu bar the default menu for a window:

```
setMenuBar(mBar);
```

For each menu name that you want to appear in the menu bar you must create a Menu object:

```
Menu m = new Menu("File");
```

The menu object can then be added to the menu bar using the add() method of the menu bar object, passing the menu object as a parameter:

```
mBar.add(m);
```

Having created the menu, items can be added to it:

```
m.add(new MenuItem("New"));
m.add(new MenuItem("Open"));
```

To add a separator line between items, the addSeparator() method is used:

```
m.addseparator();
m.add(new MenuItem("Save"));
m.add(new MenuItem("Save As"));
m.addseparator();
```

A menu item can have its own submenu by creating a another menu object, adding the new menu object to the existing menu, and then adding menu items to *that* menu. For instance, we could add a menu item "Print", with submenu items "To File" and To Printer", to the File menu as follows:

```
Menu sm = new Menu("Print");
m.add(sm);
sm.add(new MenuItem("To File"));
sm.add(new MenuItem("To Printer"));
```

Menu items that can be toggled between two states can be included in a menu. They are known as check box menu items and alternate between a checked and an unchecked state. When in the checked state a check mark is displayed next to the name. This code creates a submenu called Options, which contains two check box menu items, Bold and Italic:

```
Menu sm = new Menu("Options");
m.add(sm);
sm.add(new CheckboxMenuItem("Bold"));
sm.add(new CheckboxMenuItem("Italic"));
```

An action event is triggered when the user selects a menu item. The event target is an instance of MenuItem and the second argument, arg, contains the name of the menu item. The state of a check box menu item can be obtained using the getState() method. The item can be initialised to a checked state using the setState() method.

This example is a reworking of the previous example, using menus instead of buttons to copy the text from the text field to the text area. An extra facility is an Options submenu which contains two check box menu items, Bold and Italic, which, when in a checked state cause the text to be copied in bold, italic or both.

Listing 16.19:
Using menus in a Frame window (see Figure 16.19)

```
import java.awt.*;
import java.applet.*;
public class MenuExample extends Applet
    {
    public void init()
        {
        add(new Button("Click to display frame"));
        }
    public boolean action(Event evt, Object arg)
        {
```

```
          if (evt.target instanceof Button)
              {
              new TextFrame("Menu Example");
              return (true);
              }
          return (false);
          }
      }
class TextFrame extends Frame
    {
    TextField txtField;
    TextArea txtArea;
    CheckboxMenuItem chkBold, chkItalic;
    Font f;
    public TextFrame(String title)
        {
        super(title);

        MenuBar mBar = new MenuBar();
        setMenuBar(mBar);

        Menu m = new Menu("File");
        mBar.add(m);
        m.add(new MenuItem("Quit"));

        m = new Menu("Text");
        mBar.add(m);
        m.add(new MenuItem("Insert"));
        m.add(new MenuItem("Append"));
        m.add(new MenuItem("Replace"));
        m.addSeparator();
        m.add(new MenuItem("Delete"));
        m.addSeparator();

        Menu sm = new Menu("Options");
        m.add(sm);
        chkBold = new CheckboxMenuItem("Bold");
        sm.add(chkBold);
        chkItalic = new CheckboxMenuItem("Italic");
        sm.add(chkItalic);

        txtField = new TextField("Enter text here");
        txtArea = new TextArea();
        f = new Font("Helvetica", Font.PLAIN, 12);
```

```
            txtArea.setFont(f);

            Panel p = new Panel();
            p.setLayout(new FlowLayout());
            p.add(new Button("Quit"));
            setLayout(new BorderLayout());

            add("North", txtField);
            add("South", p);
            add("Center", txtArea);

            resize(400, 250);
            show();
            }
        public boolean handleEvent(Event evt)
            {
            if (evt.id == evt.WINDOW_DESTROY)
                {
                dispose();
                return true;
                }
            return super.handleEvent(evt);
            }
        public boolean action(Event evt, Object arg)
            {
            if (evt.target instanceof MenuItem)
                {
                int fontStyle = 0;
                if (chkBold.getState())
                    fontStyle += Font.BOLD;
                if (chkItalic.getState())
                    fontStyle += Font.ITALIC;
                f = new Font("Helvetica", fontStyle, 12);
                txtArea.setFont(f);
                if (arg.equals("Quit"))
                    {
                    dispose();
                    }
                else if (arg.equals("Insert"))
                    {
                    String s = txtField.getText();
                    txtArea.insertText(s, txtArea.getSelectionStart());
                    }
                else if (arg.equals("Append"))
```

```
                        {
                        String s = txtField.getText();
                        txtArea.appendText(s);
                        }
                    else if (arg.equals("Replace"))
                        {
                        String s = txtField.getText();
                        txtArea.replaceText(s, txtArea.getSelectionStart(),
                                txtArea.getSelectionEnd());
                        }
                    else if (arg.equals("Delete"))
                        {
                        txtArea.setText("");
                        }
                    return (true);
                    }

                if (evt.target instanceof Button)
                    {
                    dispose();
                    return true;
                    }
                return (false);
                }
            }
```

Figure 16.19: *The* MenuExample *applet (see Listing 16.19)*

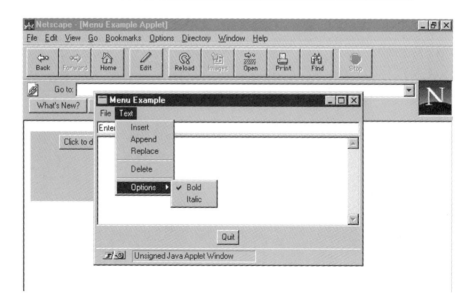

Dialogs

The other class derived from the Window class is the Dialog class. Dialog boxes are usually used either to get information from the user, or to warn the user about something or just to display some information, an *About* box, for instance.

Dialogs can be either *modal* or *modeless*. A modal dialog will not allow input to any other window of the application until the user has dealt with it. A modeless dialog, on the other hand, allows the user to interact both with the dialog and with any other window in the application.

The Dialog constructor has two forms. The first accepts two arguments:

```
dlg = new Dialog(Frame frame, boolean modal);
```

where *frame* is the parent window of the dialog and *modal* is a boolean value which, if true, makes the dialog modal, or modeless if it is false. Dialogs can therefore only be attached to frame windows that are already independent of the applet.

The other form accepts a string argument which will become the title of the dialog:

```
dlg = new Dialog(Frame frame, String title, boolean modal);
```

Dialogs, like frame windows, must be displayed using the show() method and removed using dispose().

As an example of a modal dialog, we will add a confirmation dialog box to the same example. This time, when the user clicks on the Delete menu option, a dialog box will pop up asking if they are sure. If the user clicks on the Yes button, the text will be deleted. If the No button is clicked, the dialog will be removed and the text will remain undeleted (see Figure 16.20).

Here is the source code:

Listing 16.20: *An example illustrating the use of Dialogs (see Figure 16.20)*

```
import java.awt.*;
import java.applet.*;
public class DialogExample extends Applet
    {
    public void init()
        {
        add(new Button("Click to display frame"));
```

```java
      }
   public boolean action(Event evt, Object arg)
      {
      if (evt.target instanceof Button)
         {
         new TextFrame("Menu Example");
         return (true);
         }
      return (false);
      }
   }

class TextFrame extends Frame
   {
   TextField txtField;
   TextArea txtArea;
   CheckboxMenuItem chkBold, chkItalic;
   Font f;
   ConfirmDialog dlg;

   public TextFrame(String title)
      {
      super(title);

      MenuBar mBar = new MenuBar();
      setMenuBar(mBar);

      Menu m = new Menu("File");
      mBar.add(m);
      m.add(new MenuItem("Quit"));

      m = new Menu("Text");
      mBar.add(m);
      m.add(new MenuItem("Insert"));
      m.add(new MenuItem("Append"));
      m.add(new MenuItem("Replace"));
      m.addSeparator();
      m.add(new MenuItem("Delete"));
      m.addSeparator();

      Menu sm = new Menu("Options");
      m.add(sm);
```

```
chkBold = new CheckboxMenuItem("Bold");
sm.add(chkBold);
chkItalic = new CheckboxMenuItem("Italic");
sm.add(chkItalic);

txtField = new TextField("Enter text here");
txtArea = new TextArea();
f = new Font("Helvetica", Font.PLAIN, 12);
txtArea.setFont(f);

Panel p = new Panel();
p.setLayout(new FlowLayout());
p.add(new Button("Quit"));

setLayout(new BorderLayout());

add("North", txtField);
add("South", p);
add("Center", txtArea);

resize(400, 250);
show();
}

public boolean handleEvent(Event evt)
    {
    if (evt.id == evt.WINDOW_DESTROY)
        {
        dispose();
        return true;
        }
    return super.handleEvent(evt);
    }

public boolean action(Event evt, Object arg)
    {
    if (evt.target instanceof MenuItem)
        {
        int fontStyle = 0;
        if (chkBold.getState())
            fontStyle += Font.BOLD;
        if (chkItalic.getState())
```

```
                    fontStyle += Font.ITALIC;
               f = new Font("Helvetica", fontStyle, 12);
               txtArea.setFont(f);

               if (arg.equals("Quit"))
                  {
                  dispose();
                  }
               else if (arg.equals("Insert"))
                  {
                  String s = txtField.getText();
                  txtArea.insertText(s, txtArea.getSelectionStart());
                  }
               else if (arg.equals("Append"))
                  {
                  String s = txtField.getText();
                  txtArea.appendText(s);
                  }
               else if (arg.equals("Replace"))
                  {
                  String s = txtField.getText();
                  txtArea.replaceText(s, txtArea.getSelectionStart(),
                          txtArea.getSelectionEnd());
                  }
               else if (arg.equals("Delete"))
                  {
                  dlg = new ConfirmDialog(this, "Confirm Deletion", true);
                  dlg.show();
                  }
               return (true);
               }

            if (evt.target instanceof Button)
               {
               dispose();
               return true;
               }
            return (false);
            }
         }

      class ConfirmDialog extends Dialog
```

```
{
TextFrame tf;

public ConfirmDialog(Frame parent, String title, boolean modal)
   {
   super (parent, title, modal);

   tf = (TextFrame)parent;

   Panel p1 = new Panel();
   p1.setLayout(new FlowLayout());
   p1.add(new Label("Are you sure?"));

   Panel p2 = new Panel();
   p2.setLayout(new FlowLayout());
   p2.add(new Button("Yes"));
   p2.add(new Button("No"));

   add("North", p1);
   add("South", p2);

   resize(250, 120);
   }

public boolean action(Event evt, Object arg)
   {
   if (evt.target instanceof Button)
      {
      if (arg.equals("Yes"))
         {
         tf.txtArea.setText("");
         dispose();
         }
      else if (arg.equals("No"))
         {
         dispose();
         }
      return (true);
      }
   return (false);
   }
}
```

Figure 16.20: *The* DialogExample *applet (see Listing 16.20)*

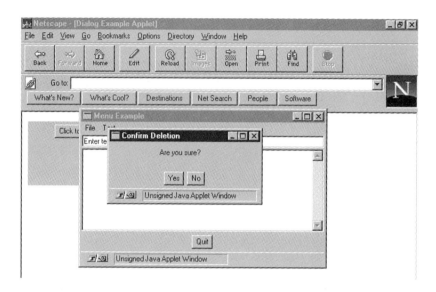

Summary

Designing a user interface in Java is not as straightforward as it is when using other langauges like Visual Basic or C++ where you have visual tools that let you design an interface on the screen very quickly and easily. In Java, it must all be done in the code. Visual Java tools are, however, now becoming available which will undoubtedly make your job a lot easier.

A Java interface is constructed from components. These components include all the usual controls that you would find in any user interface: buttons, checkboxes, lists, scrollbars and so on. Some components are also containers – you can place other components within them. Panels are the most common form of container (although an applet itself is a container).

Placement of components is controlled by a number of layout managers. These let you choose different ways of positioning components within a container, secure in the knowledge that Java will position the components correctly, no matter which platform your program is running on.

Java also provides window classes, frame and dialog, which allow you to create windows that are independent of an applet. Frames can have menus attached to them.

17

Error Handling using Exceptions

Introduction

Errors will always occur in programs. Sometimes they are the fault of the programmer, an out-of-bounds array element, for instance, or an attempt to access an object via a null pointer. Other times the errors might be caused by circumstances out of the control of the programmer, such as a full disk drive or a printer running out of paper.

A good programmer should not allow the first type of error to occur. It should be second nature to check the bounds of an array or test to see whether a variable is set to null. Guarding against the second type of error is slightly more difficult and requires a fair amount of diligence from the programmer to make the program as robust as possible under unforeseen conditions.

When something unexpected happens the aim must be to handle the error in the best way possible. It is sometimes possible for a program to handle an error in such a way that the it can return to a stable state and allows the user to correct the underlying problem and continue the process, or carry on in another section of the program. If this is not possible the program should try and save as much data as possible and then terminate gracefully.

To accomplish this aim using traditional error handling methods involves adding a great deal of extra code to the program to detect any errors that arise, report them and recover from them in a competent fashion. For instance, if you were writing a program method that that opened a file and wrote some data to it you could not simply write the following:

```
writedata()
    {
    open file for writing;
    write data to file;
    close file;
    }
```

What happens if the file the user has specified does not exist, or the user is writing to a network and doesn't have write access, or the disk becomes full half way through writing the data? At each stage of the process the programmer must check to make sure that the previous step has been completed successfully before proceeding with the next step. If an error occurs you must try to detect what kind of error it is, report the error and return a specific error code to the calling method for it to deal with in a, hopefully, orderly fashion. The above example of writing data to a file will become something like this:

```
writedata()
    {
    open file for writing;
    if (file is open)
        {
        write data to file;
        if (data write failed)
            {
            close file;
            return (WRITE_FAILED_ERROR);
            }
        }
    else
        {
        return (OPEN_FILE_ERROR);
        }
    close file;
    if (file not closed)
        {
        return (CLOSE_FILE_ERROR);
        }
    else
        {
        return (NO_ERROR);
        }
    }
```

Our code has expanded significantly and we have not included any error reporting or even dealt with all the possible errors. For example, if the open file operation fails we are just returning an OPEN_FILE_ERROR; we don't specify why the open operation failed – the file might not exist, or it couldn't be opened for writing. It is almost impossible to anticipate all the possible errors that can occur without the code becoming an unmanageable size and almost incomprehensible to anyone studying the code.

This type of error handling has other drawbacks – which method actually handles the error? How far should error codes be passed back up the method stack? Which method is actually going to report the error to the user and attempt to recover gracefully?

To provide a better solution to the perennial problem of error handling, Java (like C++) includes a more structured approach for dealing with errors, called *exception handling*. An *exception* arises when something occurs that disrupts the normal flow of control of the program.

When an error occurs in a Java program, an exception object is created, encapsulating the information regarding the error. The exception object is passed to the Java runtime system which sets about finding a handler that can deal with that particular exception. The search is carried out by moving backwards through each calling method until an exception handler for the error in question is found, and the error can be dealt with. If an appropriate exception handler cannot be found in any of the calling methods, the program will terminate.

The creation of the exception object and its transmission to the exception handling mechanism of the runtime system is called *throwing an exception*. When this happens, the method in which the error occurred immediately exits. When an appropriate exception handler is found, it is said to *catch the exception*. The exception handler method will then take control.

Exception Objects

Every object thrown by an exception must be an instance of the class Throwable or one of the classes derived from it. You can either make use of the exceptions that are built into Java or, if none of the standard ones meet your needs, you can create your own.

We draw your attention to the diagrams in Appendix A of the Java Class Hierarchies. As you can see from the java.lang class hierarchy, the Throwable class has two subclasses, Error and Exception. The Error subclass defines errors that are internal to the Java run time system. These are uncommon but are usually serious enough to cause the program to terminate. There is not a great deal you can do in such circumstances and you should not try to handle these as exceptions.

The other subclass of Throwable, Exception, is the one you must concentrate on. It contains a number of child classes. One of these, RunTimeException, contains exceptions that arise at run time due usually to errors in the program code.

Examples are ArrayIndexOutOfBoundsException, which occurs when an attempt is made to access an array element outside the bounds specified for the array, and NullPointerException, which occurs when an attempt is made to access an object through a null reference. These errors, as we mentioned at the start of the chapter, should be prevented by building proper safeguards into the program and should not be handled as exceptions. Indeed, Java does not expect you to handle them.

The same is not true of all the other subclasses that are derived from Exception. These exceptions represent errors that the programmer can and must handle – errors that can usually be anticipated and responded to in a way that either allows the program to continue operating, or saves any data and exits gracefully. The following classes are all derived from Exception:

```
IOException
InterruptedException
ClassNotFoundException
CloneNotSupportedException
IllegalAccessException
InstantiationException
AWTException
NoSuchMethodException
```

How to Catch Exceptions

The try/catch **block**

Exceptions are caught by placing the statements within which an exception might occur inside a *try* block. The try block is followed immediately by one or more *catch* clauses, which act as the handlers. This is how a try/catch combination looks:

```
try
    {
    code statement(s)
    }
catch (ExceptionType e)
    {
    handler statement(s)
    }
```

If an exception is thrown by any of the statements within the try block, the rest of the statements within the block are skipped and the code within the catch block is executed. Note: the argument for the catch statement must be the name of a class that is derived from the Throwable class. If an exception is not thrown the catch clause is ignored. If the exception thrown does not match the exception type specified in the catch clause, the method will be exited immediately and Java will search back through the calling methods to find a catch clause that *does* match the exception type.

The catch clause must follow on immediately from the try block – there cannot be any code statements in between. There is no limit on the number of catch clauses. They are placed one after the other, each handling a different exception type. The exception handling mechanism will work through the clauses until it finds an appropriate exception type. Here is an example of a try/catch block with multiple catch clauses:

```
String fileName = "testfile.txt";
    try
        {
        FileInputStream inFile = new FileInputStream(fileName);
        ...
        }
    catch(FileNotFoundException e)
        {
        System.out.println("File " + fileName + " not found");
        }
    catch(IOException e)
        {
        System.out.println("Other IOException found: "
                    + e.getMessage());
        }
```

In the above example, if the file does not exist, an exception of type FileNotFoundException will be thrown and caught by the first catch clause. If any other exceptions of type IOException are thrown the second catch clause will handle them. The first catch statement will only handle exceptions of type FileNotFoundException whereas the second catch statement is more general – it will handle any exception of type IOException or any of its subclasses. In the second catch clause the getMessage() method is used to display the error message that has been associated with the exception that was thrown.

The finally clause

The finally clause allows you to provide any clean up code that you think is necessary to ensure that the program can continue executing normally after an exception has been thrown and handled. The syntax looks like this:

```
try
    {
    code statement(s)
    }
catch (ExceptionType e)
    {
    handler statement(s)
    }
finally
    {
    clean up code statement(s)
    }
```

Whatever happens in the try and catch blocks (ie. if an exception is thrown or not), any statements within the finally clause will *always* be executed.

Note a try statement block *must* be followed by one or more catch blocks *or* one finally block.

How to Throw Exceptions

Declaring methods that throw exceptions

We have already seen examples in earlier chapters where we had to enclose a method statement in a try/catch block. This was because the declaration of the method specified that the method will throw an exception if something goes wrong during the execution of the statements within that block.

Note   *If you know that an error might occur within a method and that an exception may be thrown, you must specify the fact in the method header.*

That way, anyone using the method is made aware that an exception can be thrown and can take steps to handle the exception. (In fact, the program will not compile unless the method in question *is* enclosed within a `try/catch` block.) An example of a method declaration specifying that an exception might be thrown is the creation of a URL. In our Lists example applet we had to include the following code to create a URL:

```
try
    {
    URL u = new URL(siteURL);
    getAppletContext().showDocument(u, "_blank");
    }
catch(MalformedURLException e)
    {
    showStatus("URL error " + e);
    }
```

If we look at the declaration of the URL constructor that we have used here you will see how it should be specified that a method can throw an exception:

```
public final class URL
{
...
public URL (String spec) throws MalformedURLException
    {
    ...
    }
}
```

The method header includes the exception specification,

```
throws MalformedURLException
```

This tells the compiler that the constructor method is capable of throwing an exception of type MalformedURLException. Because this exception is not derived from the Error class or the RuntimeException class it is mandatory that you handle the exception. The compiler will consider it an error if you don't.

Note   Any exception classes inheriting from Error or RuntimeException should not be advertised in the method declaration.

If a method deals with more than one exception, all exceptions thrown must be specified in the method header. For example, if the URL constructor also threw exceptions of type FileNotFoundException (it doesn't!), the method header would look like this:

```
public URL (String spec)
throws MalformedURLException, FileNotFoundException
   {
   ...
   }
```

Throwing exceptions

Having declared that a method can throw an exception, you must also add the code that actually does the throwing. This is accomplished using the throw statement:

```
throw ExceptionObject;
```

The first thing to do is select an appropriate exception type, than at the point in the method where an error might occur, you must create an instance of that exception class and then, simply, throw it. For instance, in one of the URL constructor methods, you will find the following code:

```
if ((handler = getURLStreamHandler(protocol)) == null)
   {
   throw new MalformedURLException("unknown protocol: " + protocol);
   }
```

The string passed as an argument to the exception constructor is a message that can be retrieved by the handler using the getMessage() method of Throwable.

For example, if we return to our Lists example applet, we could have picked up the exception error message and displayed it in the Status field by changing the catch clause to the following:

```
try
    {
    URL u = new URL(siteURL);
    getAppletContext().showDocument(u, "_blank");
    }
catch(MalformedURLException e)
    {
    showStatus("URL error " + e.getMessage());
    }
```

Creating an exception class

If you cannot find a standard exception that would be suitable for a possible error situation in your method, you can create your own exception class. All you need to do is derive a new class from an existing Throwable class. This will either be the Exception class or one of its subclasses, such as IOException. For example:

```
public class MyIOException extends IOException
    {
    public MyIOException()
        {
        super();
        }
    public MyIOException(String s)
        {
        super(s);
        }
    }
```

It is normal practice to define a default constructor with no arguments, and a constructor that provides a message. Once the new exception class has been defined you can throw it in your method code:

```
public int MyGetData() throws MyIOException
    {
    ...
    if (error)
        throw new MyIOException("Error getting data");
    ...
    }
```

Summary

Errors in Java programs are dealt with by exception handlers. When an error occurs an exception is thrown. Wherever an error can occur, the code in which the error can originate must be enclosed within a try/ catch combination. The try block contains the code statements where an exception can be thrown, the catch block contains the code that will be executed if an exception of a particular type is thrown. A finally clause can also be defined which contains code that will *always* be executed, whether an exception is thrown or not.

Methods that can throw an exception must be declared with the *throws exceptionObject* statement added to the method definition header. If none of the standard exception types meet your requirements you can derive your own exception classes from the existing ones.

18

Threads and Multithreading

Introduction

In the earlier chapter on animation we introduced the concepts of threads and multithreading. Multithreading is the ability for a process to contain more than one path or stream of execution at any one time. Instead of waiting for a long calculation to be completed before continuing processing, a multithreaded program can be performing the calculation in one thread while other threads carry out other tasks, such as obtaining further user input. Within an application you can have one thread displaying an image while another thread is downloading the next image, ready to be displayed when required.

Those of you familiar with the C or C++ Fork command will know that it is used to force a process to take place. Well, with Java you can think of a thread as a lightweight example of a process. Java threads are as similar to a C/C++ process in that they are called independently or simultaneously, but are much more effective in their operation because they do not carry the system baggage that a process does.

Multithreading is different from multitasking in that threads share resources. They can all access the same objects, methods and variables within an application. This has its advantages and its disadvantages. On the positive side it provides much greater connectivity between the threads. Threads can communicate with each other to perform interrelated tasks. This is not possible with multitasking processes.

On the negative side, this ability to share resources can have undesirable results. If a thread is in the middle of a set of instructions which involves accessing a variable which another thread is in the process of updating the outcome could be that the first thread uses an incorrect value for that variable depending on when the second variable updates it. To overcome this problem, Java provides the ability to synchronise threads so that they can share resources in an orderly fashion, preventing data corruption. We talk about synchronisation later on in the chapter.

The difference between using the Thread class and the Runnable interface will be explained. We also intend to cover the creation and use of threads, including running multiple threads, of course. Threads can be in different states – new, runnable, blocked and dead – we will be discussing these in more detail as well as the different priorities that you can assign to threads to provide priority-based scheduling. Finally, we will talk about thread groups which allow you to group a number of threads together into logical groups to provide betther organisation.

Creating and Using Threads

Within the Java language there are two main reasons why you would use a thread within your application or applet. The first is very simple: they allow a programmer to do more than one thing at a time. The simple use of this is to allow one activity to take place, perhaps in the background, while the user or the software performs a second or a third task.

The second is a far more powerful reason to use a thread. By using them a programmer can concentrate upon the job at hand – writing an application – without worrying about the physical implementation of writing their own multitasking scheme. The programmer can get on with the code, spinning off multiple threads to perform various operations, without worrying about how the internal communication of the language handles such operations. Java worries about it for you. All you have to do is understand the classes which invoke a thread and away you go.

The Thread Class

A thread of execution is created by extending the `Thread` class. Within your definition of the `Thread` subclass you must override the `run()` method with the code that you want to execute within the thread. Once you have derived your `Thread` class you can create an instance of it and make a call to its `start()` method to begin execution of the thread code within the `run()` method.

Here is an example applet which illustrates the above. We will construct a `Thread` subclass, called `LineOfDots`, that will draw a line of dots across the applet display area.

Figure 18.1: *The* `DotsThread` *applet (see Listing 18.1)*

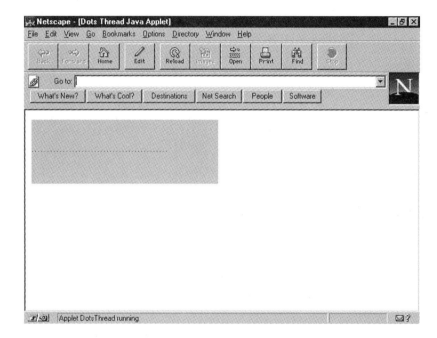

The class only has a constructor, which initialises all the instance variables, and a `run()` method, which, as we mentioned above, must contain the code that is to be executed within the thread. The code that draws the dots is very simple. A loop is set up that uses `drawString()` method to draw a dot every five pixels until the right-hand edge of the applet is reached. Notice the use of the `sleep()` method.

This provides two things:

1. It slows down the drawing by pausing for 100 milliseconds after each dot has been drawn. If there was no pause, the complete line of dots would just appear immediately, which wouldn't be too interesting.

2. By going to sleep for a period of time, the thread allows other threads to execute the code in their `run()` methods. If this wasn't done, our dot drawing thread would hog all the resources, preventing other threads from running.

The code in the applet class consists only of an init() method and a stop() method. The init() method instantiates our line of dots thread class and calls the thread start() method to begin execution of the code contained in the run() method. If the user leaves the page our applet is on, the stop() method stops the thread and sets it to null.

This will make sure that Java garbage collection function – you can think of this as an advanced memory management feature – will remove the unwanted thread object.

Here is the full source code:

Listing 18.1:
Using a thread to diaplay a line of dots (see Figure 18.1)

```java
import java.awt.*;
import java.applet.Applet;

public class DotsThread extends Applet
    {
    LineOfDots blue Dots;

    public void init()
        {
        blue Dots = new LineOfDots(this, 50, Color.blue);
        blue Dots.start();
        }

    public void stop()
        {
        if((blue Dots != null) && blue Dots.isAlive())
            {
            blue Dots.stop();
            blue Dots = null;
            }
        }
    }

class LineOfDots extends Thread
    {
    Applet theApplet;
    int appWidth;
    int currXPos;
    int yPos;
    Color dotColour;
```

```
public LineOfDots(Applet a, int y, Color colour)
    {
    this.theApplet = a;
    yPos = y;
    dotColour = colour;
    currXPos = 0;
    appWidth = theApplet.size().width;
    }

public void run()
    {
    while(currXPos < appWidth)
        {
        Graphics g = theApplet.getGraphics();
        g.setColor(dotColour);
        g.drawString(".", currXPos, yPos);
        currXPos += 5;
        try
            {
            sleep(100);
            }
        catch(InterruptedException e) {}
        }
    }
}
```

The Runnable Interface

The second way of creating and using a thread is by use of the Runnable interface. If we want to add multithreading to an applet, allowing the thread to have access to the applet's private data, we must use the Runnable interface. In the above example the thread was created from a subclass of the Thread class.

However, we now want to include a thread as part of the applet class and as we are creating the applet by deriving from the Applet class we can't derive from the Thread class as well – there is no multiple inheritance in Java. The Runnable interface provides an abstract definition of the run() method – that is all it contains. To use a thread in an applet we therefore implement the Runnable interface and define a run() method to contain the main body of the thread code.

Lets look at the line of dots applet using the Runnable interface instead of the Thread class. Here is the amended source code:

Listing 18.2:
Using the Runnable interface to create threads

```
import java.awt.*;
import java.applet.Applet;

public class DotsRunnable extends Applet implements Runnable
    {
    Thread redDots;
    int appWidth;
    int currXPos;
    int yPos;
    Color dotColour;

    public void start()
        {
        if(blue Dots == null)
            {
            blue Dots = new Thread(this);
            blue Dots.start();
            }
        }

    public void stop()
        {
        if((blue Dots != null) && blue Dots.isAlive())
            {
            blue Dots.stop();
            blue Dots = null;
            }
        }

    public void run()
        {

        yPos = 50;
        dotColour = Color. blue;
        currXPos = 0;
        appWidth = this.size().width;

        while(currXPos < appWidth)
            {
```

```
Graphics g = getGraphics();
g.setColor(dotColour);
g.drawString(".", currXPos, yPos);
currXPos += 5;
try
   {
   blue.Dots.sleep(100);
   }
catch(InterruptedException e) {}
}
}
}
```

As you can see, the code is very similar to the first example – it has just moved around a little. The first difference is that implements Runnable has been added to the first line of the class definition:

```
public class DotsRunnable extends Applet implements Runnable
   {
   ...
   }
```

The instance variables used by the dot drawing thread are now in the main body of the applet. The initialisation of these variables is now part of the run() method. This method definition overrides the abstract run() method defined in the Runnable interface. The main loop of the dot drawing thread is still included within the run() method. The only other differences are that the thread is now started in the applet's start() method and stopped in the applet's stop() method. Thus, if the user leaves the page on which the applet is situated, the thread will be stopped.

Multiple Threads

We will now show an example which illustrates how easy it is to create and run a number of threads in parallel. This applet is based on our first example, but this time three threads of type LineOfDots are created – one red, one green and one blue. The thread class is unchanged, the only difference is within the applet class:

Listing 18.3:
The use of multiple threads (see Figure 18.2)

```java
public class MultiLines extends Applet
    {
    LineOfDots redDots;
    LineOfDots greenDots;
    LineOfDots blueDots;
    public void init()
        {
        redDots = new LineOfDots(this, 25, Color.red);
        greenDots = new LineOfDots(this, 50, Color.green);
        blueDots = new LineOfDots(this, 75, Color.blue);
        redDots.start();
        greenDots.start();
        blueDots.start();
        }
    }
```

If you run this applet you will see that the three lines are drawn across the screen at the same rate, illustrating that each thread is given an equal amount of the resources.

Figure 18.2: *The MultiLines applet (see Listing 18.3)*

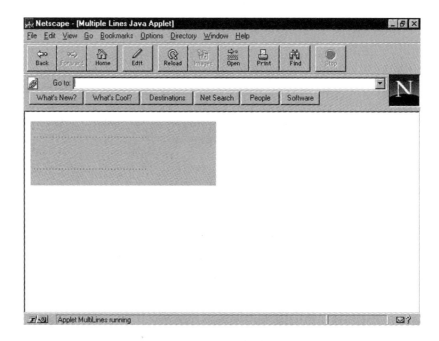

Controlling a Thread

Once a thread has been created there are many ways you can control and manage it. We will now talk about the various methods that you can utilise. The methods that we have seen so far are start(), stop() and run(). When you are deriving from the Thread class the start() and stop() methods become the default, but if you are using the Runnable interface you MUST declare these methods explicitly, otherwise the applet start() and stop() methods will be called.

start()

This method starts the execution of a thread by calling the run() method. You should determine if the thread has been created already – this is done by testing to see if the thread object is set to null:

```
public void start()
    {
    if(redDots == null)
        {
        redDots = new Thread(this);
        redDots.start();
        }
    }
```

If you try starting a thread that is already running an IllegalThread-StateException will be thrown. Note that the thread start() method is being called explicitly by specifying the redDots thread object and that the code is being run within the applet start() method.

stop()

This method stops a thread's execution. After the stop() method has been used, the thread will continue to exist within your application or applet as long as you continue to reference it. To ensure that the Java grabage collection recovers the resource allocated to the thread you must assign a value of null to the thread:

```
public void stop()
    {
    if((redDots != null) && redDots.isAlive())
        {
        redDots.stop();
```

```
            redDots = null;
            }
        }
```

run()

This method will, to C or C++ programmers, be familiar as the main function in either language. run() as a method contains the main code needed be executed by a thread.

```
public void run()
    {
  while(currXPos < appWidth)
        {
        Graphics g = theApplet.getGraphics();
        g.setColor(dotColour);
        g.drawString(".", currXPos, yPos);
        currXPos += 5;
        try
            {
            sleep(100);
            }
        catch(InterruptedException e) {}
        }
    }
```

suspend()

Suspends execution of a thread. If you want to start it running again you must use the resume() method.

resume()

Resumes execution of a suspended thread. It has no effect on a thread that has not been suspended.

yield()

This causes a thread to yield to any other runnable threads. If no other runnable threads exist, the current thread will carry on executing.

Naming Threads

Like any good language a strong naming policy is a necessity. In order to control threads that you create you can use a standard `Thread` constructor of naming them, and these names can consist of any valid Java string. Naming threads is a convenient way of tracking their usage. You can give a thread a name whenever it is created, at any point during its usage, and if needed you can also rename it.

To assign a name at creation time use the `Thread` constructor to make Java accept a string as an argument:

```
Thread testThread = new Thread("ThreadName");
```

This command creates a thread using the `new` method and then goes on to assign it a name "ThreadName".

getName()

Once a thread has been named you will need to control it during the life of the thread. If you want to query a thread for its name you can use the `getName()` method. This method will return the name that has been associated with a specified thread object.

```
System.out.println("The name of this thread is " +
                        testThread.getName());
```

setName()

Following the creation of a thread you can alter its name at any point using the `setName` method. A parent process of a thread, a thread itself or any other method that has been given access to a thread object can be used to rename a thread. For instance:

```
testThread.setName("NewThreadName");
```

This process changes the name of our previously defined `testThread` to "NewThreadName" from "ThreadName".

Thread Priorities

In Java you can give any thread a *priority*. The Java runtime system will look for the thread with the highest priority when it is scheduling threads for execution.

Priority settings range from MIN_PRIORITY (value = 1) to MAX_PRIORITY (value = 10). The standard is NORM_PRIORITY which has a value of 5.

When the runtime is looking for the next thread to be given a chance to run, it will first look for the thread with the highest priority. If all the threads have the same priority, then each will be given a chance in turn.

A thread will inherit the priority of the thread that created it. To modify the priority of a thread, you use the setPriority() method. For instance, in our multiple lines of dots example we could give the threads different priorites like this:

```
public void init()
    {
    redDots = new LineOfDots(this, 25, Color.red,
        Thread.MIN_PRIORITY);
    greenDots = new LineOfDots(this, 50, Color.green,
        Thread.NORM_PRIORITY);
    blueDots = new LineOfDots(this, 75, Color.blue,
        Thread.MAX_PRIORITY);
    redDots.start();
    greenDots.start();
    blueDots.start();
    }
```

In fact, if you try giving different priorities to threads you will get different results on different platforms. Under the Solaris operating system, the priorites will have an effect. However, Windows 95 or Windows NT, operate a time-slicing policy with threads and you will find, if you run the above example under Windows, that the lines will continue to be drawn at the same rates.

You should therefore not place too much emphasis on giving threads priorities as you will not be able to predict on which platform your applets are run. You should, however, make sure that your threads are cooperative with regard to other threads by using the sleep() and yield() methods to give other threads a chance to run.

Cooperation between Threads

You should always ensure that any threads that you include in your programs cooperate fully with other threads that may be running. During each thread loop, the sleep() or yield() methods should be called so that the thread does not hog the system resources. Threads that don't cooperate in this way are known as selfish threads.

If the purpose of a thread loop is to provide animation you would normally call the `sleep()` method once for every iteration of the loop. This has the twin benefits of slowing the animation down to a reasonable speed for viewing and allowing other threads to run. If the thread requires almost continuous operation it would not make sense to use the `sleep()` method. In this case you should call `yield()` whenever it is convenient.

Thread States

Threads can be in various states at any point in their life cycle. These are the four states:

New

When a thread is first created by the `new` operator and the `start()` method has not been called, the thread is in the new state. It hasn't had any system resources allocated to it yet and no code has been executed. If you make a call to any method other than `start()` or `stop()` when the thread is in this state an `IllegalThreadStateException` will be thrown.

Runnable

The `start()` method organises the system resources that the thread will require, schedules it and calls the `run()` method. At this point the thread is in the runnable state. This doesn't always mean that it is running, but that it is capable of being run.

Blocked or Not Runnable

A thread becomes *blocked* or *not runnable* when one of these events occur:

1. The thread's `sleep()` method is called.
2. The thread's `suspend()` method is called.
3. The thread calls it's `wait()` method.

4. The thread is waiting for an input/output operation to complete.

For example, in our examples we have used the `sleep()` method to put the thread to sleep for 100 milliseconds:

```
try
   {
   redDots.sleep(100);
   }
catch(InterruptedException e) {}
```

During these 100 milliseconds the `redDots` thread is in the blocked state. Once the time is up, it re-enters the runnable state. It still might not begin running again – that will depend upon the processor usage.

The way that a thread has become *blocked* will determine how it can be moved back to a *runnable* state:

- If the `sleep()` method was used, the number of milliseconds specified must pass.
- If the `suspend()` method was used, then someone must call the `resume()` method.
- If the thread has called the `wait()` method, then the object concerned must call the `notify()` or `notifyAll()` method. (This is covered in the section on synchronisation later in the chapter.)
- If the thread is waiting for an input/ouput operation to finish, then that I/O must complete first.

You must use the correct escape route for a blocked thread – using `resume()` on a thread that has been put to sleep will not immediately return it to a runnable state.

Dead

When the `run()` method of a thread finishes executing and exits normally, the thread will become dead. A thread will also be killed if it's `stop()` method is called.

The `isAlive()` method

This method returns `true` if the thread is either runnable or blocked, `false` if it is new or dead. You cannot, however, tell which of these states the thread actually occupies.

Thread Groups

Thread groups provide you with a way of organising the threads in your programs into groups that can be manipulated as single objects, rather than individually. This can be very useful if you want to, say, kill a number of threads in one go.

A thread group is created like this:

```
ThreadGroup myThreadGroup = new ThreadGroup(groupName);
```

where groupName is a unique string that identifies the group of threads.

Most of the Thread methods, plus a couple of extra ones, are available within the ThreadGroup class and enable you to perform group operations on threads. For example, the following slice of code uses the activeCount() method to determine whether any threads within the group myThreadGroup are still running, and, if so, kills them all by using the stop() method:

```
if (mwThreadGroup.activeCount() > 0)
    {
    myThreadGroup.stop();
    }
```

Keeping it in sync

One of the problems with threads is that they are not independent processes with a complete copy of data objects, as with a process defined in C or C++. This could therefore lead to a scenario where you are not certain which thread will access an object at any given time, complicated by the fact that multiple threads can access the same objects or methods.

The way around this potential nightmare is to use the synchronized keyword to lock an object just long enough to execute a block of code. Once used no other thread can make changes to a specified object until that block of code has been executed. Lets look at a simple example. We will use the Rectangle class that we developed in the chapter on Classes and Objects. If we are using the instance variables of a Rectangle object to update other variables, we can make use of the synchronized keyword to prevent any other threads from changing the rectangle variables while we are accessing them:

```
public void getDimensions(Rectangle myRect)
  {
  int theWidth, theHeight;
  synchronized (myRect)
    {
    theWidth = myRect.width;
    theHeight = myRect.height;
    }
  System.out.println("The width is " + theWidth);
  System.out.println("The height is " + theHeight);
  }
```

What this code does is set up a method called getDimensions() which contains a synchronized piece of code. This code, which we define as the object myRect, remains locked until the block of code making up the synchronized statement is executed. This ensures that the values of theWidth and theHeight, which are printed to screen, can both be obtained without any other thread amending the rectangle variables in the mean time.

You can also use the synchronized keyword to act as a modifier for methods, ensuring that only one thread at a time executes any given method. So our earlier example could be altered to the following construct:

```
public synchronized void getDimensions(Rectangle myRect)
  {
  int theWidth, theHeight;

  theWidth = myRect.width;
  theHeight = myRect.height;

  System.out.println("The width is " + theWidth);
  System.out.println("The height is " + theHeight);
  }
```

Now no other threads can change the rectangle values while the method is executing. When a thread enters the synchronized method it is guaranteed that no other thread can execute the method on the same object until the first thread has exited the method. A queue of threads is set up waiting for the object to become available. Any object in Java that has synchronized methods is known as a *monitor*.

wait() **and** notify()

There are times when you might want to update the instance variables of an object but only when a certain condition becomes true. For example, in the following code extract the method TransferStock() is used to transfer a quantity from one stock location to another.

Before doing so, it checks that the value held in the variable fromLocation is greater than the value of quantity. If the value of fromLocation is not sufficient the thread goes to sleep for a short while in the hope that another thread using the same method will have transferred some stock to it.

```
public synchronized void TransferStock(int fromLocation,
          int toLocation, int quantity)
  {
  while (fromLocation < quantity)
    {
    try
      {
      Thread.sleep(10);
      } catch (InterruptedException e) {}
    }
  fromLocation -= quantity;
  toLocation += quantity;
  }
```

The method has been tagged synchronized so only one thread can update the fromLocation and toLocation variables at one time. However, because the update is conditional, problems can occur. If fromLocation does not have sufficient stock to allow the transfer out then the thread that has called the method will lock up the method until it does, thus preventing any other thread from using the method to transfer stock in to that location. The result is a deadlock situation.

The answer is to use the wait() and notify() methods. Here is the above TransferStock method with these methods added:

```
public synchronized void TransferStock(int fromLocation,
          int toLocation, int quantity)
  {
  while (fromLocation < quantity)
    {
    try
      {
```

```
        wait();
        } catch (InterruptedException e) {}
    }
    fromLocation -= quantity;
    toLocation += quantity;
    notify();
}
```

When a thread calls the TransferStock() method and the value in fromLocation is not sufficient for the transfer to take place, the thread calls the wait() method. This will cause the thread to be deactivated and placed in a queue, waiting for another thread to transfer stock to the fromLocation.

When another thread calls the TransferStock() method to move stock to the location that is the fromLocation of the first thread it will call the notify() method when it has finished. This will reactivate the waiting thread and give it the opportunity to check the total held in it's fromLocation and, if the quantity is high enough, go ahead with the transfer.

You must ensure that there is a matching notify() method for every wait() method. Otherwise any waiting threads will not be released from the queue and will wait forever.

Summary

Let's take a look at what we've discussed. Java uses threads to run multiple blocks of code in parallel. It is a lightweight process which means it does not consume massive amounts of system resources, and threads do not make complete new copies of variables in the way that C or C++ does when a fork command is issued. This allows for much faster thread start up and execution. But this causes a problem because it opens the data of a thread up to any other thread, but you can get around this by using the synchronization keyword.

A thread is based on the base class of Thread and can be created by simply extending the Thread class or by invoking the Runnable interface. By using Runnable you can add threading to an existing class such as the applet class.

Java Input and Output

Introduction to Streams

The `java.io` package contains all the interfaces, classes and methods needed to implement the input and output of data in your Java applications or applets. The backbone of the `java.io` package is a technology called Streams. Streams are the heart of I/O in Java and that's why we want you to understand one of the most important parts of the Java language before you enter into handling I/O programming.

The simple idea behind a stream is that it provides a way for your Java programs to send or receive information to or from any data source. The source or destination of a stream can be almost anything – a file on disk, the memory in the computer or the internet itself. The important thing is that the methods used to accomplish all this are all pretty similar, providing a level of abstraction that makes the transfer of information consistent from any source to any destination.

It is worth remembering that the whole idea of Java is to create portable code that will run across multiple platforms. Therefore the code you generate abstracts elements like I/O in order to achieve this portability.

Streams are either *input streams*, for reading data from any source, such as a web server or a disk file, or *output streams,* for writing data to any destination, such as the screen or a printer. Data can also be exchanged between two threads, using a *pipe*, the thread writing the data being known as the *producer* and the thread reading the data known as the *consumer.*

Java makes heavy use of streams internally and they will have many uses within your Java software. Think about it. You can use streams to read and write data to all sorts of devices, databases, files, other processes and even to network sockets. Given this power you might be thinking that programming streams is going to be a nightmare. But it is not that bad. The classes for streams all use common methods, which really makes using them quite easy. To use them you must import the java.io package into any application or applet you create that needs to use any of the I/O classes.

Java defines a whole host of classes that enable you to move data around in your applications and applets and it is really down to you to choose which classes best suit your needs. The reality is that each have their own advantages and disadvantages and range of flexibility.

The I/O classes in Java are all based upon two abstract classes – InputStream and OutputStream. As they are abstract classes, the common methods that apply to all the I/O classes are defined within these classes, but the actual code to carry out the I/O is not implemented. That is left to the subclasses. We will now take a look at all the classes that are available to you for both input and output streams, starting with input.

The InputStream **Class**

This is the abstract class that contains every derivative of all types of data inputs to the Java language, with its subclasses using most or all of its methods. When dealing with input data streams inside Java you must remember that all input stream classes are based on the class InputStream. What we will do now is take a look at the various subclasses to this class, how they work, provide sample code and take a look at the methods that you can use.

Before we begin we should just mention that you need to import java.io into your application. This is done easily with the following statement:

```
import java.io.*;
```

Input streams are the data streams that you will be sending to be accepted by and processed by another process. There are a large number of different classes of input streams and each of them is extensible by a programmer. They are listed in Table 19.1.

Table 19.1: *Input stream classes*

BufferedInputStream	This is a filter input stream that reads data from a buffer to minimise the number of reads needed.
ByteArrayInputStream	This reads data from an array of bytes.
DataInputStream	A filter input stream that reads primitive data types instead of just bytes of data, as most other input streams do.
FileInputStream	Reads data from a file.
FilterInputStream	This is an abstract class that is the superclass of the input filter streams: BufferedInput-Stream, DataInputStream, LineNumberInput-Stream and PushbackInputStream.
InputStream	the superclass to all input stream classes.
LineNumberInputStream	This is a filter input stream for counting lines.
PipedInputStream	Reads data from a pipe connected to a second process.
PushbackInputStream	A filter input stream that allows you to push a single character back onto an input stream.
SequenceInputStream	This can be used to treat multiple sequential input streams as if they were a single input stream.
StringBufferInputStream	Reads data from a string of characters.

OK. We'll come back to the input stream classes in further detail shortly, but for the moment let us look at how you interact with them. There are two types of method that you can apply to these classes: ones that are guaranteed to work and ones that may not.

Those that are guaranteed to garner a result are read(), skip(), close() and markAvailable(). The ones may or may not work are available(), mark() and reset().

It may seem strange that some methods work whilst others fail to. The reason for this is that they may either not be available as valid methods or that a producer which created them returns inaccurate or inconsistent results. This odd state of affairs arises because some producers send consistent data, with others not producing data until the Java stream-handling code indicates it is ready.

Let's take a look at these methods. Remember that, although we are using InputStream in our examples, you will usually be using one of it's subclasses.

read()

This is the most common method that you will apply to an input stream. It does what its name states: read data. Several variants of the read method are available, with the differences relating to the amount of data that is read, where data starts and stops within a stream, to where data is written and so on. The method you apply to perform a read depends totally upon your applications needs at a given time.

One consistent feature of a read method is that all are based on what is known as a blocking read. This means that once a read() method has been invoked it will not return any data until all the data requested has been received or an exception occurs. The normal way around this is to assign a thread to each read so that other processing can be carried out while you are waiting for the read to complete.

Note   All read() methods deliver an IOException exception, and this must be handled by an application. You can do this with a try/catch structure or by simply adding a throws statement to a class declaration. Table 19.2 lists the read methods methods defined in InputStream:

Table 19.2: *Read methods defined in InputStream*

`int read();`	This is a simple method of reading a byte from an input stream. The byte of data read is returned by the function itself, and supplied as an `int`.
`int read(byte[] buffer);`	This reads data into a buffer, or an array of bytes. This method will attempt to read enough data until it has filled the buffer.
`int read(byte[] buffer, int offset, int length);`	This last method builds on this by looking to fill a buffer, but not before it looks at a pre-defined offset into the data stream and will only then read a pre-defined number of bytes.

In all circumstances a read method will return an integer. You can rec-ognise when there is no more data to be read from a stream because a -1 will be returned.

Here is an example that reads an input stream and counts the number of bytes:

```
int CountBytes(InputStream in)
  {
  try
    {
    int numBytes = 0;
    int c;
while ((c = in.read()) != -1)
      numBytes++;
    }
  catch (IOException e)
    {
    System.err.println("IO error reading data: " + e);
    }
  return (numBytes);
  }
```

skip()

This method can be used to bypass a set number of bytes within a input stream. The logic behind this is to give an application the ability to move quickly through a data stream avoiding data it does not want to access, or to move quickly to a pre-determined point in the stream. In the case of an input stream for a database this method can be used to skip past a series of fixed length records to get to the records wanted. C and C++ programmers will see the commonality between what skip can achieve and the action that an lseek function performs. However, this method only works in a forward direction and will not go backwards through a stream's data. It is possible to go backwards through a stream but in order to do this you need to implement the mark() and reset() methods to perform this.

As with the read() method the skip() method will also throw an IOEx-ception exception which must be dealt with using a try/catch block, or by adding throws to the class declaration. The correct syntax for this method is:

```
long skip(long num);
```

A skip method accepts a single argument of type long: the number of bytes to skip in an input stream. The fact that data streams are of a completely mixed length means that if more bytes need to be skipped than can be handled by a long, then just use more than one skip statement in your program. skip() returns the number of bytes actually skipped. This will be less than num if the end of the stream is reached.

This example outputs every numToSkip character in an input stream:

```java
void SkipData(InputStream in, int numToSkip)
  {
  try
    {
    int c;
    while ((c = in.read()) != -1)
      {
      System.out.print((char)c);
      in.skip(numToSkip);
      }
    }
  catch (IOException e)
    {
    System.err.println("IO error skipping bytes: " + e);
    }
  }
```

close()

This method is used by an application or applet to close a data stream that it no longer needs access to. Although Java always closes an input stream automatically whenever a program exits, which is why many examples do not show a close statement within them, it is always good practise to close resources whenever they are no longer needed. Here is an example,

```java
void CloseStream(InputStream in)
  {
  try
      in.close();
  catch (IOException e)
      {
      System.err.println("IO error closing input stream: " + e);
      }
  }
```

available()

This is a finger in the air method. It is used to determine if data is ready to be read without blocking the input stream and can also be used to check to see if there is enough data available in the stream for processing before some other method, such as read(), is called into use. But be careful when using this method. It does not always return valid information for all input streams it checks.

In some circumstances a stream will always return a 0, whereas other streams will return inconsistent values. This can be attributed to the unknowns associated with the producer process and the way that the underlying Java code handles the links between the producer and the consumer processes.

In other languages, such as when you deal with C or C++, it is best to ensure that the required amount of data you are requesting with a read command is available. This is done because a read command more often than not blocks until all data is needed, which is really the only way to ensure that an application does not hang while it is waiting for data. But in Java you can turn to threads to handle this issue. What you do is assign a thread to perform the reading of an input stream, which the thread can then worry about blocking, and also worries about waiting to obtain the data you requested. This way of performing the function allows other threads to continue to process instead of waiting around for data. Given that threads are easily available to Java programmers, use of the available() method is actually not that useful, and why the problems of returning incorrect or inconsistent results not that big a worry. The syntax for this method is:

```
int available();
```

The method returns an int which indicates the number of bytes in an input stream that can be accessed/read without blocking. This method does not have any parameters, and the return value is an int. Although streams can be of unlimited size, which means that more than an int's worth of data is available, only an int's worth is reported by this method. This sample shows how the available() method works:

```
boolean IsAmountAvailable(InputStream in, int amount)
    {
    boolean returnCode = false;
    try
        {
        if (in.available() >= amount)
```

```
            returnCode = true;
        }
    catch (IOException e)
        {
        System.err.println("IO error checking availabilty: " + e);
        }
    return (returnCode);
    }
```

mark(), markSupported() and reset()

The first of these methods, mark(), is used to choose a point/location within a input stream and mark it for use at a later time. This method is not, however, generic to all input streams, with a separate method called markSupported() which determines whether an individual input stream supports the function. Once it has been decided whether an input stream supports the mark() method you can then move on to use the reset() method to return to the point that has been marked with the mark() method.

The limitations of these methods – mark() and reset() – is that they are application specific, that is a program is forced to specify the maximum amount of data that can go through an input stream before the reset() method can be called. The problem is that if more than the defined amount of data passes through the input stream, the reset() method will throw an exception. Another issue is that there is no way to attach multiple marks to an input stream. If a second mark is called before reset() has ran its course then the new mark is moved to its new location with its new limit on how much data is read before a reset occurs. The syntax for the methods is:

```
void mark(int readLimit);
boolean markSupported();
void reset();
```

A mark() method will only accept a single parameter of a type int, how much data in an input stream can pass before a reset() method is called. The markSupported() method does not have any arguments but returns a boolean value to show whether a mark() function can be used against a particular stream. The last method, reset simply resets an input stream to the point that at which a mark was called.

This sample code reads some data, then marks the position, reads some more and then returns to the marked position:

```
InputStream in;
if (in.markSupported())
   {
   ...// read some data
   in.mark(512);
   ...// read some more data (must be less than 512 bytes)
   in.reset();
   ...// read the data again
   }
else
   {
   ...// do something else
   }
```

InputStream **Subclasses**

Let's now take a look at each one of the subclasses in detail, examining how each can be used to input data into your program.

FilterInputStream

A filter input stream filters the data passed to it in an input stream so that the data is changed in some way. This subclass has itself four more subclasses and these are BufferedInputStream, DataInputStream, LineNumberInputStream and PushBackInputStream. The reality is that the top level class – FilterInputStream – does not perform a function, rather its four subclasses perform the filtering of data.

The best way to think about how this class works is that the top level class provides a pipe into which data can be entered, with its subclasses performing the action of slicing and dicing the data in the pipe into sizeable chunks that can be used by an application or applet.

ByteArrayInputStream

This extension to the FilterInputStream class is used to create an input stream from a byte array. The class contains three variables that can be used to control the stream:

- buf the name of the byte array where the data is stored
- count the number of bytes to be used within the byte array
- pos the current position of a read within the byte array

This example reads in the bytes from a byte array, `alphabet`, and then outputs every other character, using the `skip()` method to jump a byte each time:

```java
import java.io.*;
public class OddLetters
  {
  public static void main(String[] args)
    {
    byte Alphabet[] = { 'a','b','c','d','e','f','g','h','i',
                        'j','k','l','m','n','o','p','q','r',
                        's','t','u','v','w','x','y','z'};
    ByteArrayInputStream in =
                  = new ByteArrayInputStream(alphabet);
    int c;
    while ((c = in.read()) > -1)
      {
      System.out.print((char)c);
      in.skip(1);
      }
    System.out.println();
    }
  }
```

This class also allows for the use of the `reset()` method which resets an input stream back to its beginning. But there is no use of the `mark()` method to mark a specific location within a stream.

BufferedInputStream

This class is a subclass of `FilterInputStream`. The object of this class is to create a read buffer full of data. The action of this class can be viewed as making a smooth stream of data which allows for continuous reading of bytes, instead of a staggered flow of data as a stream waits for data to reach it. When a request is made to read the data, the buffered stream is read rather than the original input stream. The physical size of both the buffer and the reads performed on it can be controlled via its methods. Note that is the only class to use both the `mark()` and `reset()` methods correctly. Because this is a filter stream you can use it with other stream objects, `FileInputStream` for instance, so that you can properly utilise these methods with streams that don't usually support them.

DataInputStream

This is a filter input stream that implements the `DataInput` interface. The simple action of this class is to be used to read primitive data types, and interpret them across platforms in order to make them accessible to Java no matter what platform it is running on. A list of the available `read()` methods is shown in Table 19.3.

Table 19.3: *Read methods for DataInputStream*

`public boolean readBoolean() throws IOException`	Reads a boolean from the input stream.
`public byte readByte() throws IOException`	Reads a byte from the input stream.
`public char readChar() throws IOException`	Reads a 16-bit Unicode char from the input stream.
`public double readDouble() throws IOException`	Reads a 64-bit double from the input stream.
`public float readFloat()throws IOException`	Reads a 32-bit float from the input stream.
`public int readInt() throws IOException`	Reads a 32-bit int from the input stream.
`public long readLong() throws IOException`	Reads a 64-bit long from the input stream.
`public short readShort() throws IOException`	Reads a 16-bit short from the input stream.
`public int readUnsignedByte() throws IOException`	Reads an unsigned 8-bit byte from the input stream.
`public int readUnsignedShort() throws IOException`	Reads an unsigned 16-bit short from the input stream.
`public String readLine() throws IOException`	Reads a string of characters terminated by a newline.
`public String readUTF() throws IOException`	Reads a Unicode string terminated by a newline.

LineNumberInputStream

As its title gives away, this class is used to keep track of line numbers which could, for example, be used to mark and reset data streams. It is a filter input stream that counts the number of line terminators that are encountered as it filters an input stream.

A line terminator is either a "\n", a "\r", or a combination "\r\n". Each time one of these terminators occurs in the input stream, the filter increments a counter, which starts at 1. The current count can be obtained using the `getLineNumber()` method. You can also set the current line number with `setLineNumber()`.

PushbackInputStream

The idea behind this class is to create a one-byte input buffer that can allow an input stream to backtrack one byte after it has been read. The idea being that it is possible to test the next byte of data in a stream without having to perform an action. This can be especially useful when parsing a stream so that you can determine how you want to handle the data by looking ahead to see what comes next. A byte that has already been read can be pushed back using the unread() method.

FileInputStream

The basic function of this class is to allow Java to read files. It works only with sequential files and not indexed files or hash tables. It is wise to ensure that you always close a file input stream if you plan to make subsequent accesses to it after the end of a file has been reached. The mark() and reset() methods are not available to this class. The only way to return to a position within a file input stream is to use the skip() method and then read a stream until the desired data is found.

This example uses both the FileInputStream and FileOutputStream classes. It opens an existing file, called "testfile.in", reads the contents of the file, and outputs the data to a new file, "testfile.out".

Listing 19.1:
Using the FileIn-
putStream and
FileOutput-
Stream *classes to*
copy a file

```
import java.io.*;
public class CopyFile
    {
    public static void main(String[] args)
        {
        try
            {
            FileInputStream fisFile
                        = new FileInputStream("testfile.in");
            FileOutputStream fosFile
                        = new FileOutputStream("testfile.out");
            int c;
            while ((c = fisFile.read()) > -1)
                fosFile.write(c);
                fisFile.close();
                fosFile.close();
            }
catch (FileNotFoundException e)
```

```
        {
        System.err.println("CopyFile: " + e);
        }
     catch (IOException e)
        {
        System.err.println("CopyFile: " + e);
        }
     }
}
```

PipedInputStream

The PipedInputStream and PipedOutputStream classes must be used together. They allow you to communicate between two threads that have a producer/consumer relationship. One thread sends output data to a pipe. The consumer thread receives the data by reading it from the pipe. As you have no doubt guessed, an output stream to a pipe is provided by the PipedOutputStream class.

To read the corresponding input stream, PipedInputStream must be used. Any unread data is buffered by the pipe. When the pipe is full, the output thread blocks until space becomes available again. The input thread blocks if the pipe becomes empty until more bytes are sent to the pipe.

This extract of code shows how a piped connection between two threads is set up:

```
PipedInputStream pipeIn = new PipedInputStream();
PipedOutputStream pipeOut = new PipedOutputStream(pipeIn);
```

The producer thread can now use the write() method to output data to pipeOut and the consumer thread can read the data from pipeIn.

The connection can also be set up explicitly by using the connect() method. Here is the same example using connect():

```
PipedInputStream pipeIn = new PipedInputStream();
PipedOutputStream pipeOut = new PipedOutputStream();
pipeIn.connect(pipeOut);
```

SequenceInputStream

The use of this class is to enable multiple streams to be read in sequence and then be converted into one single data stream. The first input stream is read to its end, then the next stream is read to its conclusion and so on and so forth. The output data is issued as a single stream, and the only methods available to this class are read() and close().

You could of course just read in each input stream one by one and process them that way. This class is useful, though, when you have an existing method that will only accept one input stream.

StringBufferInputStream

This class is used to create an input stream from the data stored in a string buffer. The stream of data that is accessed is controlled using three variables:

- buf the name of the byte array where the data is stored
- count the number of bytes to be used within the byte array
- pos the current position of a read within the byte array

This class is very similar to the ByteArrayInputStream, but whereas that class inputs data into a stream as an array of bytes, StringBuffer-InputStream creates an input stream as an array of characters.

The OutputStream **Class**

An output stream is simply the data stream generated by what we have defined as a producer stream. As with the input streams that we have discussed there are a number of different classes that pertain to output streams and the data within them.

You will see that just about every input stream class that we have talked about in the previous section has a corresponding output stream class. The OutputStream class is the abstract class that defines the methods that can be applied to output streams and contains all the output stream subclasses. These are listed in Table 19.4.

Now you know the classes available to you here are the three main methods that can be applied to them.

Table 19.4:

BufferedOutputStream	This is a filter output stream that writes data to a buffer in order to minimise the actual writes that need to be made.
ByteArrayOutputStream	Simply writes data to an byte array.
DataOutputStream	A filter output stream that writes primitive data types to a stream in the form of binary data.
FileOutputStream	Writes data into an actual file.
FilterOutputStream	This is an abstract class that is the superclass of the output filter streams: BufferedOutputStream, DataOutputStream, and PrintStream.
OutputStream	the superclass to all output stream classes.
PipedOutputStream	This one writes data to a pipe.
PrintStream	A filter output stream used to take primitive data types and convert them to a printable form.

write()

This is the most basic method for writing data to an output stream. As with the read() method there are a number of restrictions associated with its use. For example, all writes inside Java are based on a blocking write, which means that when data is written the write() method will not return a value until all the data has been sent and accepted or an exception has occurred. The main issue with this is the continuation of an application during the time it takes for the write to be completed. By now you should understand that this performance issue within Java is not really a problem. All you do is assign a thread to the task at hand and the application or applet will continue to run at optimum performance. As with the earlier section on input classes, all Java output classes will throw an IOException exception when used. Here is the syntax for the three forms of the write() method:

- void write(int b);
- void write(byte[] buffer);
- void write (byte[] buffer, int offset, int length)

This example copies the bytes from an input stream to an output stream:

```
void CopyData(InputStream in, OutputStream out)
  {
  try
    {
    int c;
    while ((c = in.read()) != -1)
        out.write(c);
    out.flush();
    }
  catch (IOException e)
    {
    System.err.println("IO copying data: " + e);
    }
  }
```

flush()

This method is used when you want any data that has been placed into a buffer to be forced out and written to an output device, such as a disk file. A use of this method is when dealing with a lengthy block that has been caused by a write method. Sometimes a consumer process within Java can take a long time and this can be overcome by using the flush() method to make make Java accept the data.

close()

This method is practically identical to the one described when handling the close of an output stream. You use this one to end a stream that is no longer needed by an application or applet.

OutputStream **Subclasses**

Let's now take a look at each of the OutputStream subclasses in detail, examining how they can be used to output data from your program.

FilterOutputStream

This class has three subclasses to it: DataOutputStream, BufferedOutputStream and PrintStream. Just as the FileInputStream we talked about earlier performs no real action, so this top level class also performs no action, allowing its three subclasses to perform all of the work.

BufferedOutputStream

This class implements all of the methods defined by the superclass Output-putStream. The key feature of this class is its ability to create a write buffer that takes the form of an array of bytes. It smooths out a stream of data so that a Java application or applet can perform a continuous read. The size of a buffer and the size of the reads performed on it can be controlled by its methods.

DataOutputStream

This class implements the DataOutput interface, and is a complete inverse of the DataInputStream in as much as it is used to write primitive data types. Its methods include those listed in Table 19.5.

Table 19.5:

`public final void writeBoolean(boolean b) throws IOException`	Writes a boolean to the output stream.
`public final void writeByte(byte b) throws IOException`	Writes an 8-bit byte to the output stream.
`public final void writeChar(char c) throws IOException`	Writes a 16-bit Unicode char to the output stream.
`public final void writeDouble(double d) throws IOException`	Writes a 64-bit double to the output stream.
`public final void writeFloat(float f) throws IOException`	Writes a 32-bit float to the output stream.
`public final void writeInt(int i) throws IOException`	Writes a 32-bit int to the output stream.
`public final void writeLong(long l) throws IOException`	Writes a 64-bit long to the output stream.
`public final void writeShort(short s) throws IOException`	Writes a 16-bit short to the output stream.
`public final void writeBytes(String s) throws IOException`	Writes a string as a byte sequence to the output stream.
`public final void writeChars(String s) throws IOException`	Writes a string as a character sequence to the output stream.
`public final void writeUTF(String s) throws IOException`	Writes a Unicode string to the output stream.

PrintStream

The use of this class is to write data to an output stream formatted as a string. It is the class used to perform output that you have already seen before such as:

```
System.out.print()
System.out.println()
```

When applying this class it is possible to perform autoflushing. It has two constructors:

- `PrintStream(OutputStream)` – used to create a new `PrintStream`
- `PrintStream(OutputStream, boolean)` – creates a new `Print-Stream`, with autoflushing

If the second constructor is used and the second argument set to `true`, a `flush()` is actioned after every character has been written.

The methods used by the `PrintStream` class to format primitive data types for output are listed in Table 19.6.

Table 19.6: *Methods for the PrintStream classes*

`public void print(Object obj)`	Prints an object using the string resulting from toString().
`public void print(String s)`	Prints a string in ASCII (not Unicode).
`public void print(char c[])`	Prints an array of characters in ASCII (not Unicode).
`public void print(char c)`	Prints a character in ASCII (not Unicode).
`public void print(int i)`	Prints an integer.
`public void print(long l)`	Prints a long integer.
`public void print(float f)`	Prints a floating-point number.
`public void print(double d)`	Prints a double-precision floating-point number.
`public void print(boolean b)`	Prints a boolean value.
`public void println()`	Outputs a blank line

Table 19.6: *Methods for the PrintStream classes (continued)*

```
public void println(Object obj)
public void println(String s)
public void println(char c[])
public void println(char c)
public void println(int i)
public void println(long l)
public void println(float f)
public void println(double d)
public void println(boolean b)
```

These methods print the relevant data value followed by a newline

The following example shows how the PrintStream class is used to format three different primitive types into strings. Three arrays are created, a String array, a double array and an int array. The println() method of PrintStream is used to output the data – to a file in this case – as character strings. Notice how the instance of the filter class is "wrapped" around the FileOutputStream object.

Listing 19.2: *Formatting output using the PrintStream class*

```
import java.io.*;
public class PrintStock
    {
    public static void main(String[] args)
        {
        String productName[] = { "Hammer", "Chisel", "Screwdriver" };
        double productPrice[] = { 8.99, 6.50, 3.69 };
        int productQuantity[] = { 23, 14, 38 };
        try
            {
            PrintStream prOut =
                new PrintStream(new FileOutputStream("output.txt"));

            for (int i = 0; i < 3; i++)
                {
                prOut.println("Product : " + productName[i]);
                prOut.println("Price   : " + productPrice[i]);
                prOut.println("Quantity: " + productQuantity[i]);
                }
```

```
        prOut.flush();
        prOut.close();
        }
    catch (IOException e)
        {
        System.err.println("PrintStock: " + e);
        }
    }
}
```

ByteArrayOutputStream

This acts as the counterpart to the ByteArrayInputStream and is used to create an output stream of data to an array of bytes. Or to look at it another way, you use it to push the output data from a Java application or applet into a predefined buffer. This data is controlled via two variables:

- buf – the name of a buffer where data is stored
- Count – the number of bytes that are physically stored in the buffer

FileOutputStream

This class enables Java to write data into a file. It is important that you always close a file output stream you have created after the end of a file has been reached. If you do not properly terminate it with an end of file marker you will have errors thrown up by Java.

See the FileInputStream and PrintStream examples.

PipedOutputStream

The use of this class is to move data to and from threads that have been defined and piped together using the PipedInputStream class. The two classes are intrinsically linked together and therefore must always be used together.

See the section on PipedInputStream for further details.

Miscellaneous I/O Classes

The java.io package that ships with the JDK also comes with two extra classes for dealing with files. These are File and RandomAccessFile.

File

The File class is used to represent a filename. What you cannot do with this class is read or write data to a file, but what you can do is interrogate a file to get information such as name and path. You can also interact with the underlying file system by creating directories, deleting and renaming files, obtaining file permission settings and listing the files contained within a directory. Table 19.7 lists the methods available to you.

Table 19.7: *Methods for File*

public boolean canRead()	Determines if the application can read from the specified file.
public boolean canWrite()	Determines if the application can write to this file.
public boolean delete()	Deletes the file specified by this object.
public boolean exists()	Determines if this file exists.
public String getAbsolutePath()	Generates the absolute pathname of this file.
public String getName()	Returns the filename of this file.
public String getParent()	Returns the parent directory of this file.
public String getPath()	Returns the pathname of this file.
public boolean isAbsolute()	Determines if the pathname of the file is absolute.
public boolean isDirectory()	Determines whether this is a directory.
public boolean isFile()	Determines whether this is a file.
public long lastModified()	Returns the date and time the file was last modified.
public long length()	Returns the size of the file in bytes.

Table 19.7: *Methods for File (continued)*

`public String[] list()`	Lists the files in the directory specified by this file.
`public boolean mkdir()`	Creates a directory whose path name is specified by this file.
`public boolean mkdirs()`	Creates all the directories in the pathname.
`public boolean renameTo()`	Renames the file.

The following example application uses the File class to list all the files in the current directory. As well as each file's name, the access rights, size and last modification date are included in the list.

Listing 19.3:
Using the File class to list files in a directory (see Figure 19.1)

```java
import java.awt.*;
import java.io.*;
import java.util.Date;

public class ListFiles extends Frame
    {
    List dirList;
    Button btnQuit;
    String fileDetails[];

    public ListFiles(String dirName) throws IOException
        {
        super("Directory: " + dirName);

        dirList = new List(15, false);
        dirList.setFont(new Font("Courier", Font.PLAIN, 12));
        btnQuit = new Button("Quit");

        Panel pnlButtons = new Panel();
        pnlButtons.setLayout(new FlowLayout());
        pnlButtons.add(btnQuit);

        setLayout(new BorderLayout());

        add("South", pnlButtons);
        add("Center", dirList);

        ListFilesInDir(dirName);
```

```java
        }

    public void ListFilesInDir(String dirName) throws IOException
        {
        File directory = new File(dirName);
        String files[];

        dirList.clear();

        files = directory.list();

        fileDetails = new String[files.length];

        for (int i = 0; i < files.length; i++)
            GetFileDetails(new File(directory, files[i]), i);

        for (int i = 0; i < files.length; i++)
            dirList.addItem(fileDetails[i]);
        }

    public void GetFileDetails(File f, int item)
        {
        String details;

        details = f.getName() + "    ";
        details += f.canRead() ? "r" : "-";
        details += f.canWrite() ? "w" : "-";
        details += "    ";
        details += f.length() + "    ";
        details += new Date(f.lastModified());

        fileDetails[item] = details;
        }

    public boolean handleEvent(Event evt)
        {
        if (evt.id == evt.WINDOW_DESTROY)
            System.exit(0);
        return super.handleEvent(evt);
        }

    public boolean action(Event evt, Object arg)
```

```
        {
        if (evt.target instanceof Button)
            {
            if (arg == "Quit")
                {
                System.exit(0);
                }
            return true;
            }
        return false;
        }

    public static void main(String[] args) throws IOException
        {
        String theDirectory;

        theDirectory = System.getProperty("user.dir");
        Frame lf = new ListFiles(theDirectory);
        lf.resize(400, 250);
        lf.show();
        }
    }
```

The ListFiles constructor sets up a frame consisting of a scrollable list and a Quit button and then calls the ListFilesInDir() method to obtain the files in the current directory. The ListFilesInDir() method first creates a File object of the directory passed as an argument. It then uses the File object list() method to create an array of strings to hold the file names.

We then have two for loops. The first cycles through the list of file names, calling the method GetFileDetails() for each file in the list. The first argument to GetFileDetails() is a File object created for the file being processed. Within the GetFileDetails() method, the File methods are used to obtain the required information about each file. A string is constructed and added to the fileDetails string array. We haven't bothered to format this string to any great extent as the purpose of the example is to illustrate the way the file list is constructed rather than the quality of the display.

The second for loop in ListFilesInDir() adds each description string to the scrollable list.

The only other thing worth mentioning is the line in the main() method:

```
theDirectory = System.getProperty("user.dir");
```

This returns a string containing the current directory.

Figure 19.1: *The ListFiles application (see Listing 19.3)*

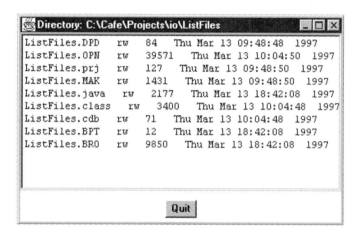

RandomAccessFile

The RandomAccessFile represents a random-access file, allowing you to read or write data from any point in a file. Files can be opened for reading only or for read/write access.

It includes methods to manipulate a file pointer, the position in the file at which an operation will be carried out. The getFilePointer() method returns the current position of the file pointer. The seek() method sets the file pointer to an offset position within the file, determined by the argument of type long that is passed to seek(). Any read, write or skip operation will take place at this point.

It uses methods defined in both the DataInput and DataOutput interfaces, thus allowing primitive data values to be written to and read from the file. All of the read() methods defined in DataInput and all the write() methods from DataOutput are available.

Summary

The simple summary is that streams are the way Java can read and write data to and from outside applications, be it a process, network device or whatever. All streams that are created by Java are 8-bit byte streams. Streams consist of two main types: input and output.

Input streams take data from any source, such as the internet or disk files. The main methods that can be applied to an input stream are read(), skip(), markSupported and close(). These work with all input streams. available(), mark() and reset() only work with some input streams.

An output stream produces data for any destination, such as the screen or a disk file. The main methods that can be applied to output streams are write(), flush() and close().

Java provides many different classes for manipulating streams in various ways. All the classes, except RandomAccessFile and File are subclasses of either InputStream or OuputStream.

These two classes are abstract classes that you would not normally derive from. Some of the subclasses provide extra methods for carrying out their own specific tasks. The RandomAccessFile class, for instance, has methods to manipulate a file pointer, and the PrintStream class contains a number of different methods for printing Java primitive data types in a text format.

The Net Class Library

Introduction

The Java language is a programming language designed to create applications and applets for use on the Internet and across networks of computers. Given this, having access to a healthy set of application programming interfaces (APIs) for network connectivity, is critical. Within Java this is catered for with the `java.net` library of classes.

`Java.net` can be viewed as a high level interface for making connections over the Internet or a network using Java-based software. You could even, if that is your passion, build multi-user games with the language, or programs that require multiple users to be connected simultaneously.

Sockets

Those of you familiar with Unix programming will be well aware of a socket when we talk about it. For a long time a socket was an almost unknown entity within the world of Windows programming. But as the Internet became pervasive, encroaching upon far more than the academic world of dusty Unix-based workstations, so the Winsock (in its various guises) became a reality.

A socket has become a very critical part of networking and the Internet so it is of little surprise that the Java language has a set of classes that deal specifically with the creation and manipulation of sockets. The `java.net` package strictly governs the use of sockets.

So what is a socket? Well the best way to think of it is as a network process that creates a link between two host computers, a sort of two-way path between which data from a server and a client can be passed. Each end of the connection uses a socket – the server software will open a socket and wait for a connection and the client software calls the server socket to begin the connection.

To start a connection a destination address and a port number are required. The destination address is the unique address that every computer on the TCP/IP network has. Each socket connection has its own port, which controls where the data is sent once a connection is established. This works by an application informing an operating system (in the case of Java this could be a JVM inside something like *Microsoft's Internet Explorer* Web browser, or indeed *JavaSoft's JavaOS* operating system) that it is waiting for activity to occur on a specific port. There are several well-known port numbers: for instance, the http protocol uses port 80, ftp uses port 21, and telnet uses port 23.

What happens next is that a waiting game begins, with the application sort of going into stasis waiting for activity to start on the port. You see the application does not need to constantly keep probing the port to see if things have started because the operating system should be performing this function. When activity does commence the application will wake up, complete its connection to a server socket and whatever action a programmer has deemed fitting will take place.

Java basically uses three classes within java.net to handle sockets. These are: `Server`, `SocketSocket` and `SocketImpl`. The first two will be the most used classes you will want to understand, with the latter being implemented by a Java-enabled operating system. This means it is there and you take advantage of it without having to ever master the technicalities of the `SocketImpl` design.

socket

The simple role of this class is the creation of a network connection. `socket` is used in conjunction with `SocketImpl` to put into action a socket operation. By using the socket class, the code is kept platform-independent – you don't have to worry about how the connection is being established on the operating system your Java program is running on.

This simple example application creates a connection to the destination address and port specified in the command-line arguments and ouputs the data from the input stream to the console:

```
import java.io.*;
import java.net.*;
public class EchoSocket
    {
    public static void main(String[] args)
        {
        String lineRead;
        int port;

        if (args.length != 2)
            {
            System.out.println("Usage: java EchoSocket
                                    <destination> <port>");
            System.exit(0);
            }

        port = Integer.parseInt(args[1]);

        try
            {
            Socket client = new Socket(args[0], port);
            DataInputStream inData =
                    new DataInputStream(client.getInputStream());

            while ((lineRead = inData.readLine()) != null)
                System.out.println(lineRead);
            inData.close();
            client.close();
            }
        catch (IOException e)
            {
            System.err.println("Error connecting to socket: " + e);
            }
        }
    }
```

The important part of this example is the following lines:

```
Socket client = new socket(args[0], port);
```

```
DataInputStream inData =
                new DataInputStream(client.getInputStream());
```

A socket connection, client, is established by the first line. Then the input data stream, inData, is opened using the getInputStream() method of the Socket class.

After that, a while loop reads the data line by line until the server disconnects. When this happens the readLine() method will return a null string. Each line read in is sent to standard output.

ServerSocket

This class is a server-side function. It waits for a connection to be requested from a client and will accept the connection and assign the requested port on a server.

Let's create an example that provides a simple server that will echo back whatever a client types in. Once started the program will wait for a client to attach to the port that is specified in the command line. The port can be anything that is not used by any of the standard services – 8765 for example.

Here is the source code:

Listing 20.2:
Using Sockets on the server

```
import java.io.*;
import java.net.*;

public class SimpleServer
    {
    public static void main(String[] args)
        {
        String lineIn;
        int port;
        if (args.length != 1)
            {
            System.out.println("Usage: java SimpleServer <port>");
            System.exit(0);
            }

        port = Integer.parseInt(args[1]);
        try
            {
            ServerSocket server = new ServerSocket(port);
```

```
        Socket client = server.accept();

        DataInputStream fromClient =
                new DataInputStream(client.getInputStream());
        PrintStream toClient =
                new PrintStream(client.getOutputStream());
        toClient.println("Hi there! Please type some text.\r");
        toClient.println("Type EXIT when finished.\r");
        while (true)
            {
            lineIn = fromClient.readLine();
            if (lineIn.equals("EXIT"))
               break;
            toClient.println(lineIn);
            }
        client.close();
        server.close();
        fromClient.close();
        toClient.close();
        }
    catch (IOException e)
        {
        System.err.println("Error in server: " + e);
        }
    }
}
```

The first thing the program does is set up a ServerSocket object to monitor the port specified:

```
ServerSocket server = new ServerSocket(port);
```

When a client establishes a connection the accept() method returns a Socket object.

```
Socket client = server.accept();
```

We then set up an input and an output stream for that socket so that we can receive data input from the client and echo that data back:

```
DataInputStream fromClient =
                new DataInputStream(client.getInputStream());
PrintStream toClient =
                new PrintStream(client.getOutputStream());
```

Once that has been done an opening message is sent to the client and a loop is entered which just echoes back to the client whatever is received on the input stream. When the client enters the word EXIT we close everything down.

Datagrams

In the examples presented in the previous section we actually established a connection between a client and a server. That connection remained until it was broken. To do this involves the use of the Transport Control Protocol (TCP). With this protocol, the sockets remain connected and data is transferred using streams. Any data sent by one end is received at the other end in the same order in which it was sent and delivery is guaranteed.

Another method of communicating using sockets is the User Datagram Protocol (UDP). A datagram is a bundle of data, a segment that contains packet length, Internet address, port and packet data all nicely packaged together. Using this communications mode, a connection does not have to be established – you simply send the datagram. The advantage is that the operation is fast, the disadvantage is that you can't guarantee that the datagram will arrive! You can't even guarantee that multiple datagrams will be received in the order in which they were sent.

Datagrams are useful when you want a fast and efficient method of sending non-critical data. If you require guaranteed deleivery then it is better to use TCP.

There are two classes associated with sending and receiving datagrams: DatagramPacket and DatagramSocket.

Sending a datagram

Here is an example program which sends a one line message as a datagram:

Listing 20.3: A simple application to send a datagram

```
import java.io.*;
import java.net.*;
public class SendDatagram
    {
    public static void main(String[] args)
```

```
   {
   String message = "This is the message we are sending";
   int port;

   if (args.length != 2)
      {
      System.out.println("Usage: java SendDatagram
                                   <host name> <port>");
      System.exit(0);
      }

port = Integer.parseInt(args[1]);

try
   {
     InetAddress address = InetAddress.getByName(args[0]);
     byte buffer[] = new byte[message.length()];
     message.getBytes(0, message.length(), buffer, 0);
     DatagramPacket sendPacket =
        new DatagramPacket(buffer, buffer.length, address, port);
     DatagramSocket socket = new DatagramSocket();
     socket.send(sendPacket);
   }
   catch (IOException e)
      {
      System.err.println("Error sending datagram: " + e);
      }
   }
}
```

The application expects the name of the destination host and a port number to be passed as a command-line arguments. It uses the InetAddress class to obtain the actual Internet address of the host.

```
InetAddress address = InetAddress.getByName(args[0]);
```

The getByName() method accepts the name, java.sun.com, for instance, and returns the IP address. If a host has multiple addresses getByName() will only return one. The method getAllByName() will retrieve all the Internet addresses for a host.

Having obtained the address we can create the datagram to be sent. This is accomplished by creating an instance of the class Datagram-Packet.

```
DatagramPacket sendPacket =
        new DatagramPacket(buffer, buffer.length, address, port);
```

The constructor requires four parameters: the message to be sent (which must be a byte array), the length of the message, the address of the destination host, and the port.

The packet is actually sent using the `send()` method of the `Datagram-Socket` class.

```
DatagramSocket socket = new DatagramSocket();
socket.send(sendPacket);
```

Notice that the destination is not specified for the socket. The address and port is held in the datagram itself.

Receiving a datagram

Receiving a datagram involves the same two classes – `DatagramPacket` and `DatagramSocket`. A `DatagramSocket` object must be created to listen to a port on the host machine. A `DatagramPacket` object is created to receive the data. Here is an example program which is the inverse of the preceding example. It will wait for a datagram message sent to the port specified in the command line and display the message on the standard output.

Here is the source code:

Listing 20.4: *A simple application to receive a datagram*

```
import java.io.*;
import java.net.*;

public class ReceiveDatagram
    {
    public static void main(String[] args)
        {
        byte buffer[] = new byte[256];
        String message;
        int port;

        if (args.length != 1)
            {
            System.out.println("Usage: java ReceiveDatagram <port>");
            System.exit(0);
            }
```

```
port = Integer.parseInt(args[1]);

try
    {
    DatagramPacket receivePacket =
        new DatagramPacket(buffer, buffer.length);

    DatagramSocket socket = new DatagramSocket(port);

    while (true)
        {
        socket.receive(receivePacket);
        message = new String(buffer, 0, 0,
                receivePacket.getLength());
        System.out.println("Message received: " + message);
        }
    }
catch (IOException e)
    {
    System.err.println("Error receiving datagram: " + e);
    }
    }
}
```

A byte array buffer is used to receive the data and this must be converted to a string to be displayed on the console. Note that when the
DatagramSocket is created the port is passed as a parameter. The DatagramSocket receive() method waits for the data and places it in the
byte array buffer when it arrives.

URL-related classes within java.net

When programming an application or an applet it may be a necessity to
send outside of your program for data, and this data could easily live on
the Internet. Therefore Java has within it classes for making links to
URLs (or Universal Resource Locator).

A URL is set up to perform a certain function when used, such as download a Web page or even a file. So Java allows you to embed these
directly into your code making access to the Internet only a line or so of
code away. A URL is similar in function to a socket, in that they allow
for easy integration of network devices into your software. But you will

find that working with URLs is a lot more easy and friendly that dealing with sockets.

The URL class

The URL class basically takes a URL string from the Internet and turns it into an object that can then be manipulated using associated methods. These methods generally perform the function of getting things like hostnames and filenames. URL also has methods that can open and maintain the data connections of an input stream. We have seen examples of the use of this class in earlier chapters. Table 20.1 lists some of the other classes relating to URLs.

Table 20.1: *URL classes*

URLConnection	This is an abstract class that is used to create and control the connection to a platform or a firewall-specific location, and is a simplified version of the connection interfaces for the URL class.
URLEncoder	This class takes a string of text and turns it into the www.xxxx.xxxx url-encoded format that is so familiar to the Internet, which is a MIME format. This can be used in conjunction with the URL class.
URLStreamHandler	Again another abstract class. The idea of this class is to create a format for opening a data stream connection to a specified URL. The class is only really concerned about the protocol of the URL, and this is really a class that an advanced programmer should worry about.

Summary

The java.net package is what gives you your connection to the outside world. It embraces URLs, TCP and other communication related technologies. The classes within it allow you to make and break connections that move data around disparate systems.

You can either use a connection-based communications protcol such as TCP, involving a client and a server in two-way communication via sockets or use a connectionless protocol like UDP, where datagrams are sent from one host to another with no guarantee that the packets of data will arrive, or what order they will arrive in.

Appendix A

Java Class Hierarchy Diagrams

java.lang **class hierarchy (1)**

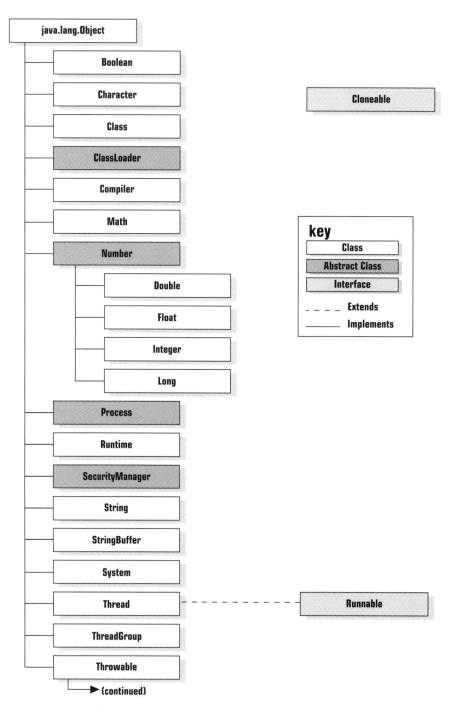

java.lang **class hierarchy (2)**

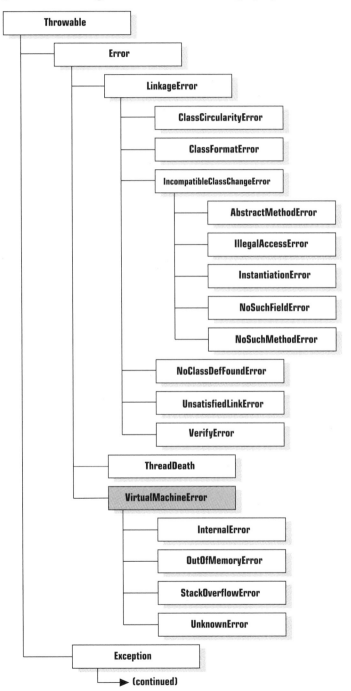

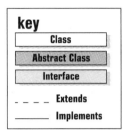

java.lang **class hierarchy (3)**

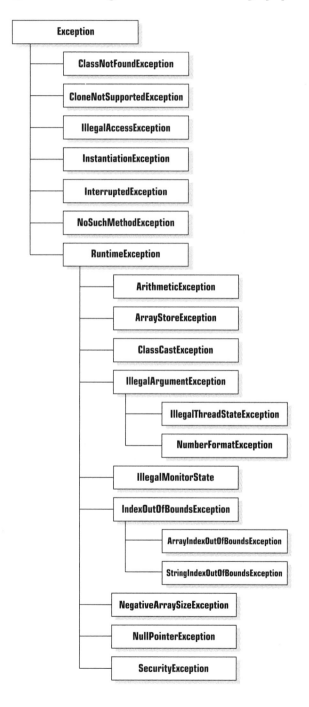

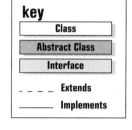

java.io **class hierarchy (1)**

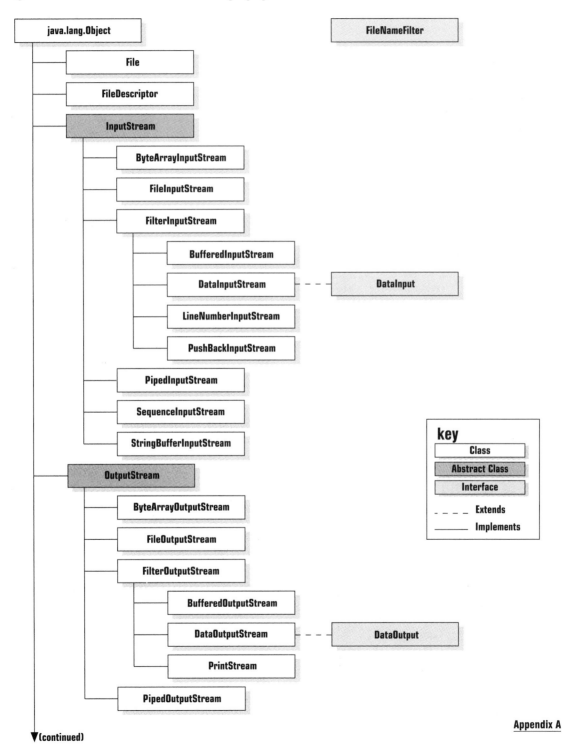

▼(continued)

java.io **class hierarchy (2)**

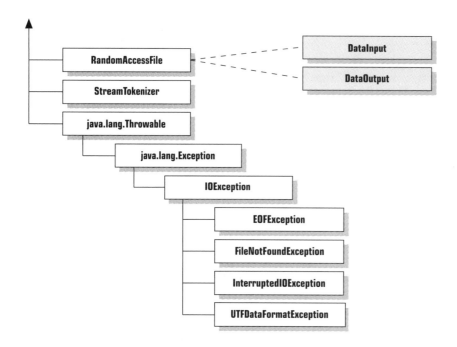

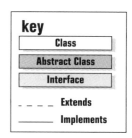

key

| Class |
| Abstract Class |
| Interface |

- - - - Extends
———— Implements

java.util **class hierarchy**

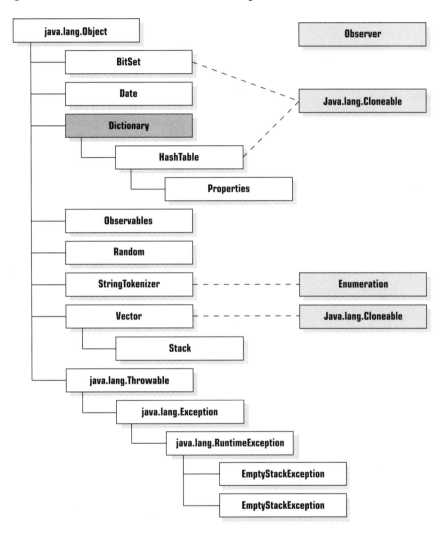

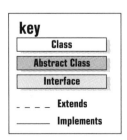

key

Class
Abstract Class
Interface

- - - - Extends
———— Implements

java.net **class hierarchy**

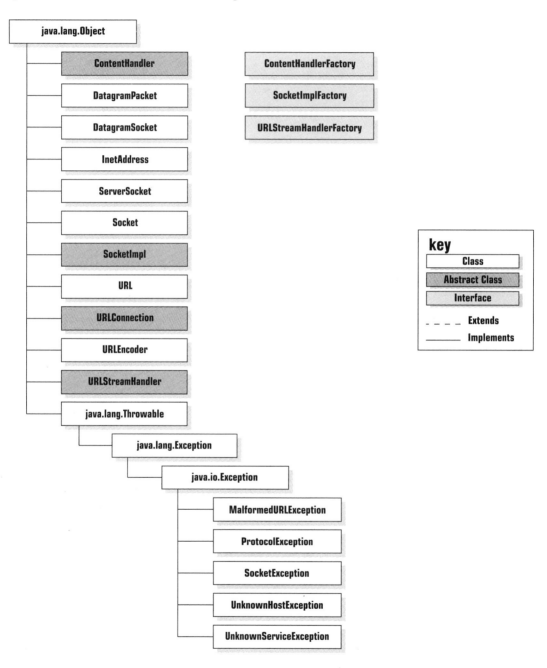

java.awt **class hierarchy (1)**

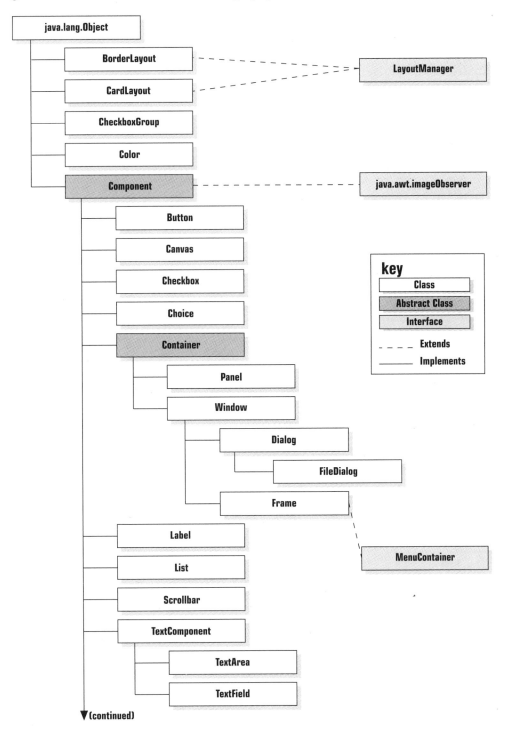

key

Class
Abstract Class
Interface

- - - - Extends

———— Implements

▼(continued)

java.awt **class hierarchy (2)**

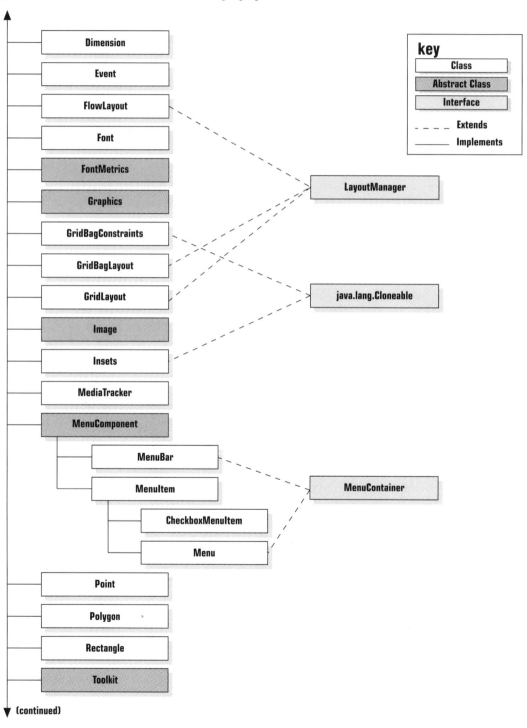

java.awt **class hierarchy (3)**

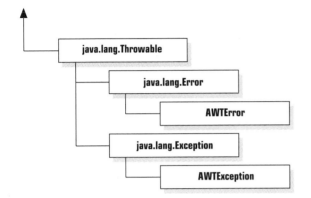

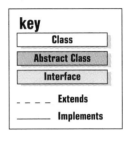

java.awt.image **class hierarchy**

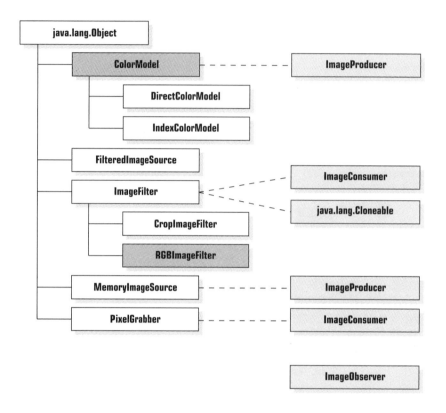

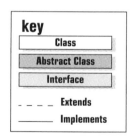

java.awt.peer **class hierarchy**

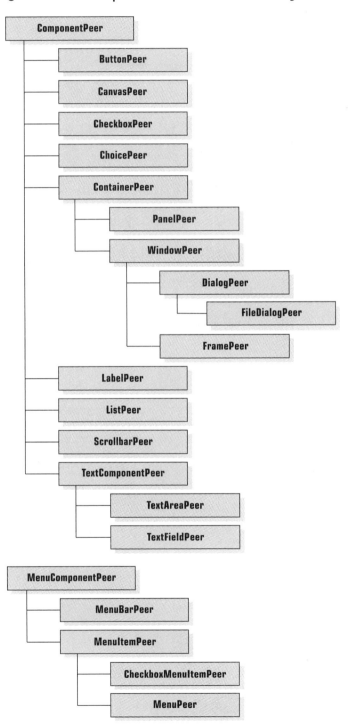

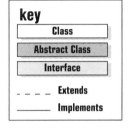

key

| Class |
| Abstract Class |
| Interface |

- - - - Extends
———— Implements

java.applet **class hierarchy**

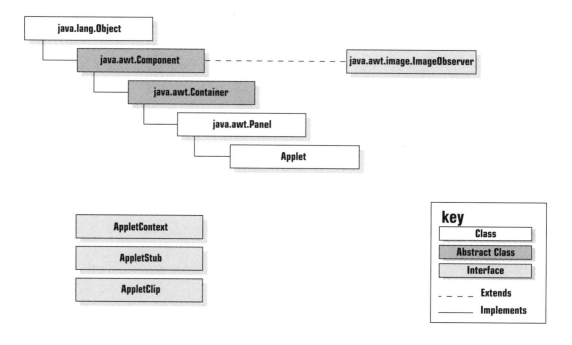

Appendix **B**

The Tools of the Trade

Introduction

When you download the Java Development Kit (JDK) you will, courtesy of those nice people at JavaSoft, obtain a number of necessary tools with which to assemble Java applications and applets. Now the JDK will give you enough to get off the ground, but you may well want to look at moving over to something like Microsoft Visual J++ or Symantec Visual café once you have go to grips with the basics of the Java language.

But for now we will assume that you only have access to the Java JDK and therefore have access to the following components:

- *Java* – the Java Interpreter
- *AppletViewer* – the Java Applet Viewer
- *Javac* – the Java Compiler
- *JavaDoc* – the Java Documentation Generator
- *Javah* – the Native Method C File Generator
- *Javap* – the Java Class Disassembler
- *JDB* – the Java Debugger

The JDK is not pretty to use and is about as basic as programming gets, but it does work and that's that: Let's take a look each component one at a time.

Java – the Java Interpreter

Java interprets (or executes) Java bytecodes that the Javac compiler creates.

Synopsis

```
java [interpreter options] classname [any program arguments]
```

Description

The java command executes Java bytecodes created by the Java compiler: javac. It basically runs Java programs.

The classname argument is the name of the class that you intend to execute. The classname must be fully qualified by including its package exactly in the name. An example being:

```
java java.lang.String
```

It is important to note that any arguments that appear after classname on the command line are passed to the class's main() method. The class specified by classname *must* contain a method main().

Java expects the bytecode for the class to be located within a file called classname.class which is generated by compiling the corresponding source file with javac. All Java bytecode files end with the filename extension.class which the compiler automatically adds when the class is compiled. classname must contain a main() method defined as follows:

```
class Aclass
    {
        public static void main(String argv[])
        {
        ...
        }
    }
```

The interpreter executes the main() method and then exits unless main() creates one or more threads. If any threads are created by main() then the Java interpreter will not exit until the last thread exits.

When you define your own classes you need to specify their location. Use CLASSPATH to do this. CLASSPATH consists of a semicolon separated list of directories that specifies the path. For example:

```
.;C:\users\dac\classes
```

The Java system always appends the location of the system classes onto the end of the class path unless you use the -classpath option to specify a unique path.

Under normal operation you would compile your source files with the javac compiler then run the program using the java interpreter. However, java can also be used to compile and run programs when the -cs option is used. As each class is loaded its modification date is compared to the modification date of the class source file. If the source has been modified more recently, it is recompiled and the new bytecode file is loaded. java repeats this procedure until all the classes are correctly compiled and loaded. You can think of its action as a kind of revision manager.

The interpreter can determine whether a class is legitimate through the mechanism of verification. Verification ensures that the bytecodes being interpreted do not violate any language constraints, such as corrupting the internal operand stack.

java_g is a non-optimized version of java suitable for use with debuggers like the Java jdb (also supplied in the JDK).

Java interpreter command line options

-debug

Allows the Java debugger – jdb to attach itself to this java session. When -debug is specified on the command line **java** displays a password which must be used when starting the debugging session. This should not be considered a secure password.

-cs, -checksource

This option tells Java to check the modification times of a specified class file. When a compiled class is loaded, this option causes the modification time of the class bytecode file to be compared to that of the class source file. If the source has been modified more recently, it is recompiled and the new bytecode file is loaded.

-classpath path

Specifies the path java uses to look up classes. Overrides the default or the CLASSPATH environment variable if it is set. Directories are separated by colons. Thus the general format for path is:

```
.;<your_path>
```

For example:

```
.;C:\users\dac\classes;C:\tools\java\classes
```

-mx x

Sets the maximum size of the memory allocation pool (the garbage collected heap) to x. The default is 16 megabytes of memory. x must be > 1000 bytes.

By default, x is measured in bytes. You can specify x in either kilobytes or megabytes by appending the letter k for kilobytes or the letter m for megabytes.

-ms x

Sets the startup size of the memory allocation pool (the garbage collected heap) to x. The default is 1 megabyte of memory. x must be > 1000 bytes.

By default, x is measured in bytes. You can specify x in either kilobytes or megabytes by appending the letter k for Kbytes or the letter m for Mbytes.

-noasyncgc

Turns off asynchronous garbage collection. When activated no garbage collection takes place unless it is explicitly called or the program runs out of memory. Normally garbage collection runs as an asynchronous thread in parallel with other threads.

-ss x

Each Java thread has two stacks: one for Java code and one for C code. The -ss option sets the maximum stack size that can be used by C code in a thread to x. Every thread that is spawned during the execution of the program passed to java has x as its C stack size. The default units for x are bytes. x must be > 1000 bytes.

You can modify the meaning of x by appending either the letter "k" for kilobytes or the letter "m" for megabytes. The default stack size is 128 kilobytes (`-ss 128k`).

-oss x

Each Java thread has two stacks: one for Java code and one for C code. The `-oss` option sets the maximum stack size that can be used by Java code in a thread to x. Every thread that is spawned during the execution of the program passed to java has x as its Java stack size. The default units for x are bytes. x must be > 1000 bytes.

You can modify the meaning of x by appending either the letter "k" for kilobytes or the letter "m" for megabytes. The default stack size is 400 kilobytes (`-oss 400k`).

-t

Prints a trace of the instructions executed (this applies to java_g only).

-v, -verbose

Causes java to print a message to stdout each time a class file is loaded.

-verify

Runs the verifier on all code.

-verifyremote

Runs the verifier on all code that is loaded into the system via a class-loader. verifyremote will be the default for the interpreter when it runs.

-noverify

Turns verification off.

-verbosegc

Causes the garbage collector to print out messages whenever it frees memory.

-DpropertyName=newValue

Redefines a property value. propertyName is the name of the property whose value you want to change and newValue is the value to change it to. For example, this command line

```
java -Dawt.button.color=blue ...
```

sets the value of the property awt.button.color to blue. java accepts any number of -D options on the command line.

javac – the Java Compiler

javac compiles Java programs.

Synopsis

```
javac [options] files
```

Description

The javac command compiles Java source code into Java bytecodes. You then use the Java interpreter – java – to interpret the Java bytecodes and execute them on whatever computing platform.

All Java source code must be contained in files whose filenames end with the .java extension. For every class defined in the source files passed to javac, the compiler stores the resulting bytecodes in a file named classname.class. The compiler places the resulting .class files in the same directory as the corresponding .java file (unless you specify the -d option).

When you define your own classes you need to specify their location. Use CLASSPATH to do this. CLASSPATH consists of a semi-colon separated list of directories that specifies the path. If the source files passed to javac reference a class not defined in any of the other files passed to javac then javac searches for the referenced class using the class path.

For example:

```
.;C:\users\dac\classes
```

Note: the system always appends the location of the system classes onto the end of the class path unless you use the -classpath option to specify a path. javac_g is a non-optimized version of javac suitable for use with debuggers like jdb.

Command line options

-classpath path

Specifies the path javac uses to look up classes. Overrides the default or the CLASSPATH environment variable if it is set. Directories are separated by semi-colons. Thus the general format for path is:

```
.;<your_path>
```

For example:

```
.;C:\users\dac\classes;C:\tools\java\classes
```

-d directory

Specifies the root directory of the class hierarchy. Thus doing:

```
javac -d <your_dir> MyProgram.java
```

causes the .class files for the classes in the MyProgram.java source file to be saved in the directory your_dir.

-g

Enables generation of debugging tables. Debugging tables contain information about line numbers and local variables – information used by Java debugging tools. By default, only line numbers are generated, unless optimization (-0) is turned on.

-nowarn

Turns off warnings. If used the compiler does not print out any warnings.

-0

Optimises compiled code by inlining static, final and private methods.

-verbose

Causes the compiler and linker to print out messages about what source files are being compiled and what class files are being loaded.

Environment variables

CLASSPATH

Used to provide the system a path to user-defined classes. Directories are separated by semi-colons, for example,

```
.;C:\users\dac\classes;C:\tools\java\classes
```

javadoc – the Java API Documentation Generator

Used to generate API documentation from source files (will create HTML files).

Synopsis

```
javadoc [options] packagename
javadoc [options] filename
```

Description

javadoc will automatically generate you a set of API documents, in a HTML format, for a specified package, or for an individual Java source code file, and can be used from the command line. Within doc comments, javadoc supports the use of special doc tags to augment the API documentation. javadoc also supports standard HTML within doc comments. This is useful for code samples and for formatting text. The package specified on the command line must be in your CLASSPATH. Note that javadoc uses .java files not .class files. javadoc reformats and displays all public and protected declarations for,

- Classes and Interfaces
- Methods
- Variables

Doc Comments

Java source files can include doc comments. Doc comments begin with /** and indicate text to be included automatically in generated documentation.

Standard HTML

You can embed standard html tags within a doc comment, but do not use heading tags like <h1> or <hr>. javadoc creates a structured document and these structural tags interfere with the formatting of the generated document.

javadoc Tags

javadoc parses special tags that are recognised when they are embedded within an Java doc comment. These doc tags enable you to autogenerate a complete, well-formatted API from our source code. The tags start with an @ character. Tags must start at the beginning of a line. Keep tags with the same name together within a doc comment. For example, put all your @author tags together so javadoc can tell where the list ends.

Class Documentation Tags

Tag	Description
`@see classname`	Adds a hyperlinked *See Also* entry to the class.
`@see fully-qualified-classname`	Adds a hyperlinked *See Also* entry to the class.
`@see fully-qualified-classname#method-name`	This adds a hyperlinked *See Also* entry to the method in the specified class.
`@version version-text`	Adds a *Version* entry.
`@author your-name`	Creates an *Author* entry. There can be multiple author tags.

Options

-classpath path

Specifies the path javadoc uses to look up the .java files. Overrides the default or the CLASSPATH environment variable, if it is set. Directories are separated by semi-colons, for example:

```
.;C:\users\dac\classes;C:\tools\java\classes
```

-d directory

Specifies the directory where javadoc stores the generated HTML files. For example:

```
javadoc -d C:\usrs\dac\public_html\doc java.lang
```

-verbose

The compiler and linker will to print out messages about what source files are being compiled and what object files have been loaded.

Environment variables

CLASSPATH

Used to provide the system a path to user-defined classes. Directories are separated by semi-colons, for example, in a Windows environment, or a colon under Unix.

```
.;C:\users\dac\classes;C:\tools\java\classes
```

javah – a Native Method C File Generator

You use this utility to produce C header files and C source code files from a Java class. Basically you can think of javah as the bonding mechanism used to make any Java code you write work with any C code you want it to.

Synopsis

```
javah [options] classnames
```

Description

Javah works by creating C header and source files that you will need to implement native methods. Any header and source files generated will be used by a C program(s) to reference an object's instance variables from native source code. The .h file contains a struct definition with a layout that will parallel the layout of any corresponding class.

The name of the header file and the structure declared within it are derived from the name of a class. If the class passed to **javah** is inside a package, the package name is prepended to both the header file name and the structure name. Underscores are to be used as name delimiters.

By default javah creates a header file for each class listed on the command line and puts the files in the current directory. Use the `-stubs` option to create source files. Use the `-o` option to concatenate the results into a single file. javah_g is a non-optimized version of javah suitable for use with debuggers like jdb.

Options

`-o outputfile`

Concatenates the resulting header or source files for all the classes listed on the command line into outputfile.

`-d directory`

Defines the directory where javah saves all header files and/or stub files.

-td directory

Sets the directory for temporary files. By default, javah stores temporary files in the directory specified by the `%TEMP%` environment variable. If `%TEMP%` is unspecified, then javah checks for a `%TMP%` environment variable. And finally, if %TMP% is unspecified, javah creates the directory `C:\tmp` and stores the files there.

-stubs

Causes javah to generate C declarations from the Java object file.

-verbose

Causes javah to print a message to stdout concerning the status of the generated files.

-classpath path

Specifies the path javah uses to look up classes. Overrides the default or the `CLASSPATH` environment variable if it is set. Directories are separated by semi-colons. The format for path is:

```
.;<your_path>
```

For example:

```
.;C:\users\dac\classes;C:\tools\java\classes
```

Environment variables

CLASSPATH

Used to provide the system a path to user-defined classes. Directories are separated by semi-colons:

```
.;C:\users\dac\classes;C:\tools\java\classes
```

javap – the Java Class File Disassembler

Used to disassemble class files.

Synopsis

```
javap [ options ] classnames
```

Description

The javap command disassembles a class file. Its output depends on the options used. If no options are used, javap prints out the public fields and methods of the classes passed to it. javap prints its output to stdout.

Options

-l

Prints out line and local variable tables.

-p

Prints out the private and protected methods and fields of the class in addition to the public ones.

-c

Prints out disassembled code, i.e., the instructions that comprise the Java bytecodes, for each of the methods in the class.

-classpath path

Specifies the path javap uses to look up classes. Overrides the default or the CLASSPATH environment variable if it is set. Directories are separated by semi-colons. Thus the general format for path is:

```
.;<your_path>
```

For example:

```
.;C:\users\dac\classes;C:\tools\java\classes
```

Environment variables

CLASSPATH

Will define a set of directories and zip files in which javap should look for class defintions. Used to provide the system with a path to user-defined classes. Directories are separated by semi-colons, for example,

```
.;C:\users\dac\classes;C:\tools\java\classes
```

jdb – The Java Debugger

jdb is designed to help you find and fix bugs in Java.

Synopsis

```
jdb [ options ] class
```

or

```
jdb [ -host hostname ] -password password
```

Description

The Java Debugger can be viewed as a dbx-like command-line debugger for Java classes. It uses the Java Debugger API to provide inspection and debugging of a local or remote Java interpreter.

Starting a jdb Session

Like dbx, there are two ways jdb can be used for debugging. The most frequently used way is to have jdb start the Java interpreter with the class to be debugged. This is done by substituting the command jdb for java in the command line. For example, to start HotJava under jdb, you use the following:

```
C:\> jdb browser.hotjava
```

or

```
C:\> jdb -classpath %INSTALL_DIR%\classes -ms4m browser.hotjava
```

When started this way, jdb invokes a second Java interpreter with any specified parameters, loads the specified class, and stops before executing that class's first instruction.

The second method of of using jdb is by attaching it to a Java interpreter that is already running. When started with the -debug option, the Java interpreter prints out a password for jdb's use.

To attach jdb to a running Java interpreter (once the session password is known), invoke it as follows:

```
C:\> jdb -host <hostname> -password <password>
```

Basic jdb Commands

The following is a list of the basic jdb commands. The Java debugger supports other commands which you can list using jdb's help command.

help, *or* ?

The most important jdb command, help displays the list of recognised commands with a brief description. When you get stuck this one saves your bacon.

print

This is used to bBrowse Java objects. The print command calls an object's `toString()` method, so it will be formatted differently depending on its class.

Classes are specified by either their object ID or by name. If a class is already loaded, a substring can be used, such as Thread for `java.lang.Thread`. If a class is not loaded, its full name must be specified, and the class will be loaded as a side effect.

dump

Dumps an object's instance variables. Objects are specified by their object ID (which is a hexadecimal integer).

threads

Lists the current threads in use. This lists all threads in the default threadgroup, which is normally the first non-system group. Threads are referenced by their object ID, or if they are in the default thread group, with the form

    t@<index>, such as t@3.

where

Dumps the stack of either a specified thread, or the current thread (which is set with the thread command). The up and down commands select which stack frame is current.

Breakpoints

Breakpoints are set in **jdb** in classes, such as "stop at MyClass:20". The source file line number must be specified, or the name of the method (the breakpoint will then be set at the first instruction of that method). The clear command removes breakpoints using a similar syntax, while the cont command continues execution.

Exceptions

When an exception occurs for which there is not a catch statement anywhere up a Java program's stack, the Java runtime normally dumps an exception trace and exits. When running under jdb, however, that exception is treated as a non-recoverable breakpoint, and jdb stops at the offending instruction. If that class was compiled with the `-g` option, instance and local variables can be printed to determine the cause of the exception.

Specific exceptions may be optionally debugged with the catch command, for example: `catch FileNotFoundException` or `catch mypackage.BigTroubleException`. The Java debugging facility keeps a list of these exceptions, and when one is thrown, it is treated as if a breakpoint was set on the instruction which caused the exception. The ignore command removes exception classes from this list.

Command line options

When you use jdb in place of the Java interpreter on the command line jdb accepts the same options as the java command. When you use jdb to attach to a running Java interpreter session, jdb accepts these options:

-host <hostname>

Sets the name of the host machine on which the interpreter session to attach to is running.

-password <password>

"Logs in" to the active interpreter session. This is the password printed by the Java interpreter prints out when invoked with the `-debug` option.

Environment variables

CLASSPATH

Used to provide the system a path to user-defined classes. Directories are separated by semi-colons, for example,

```
.;C:\users\dac\classes;C:\tools\java\classes
```

appletviewer – The Java Applet Viewer

The appletviewer command allows you to run applets outside of the context of a World-Wide Web browser.

Synopsis

```
appletviewer [ options ] urls ...
```

Description

The appletviewer connects to HTML documents or resources designated by urls in the command line. It will display each applet referenced by a document in its own window.

Options

-debug

Starts the applet viewer in the Java debugger – jdb – thus allowing you to debug the applets in the document.

Environment Variables

CLASSPATH

Specifies an ordered list of directories and zip files that appletviewer should look to provide class definitions.

Appendix C

New Features in JDK 1.1

There are a number of new features in the 1.1 release of the JDK. This appendix provides a summary.

1   Internationalisation

A complete set of Internationalisation APIs have been included in the new release to allow Java software to be developed independently of any country or language.

The following enhancements are included:

- the display of UNICODE characters
- a locale mechanism
- localized message support
- locale-sensitive date, time, time zone and number handling
- collation services
- character set converters
- parameter formatting
- support for finding character/word/sentence boundaries

2   Security and Signed Applets

A new API for Java Security has been designed to allow the inclusion of low-level and high-level security functions in Java applications. Cryptography, key management and access control will be included.

JDK 1.1 only includes a subset of the complete package and includes APIs for the following:

- digital signatures
- message digests
- key management
- access control lists
- utilities
- the ability to sign classes and other data (such as images and sounds).

3 AWT Enhancements

The quality and performance of the AWT package has been addressed in the new release. The aim is to provide a richer infrastructure to make large-scale GUI development easier in Java. This process has begun in version 1.1 with the following enhancements:

- APIs for printing
- easier/faster scrolling
- popup menus
- clipboard
- cursors per component
- a delegation-based event model
- imaging and graphics enhancements
- more flexible font support for internationalization

The Windows (Win32) version of AWT has been completely re-written to improve the speed, quality, and consistency with other platforms.

4 JavaBeans

JavaBeans allows developers to write reuseable components that end users can include in their own applications. The JavaBeans API is included in version 1.1 of the JDK.

5   Networking enhancements

The java.net base classes now include support for selected BSD-style socket options. Socket and ServerSocket are non-final, extendable classes.

The reporting and handling of network errors has been improved by adding new subclasses to SocketException and the class Multicast-Socket has been moved from sun.net to java.net.

Performance improvements and bug fixes are also included.

6   IO Enhancements

Character streams, which are like byte streams except that they contain 16-bit Unicode characters rather than 8-bit bytes, have been added to the I/O package. They will make it easier to internationalise applications because they will no longer be dependent upon specific character encoding.

7   JAR Files

JAR stands for Java ARchiveand is a platform-independent file format based on the popular ZIP file format. It is used for aggregating many files into one and therfore allows multiple Java applets and their required components (.class files, images and sounds) to be placed in a JAR file and downloaded to a browser in a single HTTP transaction. This and the fact that the JAR format supports file compression improves the speed of the download. Also, the individual entries within a JAR file can be digitally signed by the applet author for authentication purposes.

It is fully backward-compatible with existing applet code and is fully extensible.

8   Remote Method Invocation

Remote Method Invocation lets a programmer create distributed Java-to-Java applications, in which the methods of remote Java objects can be invoked from other Java virtual machines, even on different hosts.

A Java program can make a call on a remote object once it obtains a reference to it, either by looking it up in the bootstrap naming service provided by RMI or by receiving the reference as an argument or a return value.

A client can call a remote object in a server, and that server can also be a client of other remote objects.

RMI uses Object Serialization to marshal and unmarshal parameters and does not truncate types, supporting true object-oriented polymorphism.

9   Object Serialization

Object Serialization adds support for objects to the core Java IO classes. It supports the encoding of objects and the objects reachable from them into a stream of bytes and the complementary reconstruction of the object graph from the stream.

Serialization is used for lightweight persistence and for communication via sockets or Remote Method Invocation (RMI). The default encoding of objects protects private and transient data, and supports the evolution of the classes. A class may implement its own external encoding and is then solely responsible for the external format.

10   Reflection

Reflection enables Java code to discover information about the fields, methods and constructors of loaded classes. Reflected fields, methods and constructors can be used to operate on their underlying counterparts on objects, within security restrictions. The API accommodates applications that need access to either the public members of a target object (based on its runtime class) or the members declared by a given class.

11   JDBC – Java Database Connectivity

Java Database Connectivity is a standard SQL database access interface and provides uniform access to a wide range of relational databases. It also provides a common base on which higher level tools and interfaces can be built. It comes with an "ODBC Bridge" (except on

Mac 68K), a library which implements JDBC in terms of the ODBC standard C API.

12 Inner Classes

Provides a simpler syntax for the creation of adapter classes. An adapter class is a class that implements an interface (or class) required by an API, and delegates the flow of control back to an enclosing "main" object. The new language features apply to Java the concepts of lexical scoping and block structure found in many languages.

13 New Java Native Method Interface

This is a standard programming interface for writing Java native methods. The primary goal is binary compatibility of native method libraries across all Java virtual machine implementations on a given platform.

14 Performance Enhancements

The following performance enhancements are included:

- Interpreter loop in assembly code on Win32 and Solaris/Sparc.
- Non-contiguous heap support on Mac.
- Monitor speed-ups.
- Garbage collection of classes.
- AWT peer class re-write for Win32.
- JAR (Java Archive) bundling of resources for a single HTTP transaction

15 Miscellaneous

`Byte, Short` and `Void` Classes

Two new classes, `Byte` and `Short`, are added to accommodate bytes and shorts as wrapped numbers. The abstract class `Number` gets two new concrete methods: `byteValue` and `shortValue`; the default implementations of these use the `intValue` method. An uninstantiable place-holder class, `Void`, is also included.

`BigInteger` **and** `BigDecimal` **Classes**

`BigIntegers` are immutable arbitrary-precision integers, which provide analogs to all of Java's primitive integer operators, and all relevant static methods from `java.lang.Math`. Additionally, `BigIntegers` provide operations for modular arithmetic, GCD calculation, primality testing, prime generation, and single-bit manipulation. `BigDecimals` are immutable, arbitrary-precision signed decimal numbers, suitable for monetary calculations and provide operations for basic arithmetic, scale manipulation, comparison, format conversion and hashing.

The `@deprecated` **tag**

This is used in documentation comments for unambiguously marking classes, methods and fields that have been superseded by new APIs. The compiler issues a warning when it processes source code that uses a deprecated API feature.

Accessing Resource Files

APIs that provide a mechanism for locating resource files in a way that is independent of the location of the resources. For example, this mechanism can locate a resource file whether it is an applet loaded from the net using multiple HTTP connects, an applet loaded using JAR files, or a "library" installed in the `CLASSPATH`.

Additions to `APPLET` **Tag (HTML)**

Enhancements to the `<APPLET>` tag used in HTML are included.

16 Converting 1.0.2 source files to the Java 1.1 AWT API

Programs that use Java 1.1 features do not run within browsers containing runtime systems that are based on the Java 1.0x release. The next versions of Internet Explorer and Netscape Navigator, version 4 in both cases, will be able to run 1.1 based applets. Runtime systems based on 1.1 will run programs compiled under 1.0x, however.

You can compile programs that use only 1.0.2 features using the 1.1 compiler but JavaSoft will not guarantee that they will run error-free in 1.0x runtime systems.

The main changes that affect the code examples in this book are in the AWT API. Changes to the architecture of the AWT has meant that certain ways of doing things under 1.0.2 have been deprecated (no longer recommended). In most cases this means that a method name has been changed to standardise on naming conventions. Because of this, if you compile the code examples using the 1.1 compiler, you might get a message warning you that the program uses a deprecated API. Don't panic. This is just a warning to inform you that at some point in the future (likely to be a long time), the code might not run properly unless you convert it to the 1.1 API.

The 1.1 API documentation explains how you can convert your programs to the 1.1 API (see file Updating 1.0 source files to 1.1) and conversion utilities are provided.

Appendix **D**

The *Java: A Practical Guide* CD-ROM

System Compatibility

You must have Windows 95 or Windows NT to use the JDK and view the HTML documentation. Long file names are used extensively on this CD-ROM so Windows 3.1x users will only be able to view the Microsoft Viewer version of the Java documentation.

CD-ROM Contents

Example Files

All the example code listings are included on the CD-ROM in the **Examples** directory. Each chapter's examples are in separate sub-directories.

Java Developer's Kit

Versions 1.0.2 and 1.1.1 are both included on the CD-ROM in the directory **JDK**.

To install version 1.0.2 copy the file **jdk-1_0_2-win32-x86.exe** to the root directory of your C: drive and run it. The JDK will be unpacked into a directory called \java.

To install version 1.1.1 copy the file **jdk1_1_1-win32-x86.exe** to your C: drive and run it. Follow the instructions that the setup program gives you.

Java Documentation (HTML Format)

The documentation for the API of both versions of the JDK in HTML format is situated in the **APIDocs** directory. The files are **jdk-1_0_2-apidocs.zip** and **jdk1_1_1-docs_html.zip**. You will need a copy of the WinZip software to uncompress these files.

Java Documentation (Microsoft Viewer 2 Format)

The documentation for version 1.0.2 of the JDK API is available in Microsoft Viewer 2 format. This has the advantage of a full text search capability as well as the standard hyper links between packages, classes and methods.

To install, choose **Run**, enter **D:\SETUP** and click **OK**. (If your CD-ROM drive is not D: substitute the correct letter.)

Note: Please read the **readme** file on the CD-ROM for any changes to the install procedures.

Operators

-- operator (decrement) 56
!= operator (not equal) 56
%= operator 55
& operator (bitwise AND) 57
&& operator (logical AND) 57
*= operator 55
++ operator (increment) 56
+= operator 55
/= operator 55
-= operator 55
== operator (equality) 57
> operator (greater than) 56
>= operator (greater than/equal to) 56
>> operator (right shift) 58
>>> operator (zero fill right shift) 58
? : operator (conditional) 66
^ operator (bitwise XOR) 57
^ operator (logical XOR) 57
| operator (bitwise OR) 57
|| operator (logical OR) 57
~ operator (bitwise XOR) 58

A

D

E